Wellington's Highland Warriors

Arthur Wellesley, Duke of Wellington,
print after Sir Thomas Lawrence

Wellington's Highland Warriors

From the Black Watch Mutiny to the Battle of Waterloo, 1743–1815

Stuart Reid

Foreword by Philip Haythornthwaite

Frontline Books, London

Wellington's Highland Warriors:
From the Black Watch Mutiny to the Battle of Waterloo, 1743–1815

This edition published in 2010 by Frontline Books,
an imprint of Pen & Sword Books Limited,
47 Church Street, Barnsley, S. Yorkshire, S70 2AS
www.frontline-books.com, email info@frontline-books.com

Copyright © Stuart Reid, 2010
Foreword © Philip Haythornthwaite

The right of Stuart Reid to be identified as Author of this Work has been asserted by him in accordance with the Copyright, Designs and Patents Act 1988.

ISBN: 978-1-84832-557-9

All rights reserved. No part of this publication may be reproduced, stored in or introduced into a retrieval system, or transmitted, in any form, or by any means (electronic, mechanical, photocopying, recording or otherwise) without the prior written permission of the publisher. Any person who does any unauthorized act in relation to this publication may be liable to criminal prosecution and civil claims for damages.

A CIP data record for this title is available from the British Library.

For more information on our books, please visit www.frontline-books.com, email info@frontline-books.com or write to us at the above address.

Typeset by JCS Publishing Services Ltd, www.jcs-publishing.co.uk

Printed in the UK by MPG Books Limited

Contents

List of Illustrations		vii
Foreword		ix
Preface		xv
Introduction		1
Technical Notes		7
1	Brave Highland Men – A Prologue	13
2	The Black Watch and Mr Pitt's Army	35
3	The Highland War Begins: The Cameron Highlanders	55
4	High Jinks and Whisky: The Gordons	76
5	Mutiny: The Strathspey Fencibles	97
6	Castlebar Races: The Fencibles at War	117
7	The Tiger and the Elephant	138
8	The Glasgow Highlanders and the Corsican Ogre	159
9	Scotland Forever	180
Epilogue		203
Appendix 1: The Beautiful Highland Regiments		208
Appendix 2: The Gordons at Waterloo		215
Endnotes		217
Archival Sources		230
Index		250

For Chris and Linda with thanks for everything

Illustrations

Frontispiece

    Arthur Wellesley, Duke of Wellington   ii

1. Major General Simon Fraser — 29
2. Sir Ralph Abercromby — 68
3. General David Dundas — 70
4. Gerard Lake — 134
5. Major General Sir Thomas Picton — 184
6. The murder of Colonel Macara at Quatre Bras — 187
7. The Gordons and the Greys charging at Waterloo — 197
8. The same incident from a slightly different angle — 197
9. 74th Highlanders in the 1840s — 205

Plate Sections

I. Highland officer c.1760
II. *The Advantage of shifting the LEG*
III. Grenadiers of the 42nd and 92nd Highlanders
IV. 42nd officer, 1750s
V. Colonel Francis Grant
VI. Highlanders
VII. The de-kilted 72nd Highlanders
VIII. Wellesley at Assaye
IX. Officer and sergeant of the 43rd Highlanders
X. An eighteenth-century view of Dublin
XI. Piper Clarke of the 71st at Vimeiro

XII Rebels drilling by Gilray
XIII Troopers of the Royal Scots Greys
XIV *Landing Troops and Guns*
XV   Officers of the 92nd Highlanders
XVI The Battle of Toulouse

Foreword

Scottish regiments formed a relatively small proportion of the infantry of the British Army in the era of Wellington, and Highland regiments represented an even smaller part; yet the influence they exerted upon the popular perception of the army was out of all proportion to their limited numbers. At the time and in subsequent years, Highland troops featured most prominently in accounts of the campaigns and in other sources such as popular prints, even to the exclusion of others, and the reasons are not difficult to discern.

From the beginning of the French Revolutionary wars, the Scottish Highlands formed an important recruiting ground, especially in the early expansion of the army to meet the challenges of a prolonged conflict; yet at the conclusion of the Peninsular War, there were only five out of 104 numbered line regiments that bore the appellation 'Highland' and that wore the Highland uniform. There had been a considerable number of Scottish fencible regiments that could be considered 'Highland', but none survived the reduction of the army following the Peace of Amiens in 1802; and of the line regiments, six were ordered to relinquish Highland dress in 1809, as it was thought to discourage the enrolment of Lowlanders and Englishmen. That such men from other regions were required demonstrates the fact that the Highlands never provided sufficient recruits to fill all the Highland regiments, so that they had to recruit from other parts of the kingdom, notably from Lowland Scotland. That such a relatively small proportion of the army should have such an influence was a combination of several factors.

In some ways – though not as markedly as some subsequent statements – the Highland regiments represented the last vestige of the old clan system, in which a clan chief would call upon his kinsmen and their retainers to provide military service in time of need. An element of this was retained when some of the Highland regiments were first formed, to varying degrees: for example, when Sir James Grant of Grant raised his Strathspey Fencibles in 1793, no less than eighty of his 'other ranks' bore his name, and of the officers who served in his regiment, thirty-six out of seventy were named Grant. Other traces of ancient customs were also discernible: for example, John Cameron of Fassfern of the 92nd, one of the best-known battalion commanders of the period, was accompanied on his campaigns by his foster-brother Ewen Macmillan, a private in Fassiefern's regiment, evidence of the perpetuation of a traditional practice. Macmillan it was who carried away the mortally wounded Cameron at Quatre Bras, and despite his lowly rank, Macmillan presided over his burial on the field of battle.

It was believed at the time, and subsequently, that Highland soldiers were unlike any others in the army, a difference arising from their inherent national characteristics and background. An example of such beliefs is provided by a writer in Colburn's United Service Magazine in 1846,[1] who advanced the theory that not only was the Scottish soldier markedly different from the English, Irish and Welsh, but that the Highlander possessed additional characteristics to the Lowland Scot:

> The habits of the Scottish are more frugal and less luxurious; he is brought up from infancy on coarser and less nutritious diet, accustomed from an early period to hardships, fatigue, and privation, which neither the English peasant nor artisan care to endure; he is thus presumptively better calculated to submit to the toils and wants incident to the profession of a soldier ... The earlier history of the Scots is a history of successive wars ... [the] martial spirit, which had been thus excited, was cherished and handed down to successive generations. The encouragement of this spirit in the minds of Scotsmen is mainly to be attributed to a strong feeling of nationality inherent in their character [which] combined with the system of feudalism which prevailed till a recent period, all impressed a warlike stamp on the character of the people, which, whatever time and circumstances may have done, has not been entirely effaced ... The principles of religion which were at an early period inculcated in the minds of the youth of the poorer classes, added to the natural causes which engrafted a warlike spirit on their habits, gave to their character that firmness and undaunted courage which may be said to be characteristic of the people ... The Scot is superior to most others in intelligence, prudence, and caution

... his judgment is not rash, he is brave without being impetuous, and firm in the hour of danger, and perhaps it may be said that his conduct in action is characterized by too much ardour ... The Highlanders are a distinct class of people in origin, manners, and language. [The Highland soldier] may be said to be a soldier by instinct ... remarkable for courage at the most trying moment. He is more impetuous than the Scot or English, and is apt to manifest a degree of ardour and enthusiasm requiring vigilance and control on the part of commanders; his feelings are easily roused, and the sound of the national instrument calling forth all his energy and independence under circumstances of despondency or retreat.

In addition to such contemporary attitudes about the Highland soldier, the author made a point that was undoubtedly valid, in stating that 'not one of the regiments termed 'Highland' can preserve the complement of rank and file, from the district of country north of Perthshire', due in part to a diminished population as communities were replaced by sheep farms, and to the 'advance of civilization, commerce and improvement in agriculture ... and the consequent decay of feudalism and submission to chiefs'.

Other factors reinforced the image of the Highlanders as a quite unique military force, not least their distinctive uniform, most notably the kilt, a garment regarded as part of the national identity, even though, as with other 'traditional' aspects, it was generally a modernisation (from the original 'belted plaid'). Defenders of the kilt, such as Alan Cameron, colonel of the 79th, claimed that not only did it aid the soldier's health by permitting the 'free congenial circulation of that pure wholesome air which has so peculiarly benefited the Highlander', and was easily dried when wet, but that its very sight 'struck the enemy with terror and confusion'.[2] Highland dress must have had a positive effect on recruiting in some cases, despite its supposed disadvantages in discouraging Lowlanders and others: for example, Robert Eadie, one of the 'other ranks' who wrote an account of his military experiences, recalled how he went to Glasgow in 1806 intent on enlisting, and was so impressed by the tartan and bonnets of a recruiting party that he enrolled immediately in the 79th. Conversely, the kilt had its disadvantages, as recorded by another of the contemporary memorialists, James Anton of the 42nd, who described how at Waterloo his battalion had difficulty passing through hedges, because 'our bare thighs had no protection from the piercing thorns', and that to have advanced then would have been 'self-inflicted torture'; while in very icy weather 'our Highlanders had their flesh laid open and bleeding by the ruffling of the kilts against their thighs'[3] as the fabric froze.

Yet another singular aspect of the Highlanders, that attracted much attention, was the presence of bagpipers, even though at this period they were not officially sanctioned. They were not exclusive to Highland corps: the 25th Foot, for example, a Lowland regiment, certainly had a piper in 1768 as he is mentioned in the inspection return of that year as well as featuring in one of the paintings of the regiment at Minorca about three years later. The First Battalion of the 1st Foot (Royal Scots, another Lowland regiment) had a piper at least as early as 1768, and the 20th (an English regiment, then bearing the county title of East Devon) had a piper in the Peninsular War. Pipers were, however, most associated with the Highland regiments, and in some cases were retained even after Highland dress was abolished (the 71st, for example, kept theirs after conversion to light infantry). The very presence of the piper was another relic of the old clan organisation of previous years, and as custodians of their national music and tradition, pipers probably regarded themselves as occupying a much more exalted position than that of the ordinary 'ranker'. In consequence, a number of heroic deeds were performed by pipers, like George Clarke[4] of the 71st who continued to play his pipes at Vimeiro even after being shot in both legs, or Kenneth Mackay of the 79th who cheered his battalion at Waterloo by calmly walking in front of them playing 'Cogadh no Sith' ('Peace or War'). Such conduct presumably connected with an element of Highland tradition appreciated by the soldiers and perhaps deliberately fostered by their regiments – as explained by Pipe-Major John McLeod of the 93rd when complimented on playing his battalion into the charge at the Secunderabagh in the Indian Mutiny: 'I thought the boys would fecht better wi' the national music to cheer them'.[5] (Clarke reputedly said something similar, if rather more colourful, at Vimeiro: 'Diel hae my saul, if ye sal want music!') These and similar features – even the fact that many Highlanders spoke Gaelic as their natural tongue – helped to distinguish the Highland regiments from the remainder of the army, and gave them an aura of the exotic that helped shape contemporary opinion. Sometimes these perceptions blur the distinction between myth and reality, but they make aspects of the Highland regiments at this period a most suitable subject for this new study.

Philip Haythornthwaite

Notes

1. Charles Holland Macpherson, 'On the Recruiting of the Army', in *Colburn's United Service Magazine,* 1846, Vol. I, pp. 111–15.
2. *Historical Records of the Queen's Own Cameron Highlanders,* Edinburgh, 1909, Vol. I, pp. 45–6.
3. James Anton, *Retrospect of a Military Life,* Edinburgh, 1841, pp. 210, 234.
4. His name is sometimes spelled 'Clark', but 'Clarke' is the version given on the engraving of his portrait by J. F. Manskirch published in 1816.
5. William Forbes-Mitchell, *Reminiscences of the Great Mutiny,* 1857–59, London, 1897, p. 48.

Preface

While this latest history of the Highland Regiments cannot claim to be comprehensive, since each chapter could easily have been expanded into a book in itself, it will I hope provide for the first time a balanced account of how the regiments came to be raised, why they were to be different from ordinary regiments and why they came to represent not just the Highlands, but became synonymous with Scottish soldiers.

It has been my pleasure in writing this book to address a number of the myths attaching to these Highland Warriors: not with any view to iconoclasm but rather to explaining what lay behind them, why those events occurred and, in the case of the Gordons' celebrated 'stirrup charge' at Waterloo, to examining how it happened. Inevitably, in order to cover so much ground it has been necessary to focus on certain themes in each chapter; if some regiments and individuals receive more than their fair share of coverage then that is because their stories are important to understanding the whole.

It is customary to unreservedly acknowledge the author's ultimate culpability for any errors that pass undetected through the writing and editorial processes, and, rather more agreeably, to record the assistance of those who helped it to see the light of day at all: the first and foremost being Tim Newark, who had faith in it; Michael Leventhal, who listened to him; and Philip Haythornthwaite, who read it, made some constructive suggestions, and not only pronounced it fit to be read but was also prevailed upon to write a foreword.

Otherwise the usual suspects who deserve to be mentioned include Dr John Houlding; David Ryan of Caliver Books; the staff of the National Archives at Kew; the libraries of the Scottish War Museum in Edinburgh Castle and the Literary and Philosophical Society of Newcastle upon Tyne.

Introduction

Wellington's Highlanders

On 7 March 1787 a young Anglo-Irishman, the Hon. Arthur Wesley, entered the British Army as an ensign in the 73rd Highlanders. The regiment was serving in India at the time so there was nothing in the least unusual about the fact that at Christmas he would purchase his next promotion into an entirely different regiment – or that in the meantime young Arthur would not have done a single day's soldiering with the 73rd or ever worn the belted plaid-and-feathered bonnet of a Highland officer. Had he done so, it would have made a beguiling picture, for he was of course the future Duke of Wellington.

However, although he himself may never have worn the kilt, Highland regiments were to march with Wellington every step of his career, from the day he received that first commission until their mutual apotheosis on the blood-soaked ridge at Waterloo.

At the commencement of that journey there were just four Highland regiments in the British Army, but over the next few years those four regiments would briefly become no fewer than sixteen numbered regiments of the line, besides twenty-six more Highland fencible regiments raised for home service; and whilst this number was soon trimmed back to a more manageable eleven, it represented a remarkable contribution, which makes it all the more remarkable that the genesis of those regiments ultimately lay with just six Independent Companies of Highland Men, who had been raised barely a century earlier, and who were originally recruited not as soldiers at all, but as a semi-irregular police force on a wild frontier.

Remote from the centres of power and trade, and possessing a language and a culture all of their own, the Scottish clans were once widely regarded on both sides of the border as enigmatic, dangerous, if not downright savage – and intractably lawless. In a carefully considered memorandum, Duncan Forbes of Culloden, who was both the Lord President of the Court of Session, and a Highlander himself, provided what is probably the clearest and most succinct contemporary description of the clans, whom he characterised as:

> ... a set of men all bearing the same surname and believing themselves to be related one to the other and to be descended from the same common stock. In each clan there are several subaltern tribes who owe their dependence on their own immediate chief, but all agree in owing allegiance to the Supreme Chief of the Clan or Kindred and look upon it to be their duty to support him in all adventures. As those Clans or Kindreds live by themselves, and possess different Straths, Glens or districts, without any considerable mixture of Strangers, it has been for a great many years impractical (and hardly thought safe to try it) to give the Law its course among the Mountains.[1]

In time, as we shall see, the British Government would take full advantage of the clansmen's supposed sense of duty to their chiefs, but in the wake of the failed Jacobite rising of 1715, giving the Law its course was far and away the more pressing priority and so on 12 May 1725 those six companies were ordered to be raised as a sort of local gendarmerie. Colloquially they would soon be variously known as the Watch, the Highland Watch or, less formally, as *am Freiceadan Dubh* – the Black Watch – and whether the latter title referred to their clothing or to their character or to both is still open to question. Like the earlier independent companies that had preceded them at various times during the previous century, they certainly acquired a reputation for corruption and inefficiency, but then in 1739 they suddenly found themselves transformed into a regular regiment of the line. It was, as it turned out, a somewhat traumatic experience for most of them, but nevertheless the new regiment soon acquitted itself well in this very different role and it was to be only the first of many others like it raised in Scotland in the years that followed.

They were remarkable regiments, and as a surgeon who served in the 93rd during Queen Victoria's time, recalled: 'there was a friendly intimacy between Officers and men, which by strangers might be looked upon as familiarity, but which was in reality the evidence of esteem and confidence in each other which knew no fear and was the result, not only of long companionship, but of a feeling of nationality.'[2]

That expression of mutual respect could partly be explained as a reflection of Scotland's culture and in particular of the clan system, which at its very best tied leaders and followers in a mutual and willing bond of service and obligation. That bond might often be abused, sometimes shamefully so, and ancient loyalties could be strained past breaking point, but it existed none the less and should neither be dismissed nor underestimated. However, Surgeon Munro's other, less tangible, point was the more important, for in the longer term it was certainly that common 'feeling of nationality' that underpinned the mutual respect and ultimately proved the most potent factor in forming the character of these regiments.

The Union between England and Scotland in 1707 was bitterly resented by most Scots at the time, forced as it was upon an unwilling nation by bribery on the one hand and the threat of English bayonets on the other. Consequently it immediately provided the impetus for an abortive uprising in 1708 and for an actual one in 1715 that came tantalisingly close to success. Even in the final and bloodiest Jacobite Rising, the 'Forty-Five', most of those Scots who followed Bonnie Prince Charlie did so not simply to restore the ancient and, in truth, much-decayed house of Stuart, but because by doing so they sought thereby to encompass the dissolution of the Union. Not for nothing did many of them carry broadswords inscribed with the words 'Scotland and No Union', but sadly it was a point never conceded by a leader whose eyes were ever fixed upon the English throne abandoned by his grandfather.

In the end the Rising failed, not just upon the bloody battlefield of Culloden but in the hearts and minds of those other Scotsmen who either stayed at home or rallied behind King George, the Protestant Succession and the Union. Nevertheless, at the same time there was a growing emphasis upon a distinct Scottish identity within that Union and a corresponding effort on the part of those Scots who supported it to ensure that it was henceforth to be properly recognised as a political marriage between equals; a true union rather than as a takeover by the senior partner. They were to have no qualms about serving in a British army and they were already positioning themselves to play the leading role in the creation of what would become the British Empire, but they were going to do it on their own terms – as Scots.

James MacPherson's poem cycle *Ossian*, a mighty epic of Gaelic heroes supposedly conjured from the mists of antiquity and first published in 1762, not only capitalised on this determined upsurge in nationality, but at the time exercised an enormous influence little appreciated today. Now all but forgotten, it was MacPherson, rather than Sir Walter Scott, who was the man who first turned those savage Highland clansmen into romantic warriors in the Arthurian mould. In the process, consciously or unconsciously, he provided a culturally insecure Scotland with both a highly distinctive creation myth and a romantic literary heritage firmly rooted not in the douce, respectable Lowlands of John Knox, David Hume and Adam Smith, or even in Scott's beloved wild borderland, but in the infinitely wilder Highlands.

Unsurprisingly, MacPherson, a genuinely talented Gaelic scholar, was denounced at the time as a fraud by no less a figure than Samuel Johnson, and was even more vigorously condemned in the next century by the great historian Thomas Babington Macauley. It was the latter who scathingly wrote of how, thanks to the 'fabrications' of MacPherson, Scott and David Stewart of Garth, 'the vulgar imagination was so completely occupied by plaids, targets and claymores that by most Englishmen, Scotchmen and Highlanders were regarded as synonymous words.' In more recent times, other writers such as John Prebble have also hastened to join with Macauley in uncompromisingly denouncing the 'sweet smell of romantic anaesthesia' associated with the Highland revival and unduly emphasising the negative aspects of service in the army. However, whilst it is so very easy to criticise the Victorian mania for tartans and everything that went with them, it is also true that long before Sir Walter Scott ever put pen to paper, and long before fat old King George IV waddled amongst Edinburgh society in a kilt and Colonel David Stewart of Garth published his hagiography of the Highland regiments, it was the Scots themselves, of all degrees, who most eagerly embraced this swaggering synonymity of tartans and Scottishness.

Indeed by the end of the eighteenth century, with very few exceptions, any infantry regiment raised anywhere north of Edinburgh was considered a Highland one as a matter of course, without any regard to whether its recruits were actually to be found in Lochaber or in Laurencekirk. That 'Highlandism', so much derided by Macauley, Prebble and by all the other critics, ancient and modern, was not merely a romantic fancy indulged by an Anglicised elite, but a widespread and genuinely popular affirmation that those who wore the kilt and the tartan, like Surgeon Munro and his comrades in the Argylls, were not merely North Britons, but *Scots*.

This then is the story of Wellington's Highlanders; of all those 'beautiful Highland Regiments,' and of those who raised them and those who marched in them. A fascinating story, not just of battles in far-off India, Spain and at Waterloo, but one that reveals the very different expectations and experiences of Highland soldiers; a story filled with engaging rogues such as Simon Fraser and Allan Cameron of Erracht; and of the bitter feuds as rival chieftains and Highland proprietors battled each other for recruits. It is also the story of those recruits themselves, who by and large were more than capable of giving as good as they got: demanding and receiving legally binding concessions from their landlords turned recruiters, and then, like George Gordon from the Cabrach, striding forth 'in high dress with his sword by his side to announce his new profession', proudly taking to soldiering in a calculated display of swank incomprehensible to their English counterparts.

Technical Notes

Names

Army Lists and other official records and publications such as the *London Gazette* and the commission registers simply recorded officers by name, but in Scotland the fact that so many individuals bore the same surname – and displayed a lamentable lack of originality when it came to given names – meant that it was more common for men to be known by their home, being a more unique identifier. For the sake of clarity, that convention is also generally used in these pages and Colonel Allan Cameron of Erracht, to name but one, will usually be referred to as Erracht rather than Cameron.

Regimental Organisation

The British Army's infantry regiments, including the Highland ones, normally had just one battalion during this period: comprising ten companies, each mustering anything between thirty and a hundred men. Each of those companies was normally run by a captain, although at first three of them 'belonged' to what were termed the field officers, i.e. the colonel, the lieutenant colonel and the major. Although the colonel was the notional commanding officer, he was rarely seen at headquarters and to all intents and purposes the battalion was normally led by the lieutenant colonel, assisted by the major. In practice either of them might be assigned to other duties outside the battalion – or be taking it in turn to go on leave – and so on 1 September 1795 an additional lieutenant colonel and major was added to the establishment of each battalion. In practice these supernumeraries normally served on the staff rather than with their parent battalions, and on 27 May 1803 a War Office circular added three more captains to the establishment and announced that in future field officers were no longer to have any responsibility at all for commanding companies. Thus from that date onwards there were to be four field officers (not including the colonel) and ten captains in each battalion.

The junior officers in each company normally comprised a lieutenant and an ensign. However, in the case of the colonel's company, his permanent absence meant that his lieutenant was dignified by the curious title of captain-lieutenant and ranked socially as the junior captain rather than the senior lieutenant. This rank was of course abolished when colonels were relieved from notional command of their companies in 1803.

The regimental staff comprised just four commissioned officers: the adjutant, who acted as an assistant to the major and looked after most of the routine administration; the quartermaster who was primarily responsible for the battalion's 'quarters', which could be a camp ground, a billet or a garrison. He would also, generally speaking, be responsible for route planning on marches, and looking after the regimental baggage train. He was, however, not directly responsible for stores or supplies, which fell to a civilian commissariat answering directly to the Treasury rather than to the War Office. In the early days both officers might hold also hold line commissions as ensigns or lieutenants in addition to these staff appointments, but this became frowned upon – particularly in the case of quartermasters, who, the King decided, were not gentlemen. The third staff officer was the surgeon, who was of course the battalion's medical officer and was assisted by a mate, who was not a commissioned officer, while the fourth staff officer – until abolished in 1796 – was the chaplain, who did hold the King's commission but rarely if ever appeared at headquarters, let alone held services.

One of the battalion's ten companies was designated as the grenadiers, and one as the light company. On parade they stood on the right and left flanks of the battalion, and were therefore designated as flank companies, while the others were normally referred to as centre companies. The flank companies were the elite of the battalion and it was a rough rule of thumb that the younger and fitter of them first served in the light company before eventually going on to join the old and bold in the grenadiers or 'grannies'. In newly raised battalions, as so very many of the Highland regiments were at the outset of this story, the veterans – who would normally be the mainstay of the grenadier company – were obviously few and far between, and in the absence of any other criteria, tall and 'good looking' men were often chosen, for the sake of show rather than stability.

Purchase and Promotion

A young gentleman intending to purchase a commission in the army first had to obtain the approval of the regimental colonel, and then deposit the required sum of money with the regimental agent. Once upon a time the agent had simply been an individual clerk acting for the commanding officer as his 'man of business' in dealing with the financial administration of the regiment. However, by 1790 the business had become so specialised that the agents were forming partnerships and taking on staff of their own, so that in that year there were just fourteen agencies operating in London and eight in Dublin, and between them they were looking after the affairs of 108 regiments of infantry and cavalry. The various functions of an agent were admirably described in 1798, as being:

> ... to apply for, receive, disburse and account for public money advanced to him under general regulations or by particular orders. He is the ordinary channel of communication between the Regiment and the Public Departments, and is resorted to not only for providing and forwarding of arms, clothing and other regimental supplies, but also in the business, public or private, of the individual officers.

Consequently agents were very largely responsible for administering the purchase system, which in principle was no different from any other profession at the time in requiring a capital investment, whether it be to join a medical practice or a law firm, or indeed any other kind of business.

The process was straightforward enough. In the 1790s the regulation price for an ensign's commission was £400, while the next step up, a lieutenant's commission, was valued at £500. However, all that actually changed hands in purchasing that step was the 'difference' of £100, and similarly, with a captain's commission valued at £1,500, a lieutenant wanting to buy his way up only had to find the difference of £1,000. In other words, the notional purchase price actually represented the absolute or accrued value of all his commissions – should he then decide to realise his investment by selling out, the nest-egg for his retirement was made up by reversing the process. His immediate successor paid him £1,000 for his captaincy, another £100 came from the ensign purchasing the lieutenancy, and the balance from the young gentleman buying his first commission as an ensign. Although at first sight the series of transactions might seem cumbersome, all of the paperwork and money transfers were handled by the regimental agent.

It should also be emphasised that a good many commissions were obtained without purchase and indeed could not be purchased at all in fencible regiments. Non-purchase commissions were fairly freely bestowed when regiments were first raised: either to gentlemen intending to pay their way by producing recruits rather than hard cash, or by promoting deserving NCOs to provide an experienced backbone to the officer corps. Alternatively a young man could also go out as a volunteer with an established unit, serving in the ranks but messing with the officers in the hope of being on hand when a free vacancy became available. Those vacancies normally came about through the death of an officer (commissions were not heritable properties), or the retirement of a non-purchase officer, for if an officer had not purchased his commission he was not allowed to sell it. Instead, however, such officers were allowed to retire on to what was termed the 'Half-Pay'.

Half-pay was originally granted as a compensatory pension to the officers of regiments disbanded at the end of a war who would be unable to provide for themselves by selling their commissions. The polite fiction was maintained that their regiments were only 'reduced' to a cadre of officers, rather than actually disbanded, and so continued to be carried on the Army List. Naturally enough, over time the officers belonging to those phantom regiments died or found other employment, creating notional vacancies that could then be filled by retiring non-purchase officers. There was also a two-way traffic whereby an officer on half-pay who wished to return to active duty could exchange with a 'non-purchase' officer who wished to retire, particularly since the Government generally required those gentlemen raising new regiments to employ as many old officers as possible from the half-pay lists; which is why of course so many veterans of the American War helped form the officer cadres for the Highland regiments raised in the 1790s.

Money

Establishing the equivalent value of money over two hundred years ago is difficult, particularly as the currency itself has completely changed. It is important, however, to understand how that currency worked; large sums were commonly expressed in guineas, of which more in a moment, but more mundane ones were expressed as pounds, shillings and pence, often rendered as £sd. There were twelve pennies to the shilling and twenty shillings to the pound. Until the withdrawal of gold coinage during the 1790s, the pound was, however, an entirely notional concept and for actual transactions guinea pieces were preferred – gold coins, each worth twenty-one shillings (or £1 1s).

~ 1 ~

Brave Highland Men – A Prologue

The six Black Watch companies who started it all off in May 1725[3] were more than a little different from the majority of King George's soldiers – and not only because they happened to wear bonnets and plaids rather than hats and breeches. For whilst those men who were enlisted into the army's ordinary 'marching regiments' of foot could be sent anywhere that His Britannic Majesty, or rather His Majesty's ministers, desired, the Watch were raised specifically for service in the Scottish Highlands. In practice this generally meant in Perthshire, Badenoch and around the Great Glen for the most part, where they were intended to act as a quasi-military police force in their own right and also to provide guides for any of the regular troops venturing off General Wade's new roads. For what seemed good and sufficient reasons at the time, command of the individual companies – three of them initially to be led by captains and three by lieutenants – was therefore entrusted not to some of the unemployed veteran officers then languishing on the half-pay lists, but to supposedly well-affected Highland gentlemen resident in those parts. They, it was fondly imagined, would have a proper stake in ensuring the peace and tranquillity of their own districts – and would also have a thorough knowledge of the local troublemakers, criminals and political dissidents most likely to disturb that peace. This might have looked like a good idea in theory, and at first there was indeed a commendable display of zeal on the part of those chosen to demonstrate that the Government's faith in its new-found servants was not misplaced. The old ways, however, had not been forgotten and in practice all too many of the officers, and in particular that notorious old rogue, Lord Lovat, very clearly regarded their companies first and foremost not as a badly needed police force, but rather as a bounteous source of patronage and income for themselves and as a form of outdoor relief for their equally needy friends and relations.

In effect the Watch very quickly became a rather agreeable gentlemen's club. 'Many of the men who composed these companies were of a higher station in society than that from which soldiers in general are raised,' gushed their earliest historian, Colonel David Stewart of Garth. 'Cadets of gentlemen's families, sons of gentlemen farmers and tacksmen[4], either immediately or distantly descended from gentlemen's families . . . Hence it became an object of ambition with all young men of spirit to be admitted, even as privates, into a service which procured them the privilege of wearing arms.' Garth's almost idyllic picture of the Watch and its finely dressed young gentlemen soldiers, casually riding on horseback to the periodic musters, each accompanied by his own gillie or manservant, to carry his uniform and his kit, needs to be treated with a proper degree of caution of course. But there is no doubt that to those fortunate enough to serve in it, *am Freiceadan Dubh* was, to use that wonderfully evocative eighteenth-century expression, a 'job'.[5]

As in the regular army, the commanding officers of the companies received a bewildering variety of financial allotments and allowances from the Government for clothing and equipping their men, and the profits to be made on supplying the jackets, plaids, shirts, belts, pouches and everything else their men needed were accounted one of the legitimate perquisites of their rank. Rather less legitimately, but perhaps no less inevitably, some of those official funds were also shamelessly embezzled by many of the Black Watch officers: drawing allowances for men who did not exist, and granting lengthy furloughs to those men who did, in order that the captains might in the meantime draw their pay. Of themselves these pecuniary transgressions might not have been considered entirely damning by the authorities, for it was still a venal age when public service and private profit were not yet considered incompatible. However, the scale of it became scandalous and there were also well-founded rumours of protection money occasionally being demanded from farmers – the old 'black-meal' – in return for carrying out the very policing duties that the companies were supposed to be providing at the King's expense!

In fact, taking into account the scale of the various financial irregularities, the disturbing tendency to supplement official income streams by unorthodox means, and the rather casual attitude to service in the Watch in the first place, it eventually became such a notorious 'job' that the Government finally bestirred itself to assert some proper control over the six companies. Narrowly anticipating the outbreak of war with Spain over the curious matter of Captain Jenkins's ear in 1739, it ordered their consolidation into a proper marching regiment of foot under the command of John, Earl of Crawfurd, on 25 October 1739, just two days before the war officially began on 27 October. Obviously such a dramatic conversion could not take effect overnight, for not only did four completely new companies need to be raised, but the six existing ones also had to find another forty recruits apiece in to order to bring the battalion up to its full wartime establishment. Therefore it was not until some six months later, in May 1740 that His Majesty's 43rd Regiment of Foot was formally embodied as such at Taybridge, Aberfeldy, and kitted out in short red jackets with buff-coloured facings, as well as the now famous Black Watch tartan.

The frequent furloughs disappeared at once and, as regular soldiers, they now had to become accustomed to some proper military discipline, which was doubtless something of a shock to the system after the easy ways of the Watch. They still kept their officially sanctioned Highland broadswords, and their dirks and their pistols, many of them personally owned, but the elaborately decorated round shields, or targes, and the elegant gold-laced tartan clothes, which they had been accustomed to wear away from the parade ground, were soon discarded as they learned how to form and march in line; to manoeuvre by companies, divisions and wings; to deploy from column into line and back again into column; and, above all, relentlessly practised the platoon firing drills that were then at the core of British tactical thinking.

Predictably enough, while the conversion from a rural gendarmerie into a regular regiment of the line at first appeared to go very smoothly, there was some trouble in the end. Nevertheless, in the cold hard light of day it is rather difficult to avoid the impression that the infamous Black Watch mutiny of 1743 has been somewhat overblown (and perhaps wilfully misunderstood) both by contemporary propagandists trying to make political capital out of the affair, and by later historians all too eager to portray the Highlanders as the cruelly exploited victims of an alien regime.

In outline the basic facts of the affair appear to be straightforward enough. Britain, while still rather half-heartedly at war with Spain, had by that time also contrived to become involved in the quite unrelated War of the Austrian Succession. Strictly speaking, it was the Electorate of Hanover that had entered the war in support of the Hapsburg claimant to the Imperial throne, Maria Theresa. However, as the Elector of Hanover also quite fortuitously happened to be King George II of Great Britain, it was inevitable that British troops should soon find themselves sent to the Continent. Equally inevitably, as the war grew in intensity and spread to involve France and most of the other European powers, more regiments soon followed that first expeditionary force. Amongst them, on 11 March 1743, three Scottish units; 1/1st Royals, the 25th Foot and the 43rd Highlanders were all given their marching orders for Flanders. As might be expected of regular units with a long and glorious pedigree – much of it earned fighting in those same Low Countries – both the Royal Scots and the Edinburgh Regiment (as the King's Own Scottish Borderers were then known) went without a murmur, but the Black Watch, now commanded by Lord Sempill, reacted rather differently.

On 14 May they were reviewed by their old mentor, General Wade, at Finchley, which was then just a small village north of London, and there too they received their final embarkation orders. Notwithstanding all the supposed warning signs helpfully dredged up afterwards, the new regiment's behaviour during its long march from Scotland had been quite unexceptional. But now the trouble began, with rumours quickly spreading through the ranks that the regiment was not to be shipped to Flanders after all, but to the West Indies.

In the wake of the disastrous Carthagena expedition three years before, in which more than half the troops involved – including two commanding generals in quick succession – had succumbed to the dread Yellow Fever, it was understandable enough that rumours of a Caribbean posting should be greeted with dismay by the soldiers. Nevertheless, whilst the sudden fear that they were to go to the Fever Islands may well have provided the trigger for the mutiny, the real underlying problem that emerged in the subsequent courts martial was actually a combination of otherwise quite mundane grievances arising from unpaid bounties and allowances, and the startling possibility that a significant number of the men in the ranks may never have been properly enlisted in the first place. In simple terms some of the longer-serving soldiers took the view that they had joined the part-time Highland Watch, not His Majesty's 43rd Regiment of Foot. Some of them also claimed at the courts martial that they had done so without going through the usual tedious formalities of oaths, and the ritual, but very necessary, reading of the second and sixth clauses of the Articles of War relating to obedience to officers and the penalties for desertion.[6] Just how much truth there might have been in these mitigating claims still remains unclear, although they are certainly consistent with the casual, almost sociable way in which the Watch was being run before its embodiment as a regiment of the line. At any rate, shortly before midnight on 17 May 1743 some of those reluctant heroes dramatically took matters into their own hands by embarking upon a mutiny.

Surprisingly perhaps, it should be noted that there was nothing at all unique or even particularly unusual in this. Far from being confined to the Highland regiments, as sometimes seems to be suggested, mutinies in the eighteenth-century British Army were astonishingly common affairs and generally tended to follow certain unwritten rules, which were clearly understood by both officers and men. In the first place, mutiny was normally only resorted to in pursuit of certain clearly defined and usually quite limited objectives – sanctioned as it were by the immemorial custom of the service – such as those unpaid allowances and arrears. Secondly, a mutiny almost always took place at home, not in the middle of a campaign or out in some lonely garrison, and usually at the point of departure or embarkation to foreign parts. Thirdly, when it did occur, a mutiny normally amounted to little more than a fairly polite but robust refusal by the troops involved to march or to embark until their grievances were addressed, however inconvenient that might be from an operational or a bureaucratic point of view. Depending upon the particular local circumstances their demands might occasionally be accompanied by some noisy shouting and tumult – sometimes a particularly unpopular officer could even be beaten up if he was unlucky enough to be encountered without his friends, but otherwise real violence was almost unheard of. Consequently most mutinies ended quite quickly with senior officers giving in to the mutineers' demands and only very rarely punishing those involved. Far from being bloody rebellions against established authority, mutinies by both British soldiers and sailors at this period were in effect tacitly recognised by all concerned as nothing more than relatively routine industrial disputes conducted according to familiar, albeit sometimes rowdy, eighteenth-century grievance procedures.

In May 1750, for example, Lieutenant Colonel James Wolfe was grumbling that: 'If any man of the party for the roads presumes on any occasion, or for any cause whatever, to shew the same sort of disposition to mutiny and disobedience, as was observed in some soldiers of the last year's detachment . . . the officers ordered to command them are to make an immediate and severe example of the offenders.' However, notwithstanding the emotive use of the words 'mutiny' and 'severe example', he then went on to say that offenders were to be immediately returned to the regiment. Road work was apparently regarded as something of a holiday and the punishment threatened was therefore a withdrawal of privileges rather than the prospect of the lash or firing squad.[7]

That is not to say that violence was unknown, but what made the Black Watch mutiny of 1743 different from most disputes of this kind was that instead of simply sitting tight and holding out for a proper resolution of their complaints, many of those involved attempted to march off in a body and return home to Scotland. It was, of course, hopeless. Since no-one actually wanted to fight anybody, far less to embark upon the brisk massacre of tyrants popularly associated with such revolts, the regiment's officers and senior NCOs quickly regained control. Within less than an hour it was all over. The greater part of the regiment was paraded under their watchful eyes on Finchley Common and when the rolls were called at daylight it was found that only some 120 men had gone. The mutineers initially made good speed first by way of St Albans and thereafter across country, but lacking provisions they then went to ground in a Northamptonshire wood and were persuaded to surrender a few days later. Normally mutiny might be condoned by the authorities with a certain weary tolerance, but premeditated and organised mass desertion was a different matter entirely and called for exemplary punishment. Thus three of the ringleaders, Samuel and

Malcolm MacPherson, and Farquhar Shaw, were condemned to death by a court martial and duly shot by a firing squad on Tower Hill, while their followers were all drafted away from the Watch and into other units – some of them, ironically enough, serving in the West Indies! In the meantime the rest of the regiment quietly embarked for Flanders, just as the Government had intended all along; they underwent a very creditable baptism of fire at the great battle of Fontenoy, near Tournai, on 11 May 1745 and thereafter, as they say, never looked back.[8]

While much has been made by both contemporaries and historians of the 'heroic' or even the romantic nature of the mutiny and its supposed long-remembered legacy of distrust in the Highlands, it actually appears to have had very little, if any, real effect on recruiting in the years that followed. Just two years later in 1745 not only were three additional companies of the 43rd formed in order to provide reinforcement drafts for the regiment, but letters of service were granted to a regular officer, Colonel John Campbell, Earl of Loudoun, for the raising of a second Highland regiment. This time there was to be no ambiguity about its status, and from the very outset it was clearly understood that, while wearing the Highland dress, the new 64th Regiment of Foot was otherwise going to be regarded in every respect as an ordinary regiment of the line.

As it turned out, both Loudoun's regiment and the additional companies got off to a rather unlucky start, for it was of course in the late summer of that year when the last Jacobite rising erupted in Scotland, and to the Earl's chagrin a number of officers and men, including at least one complete company led by Cluny MacPherson, promptly defected to the rebels.[9] Nevertheless the majority of his men remained faithful to King George and three companies commanded by Lieutenant Colonel 'Jack' Campbell of Mamore and Captain Colin Campbell of Ballimore fought at Culloden in a composite Highland battalion that even included one of the Black Watch 'additional' companies commanded by Captain Dugald Campbell of Auchrossan.[10] Afterwards both Highland regiments went on to fight bravely in Flanders, but nevertheless when peace was signed in 1748 there was a decided feeling in some quarters that care should be taken to ensure they were included amongst those units marked for disbandment in the inevitable post-war cutbacks.

Even in Scotland, an apprehensive Lord Findlater, professing himself to be greatly disturbed by the rumour of 'an intention to turn the two Highland Regiments into Independent Companies to be sent to the Highlands ...' anxiously informed the prime minister, the Duke of Newcastle, that he was sure 'it wou'd prove a most pernicious scheme, for it wou'd effectively spread and keep up the warlike spirit there and frustrate all measures for rooting it out ... It wou'd be dangerous to scatter such a number of military Highlanders in their own country.'[11] Instead, although Loudoun's 64th were indeed doomed to be 'broke' along with all the other high-numbered regiments, the Black Watch survived to be famously re-numbered as the 42nd (Highland) Regiment of Foot.[12] Findlater, nevertheless, no doubt took some satisfaction in the fact that instead of returning home to police the Highlands, as he feared they might, the regiment was sent first to do garrison duty in Ireland in 1749 and then went overseas to the wilds of the New York frontier in 1756.

Nevertheless, notwithstanding General Wolfe's unfortunate gibe about the Highlanders being 'hardy, intrepid, accustomed to a rough country, and no great mischief if they fall',[13] which tends to be rather too freely quoted by historians both in and out of season, the Duke of Cumberland certainly did not regard the Black Watch as expendable. Indeed when the idea of sending them to the colonies was first mooted by the King two years earlier, in 1754, it was Cumberland himself who objected to the army's only Highland regiment being transferred to a putative American establishment, since it 'would be losing the corps were the men to remain in America'.[14] The Duke had no objection, however, to a routine rotation. Although sharing a common sovereign, Britain and Ireland were administered quite independently at this time. One of the curious results of this constitutional split was that British Army regiments serving in Ireland were actually paid for through the quite separate Irish exchequer, which maintained a fixed military establishment of no less than fifteen thousand men throughout the eighteenth century. This garrison, enshrined by law in Dutch William's time to defend the Protestant ascendancy, could not be reduced and so it was customary for units that were surplus to immediate requirements in Britain to be stripped down to little more than a cadre and transferred to the Irish establishment as an alternative to disbanding them. Then, when they were required for active service again, the Irish cadres – including, in this case, the 42nd – were hastily brought back up to strength by drafting in men from other units, transferred back onto the English establishment and shipped overseas.[15]

That North American posting for the Black Watch was in fact just a part of the steady escalation of low-level hostilities along the New England frontier with Canada, which erupted into another full-scale war with France later that year. Not surprisingly, as it turned out, what would eventually become known to historians as the Seven Years' War also saw an unprecedented increase in the size of the British Army. No longer was it to be confined to the old battlegrounds of Flanders and Germany: now it would fight in the Americas as well, and in both the East and West Indies, for it was an army on the verge of creating an empire.

To win such a far-flung conflict (and to gain that empire) the army obviously needed to find far more men than ever before, and it therefore looked with considerable interest to the Highlands of Scotland. Notwithstanding the earlier difficulties with the Black Watch and Loudoun's 64th, the Government had not forgotten that in 1745 some of the Highland chiefs had seemingly raised whole regiments of their clansmen for the Pretender's service in just a matter of days, while the loyal chiefs had patriotically responded in turn by providing hundreds of men to serve in the ranks of both the Argyle Militia, and in upwards of eighteen other Highland independent companies, as well as a number of less formal volunteer militias besides. Now, despite the passage of various laws in the wake of the rebellion, wisely intended to bridle the powers of the chiefs, it was believed that they still enjoyed sufficient influence over their people to enlist them for the service of King George in return for the customary marks of royal favour – or forgiveness.

This attractive assumption – that the chiefs could still exact unquestioning obedience from their people – would eventually prove to be rather more optimistic than accurate, but in the meantime it was William Pitt the Elder who claimed the credit for the idea: 'I sought for merit wherever it was to be found,' the great statesman pompously declared to an obligingly attentive House of Commons in 1766.

It is my boast that I was the first minister who looked for it and found it in the mountains of the north. I called it forth and drew into your service a hardy and intrepid race of men, who when left by your jealousy became a prey to the artifice of your enemies, and had gone nigh to have overturned the State in the war before the last. These men in the last war were brought to combat on your side; they served with fidelity as they fought with valour and conquered for you in every part of the world.[16]

In fact the quest for that merit properly began with a cautious experiment; two letters of service were granted on 4 January and 5 January 1757 respectively, not for recruiting proper regiments of the line but for the very temporary-sounding 1st and 2nd Highland Battalions. At this early stage the Government was committing itself to nothing, because both were to be 'raised for rank'. That is to say the officers had to earn their commissions by recruiting the requisite number of men. Were they to be successful the officers would then be rewarded with a permanent rank in the army and the two battalions would be taken into the line as numbered regiments of foot; fail and the experiment would be terminated by drafting their few recruits into other regiments.

The two men charged with discovering whether that merit was indeed to be found in the mountains of the north presented an interesting contrast. Both were thirty-one years old and both represented ancient houses, but there the resemblance ended. Far from being a Highlander, the first of them, Major the Honourable Archibald Montgomerie, was a scion of one of the oldest noble families in south-west Scotland, and in due course he would become the 11th Earl of Eglinton. Of covenanting stock, he had fought against the Jacobites at Culloden in 1746 as a captain in Fleming's 36th Foot, and was currently serving as the second-in-command of that regiment. He was, in short, regarded as a very safe pair of hands.

The second of the two was a different proposition entirely. While Montgomerie was a professional soldier from an old Lowland family with a reasonably solid pedigree of loyalty to the Crown and firm support for the Protestant Succession, Simon Fraser was unquestionably a Highlander and his only previous military experience had been gained as a colonel in that very same Jacobite Army that 'had gone nigh to have overturned the State'! As the Master of Lovat, the eldest son and heir of the infamous Lord Lovat, he had abandoned both his law studies at the

University of St Andrews and the patronage of the Duke of Argyll, to don a white cockade and lead his father's people at the battle of Falkirk in 1746. However, in rather mysterious circumstances he then managed not to lead them anywhere at all at Culloden, and soon afterwards surrendered himself to the Government. He may indeed have contrived to change sides during the battle and, while his poisonous old father went to the block, Fraser quickly re-positioned himself once more as a loyal protégé of Argyll's, resumed his legal career and underlined his happy return to the fold by assisting the prosecution in the infamous Appin murder trial of 1752. However, while he might unquestionably be 'McShimi', the chief of the Frasers, the Lovat title and the lands attached to it were still forfeit – if he was to win them back some signal service would have to be rendered to the Crown. Raising a regiment was the most obvious way to do it and it was through the Duke of Argyll's patronage that this *soi-disant* Jacobite and very amateur soldier obtained his letters of service.[17]

Both regiments were substantially raised in the Highlands. According to an early inspection return, Montgomerie's regiment was partly raised in the far north and west, in Caithness, Sutherland, Ross-shire and the Isle of Skye, but the majority of the recorded recruits actually came from Strathspey and Urquhart, from Atholl and Strathdearn, from Aberdeenshire, and quite inevitably from Edinburgh and Glasgow, as well as from his native Ayrshire.[18] For his part, Fraser proceeded, at least according to popular legend, to recruit a whole regiment of former rebels from all the way along the Great Glen. To Stewart of Garth and other romantically inclined historians this supposed 'Jacobite' regiment perfectly symbolised the happy reconciliation of the former supporters of the House of Stuart with the ruling House of Hanover: 'Frasers, Macdonalds, Camerons, Macleans, Macphersons, and others of disaffected names and clans, were enrolled,' declared Garth, supposedly quoting a conveniently anonymous friend of Pitt, 'their chiefs or connections obtained commissions, the lower class, always ready to follow, they with eagerness endeavoured who should first be enlisted.'[19] Sadly, the story, although an attractive and superficially plausible one, is a myth, for in reality Fraser's original captains were hardened professional soldiers brought in from the Scots regiments in the Dutch service. It is true that there *were* indeed a number of former Jacobites or their sons to be found amongst the more junior officers, but they were very much in a minority. While there is anecdotal evidence that some of the rank and file may also have followed the Stuart banner in 1745, very few of the eighteen- and nineteen-year-olds who accounted for the majority of the regiment's recruits can have done so.[20]

The fact of the matter was that neither battalion was the old-fashioned clan levy that Pitt, Argyle and their other sponsors fondly expected or pretended, and the far-flung origins of their men reveal all too clearly how neither commanding officer was able to summon them forth without, as McShimi put it, 'the concurrence and aid of friends – Gentlemen of the country with proper connections'. MacDonald of Sleat encouraged his tenants' sons to enlist with Montgomerie because the colonel was his brother-in-law, while similarly the Gordon gentry exerted themselves to help Captain John Gordon of Glentanar complete *his* company. Sir Ludovick Grant of Grant, otherwise known as the Laird of Grant, likewise instructed his tenants to see that any young men 'who incline to the army' went into his own brother-in-law's company in Montgomerie's battalion and ominously concluded by remarking that: 'I hope by your conduct at this time you'll give me reason to continue your affectionate friend and humble servt' – an implied threat that no doubt accounted for Major James Grant's company being the strongest in the battalion, with no fewer than 230 men raised in Strathspey and Urquhart.

What was more, recruiting for the two regiments was by no means confined to the Highlands. Some of those who were picked up by Montgomerie's recruiters in the narrow streets, wynds and vennels of cities like Edinburgh and Glasgow might well have been Highland in origin, but there were also inevitably some undoubted Lowlanders amongst them, including men like Robert Kirkwood from Ayrshire. Nevertheless, although Kirkwood himself claimed the majority of those whom he served with were indeed 'impress'd men from the Highlands' and a return of the regiment's 1,060 men who arrived at Charlestown, South Carolina in September 1757 officially showed only fifty-nine 'Lowland Scotch', the Earl of Loudoun, who ought to have known what he was talking about, was moved to comment that there were actually 'a good many low Countrymen alongside the Real Highlanders'.[21]

Similarly, while it was undoubtedly built around a solid core of 'real' Highlanders from the Inverness area, Fraser's regiment also had more than its share of Lowlanders, and in particular Major Clephane seems to have picked up a fair number of them around Aberdeen and Dundee: men such as Alexander Bell, nineteen years old and born in Kirriemuir; Peter Moody from Glamis and John Molyson, simply described as coming from the Mearns. Consequently, it would be fair to say that both regiments were literally recruited from everywhere in Scotland between Lochaber and Laurencekirk.

Although a quite astonishing number of Montgomerie's genuine Highland recruits were at first rejected by an inspecting officer for one reason or another, the ranks were quickly filled – and indeed oversubscribed – and his battalion was duly taken into the line, first as the 62nd Regiment of Foot and then as the 77th, before going overseas to serve very creditably indeed against the French and the Indians in the North American wilderness.[22] Fraser's, rather more famously, went to Canada; they helped take the coastal fortress of Louisburg in 1758 and in the following year followed General Wolfe to Quebec and the surprisingly brief battle on the Plains of Abraham that secured Canada for the British Empire. Despite the fact that the two battalions were not quite as advertised, from the Government's point of view the experiment was turning out to be a considerable success, for it did indeed appear to be remarkably easy to raise large numbers of men in Scotland. Consequently, as the war gathered pace, other Highland battalions quickly followed, their ranks filled with yet more footloose young men from the glens – and from the streets of Lowland burghs.

A second battalion for the far-from-expendable Black Watch was the next to be raised, as an un-covenanted dividend to accompany its glorious translation into the 42nd (Royal Highland) Regiment on 20 August 1758. Partly recruited in Glasgow, it was embodied at Perth in October 1758 before being shipped out to join the first battalion in America – where it helped fill the awful gaps torn in the regiment's ranks in the heroic but futile attempt to storm the French fortifications at Ticonderoga earlier that summer.[23] To ensure that the two service battalions were kept up to strength in future, three more 'additional' companies, like the one which Dugald Campbell of Achrossan once led at Culloden, were also thoughtfully authorised for the regiment.

However, no sooner were they fully recruited and awaiting passage to America than they were re-assigned instead as the nucleus for two completely new Highland regiments; Robert Murray Keith's 87th and John Campbell of Dunoon's 88th, both of which were urgently wanted for service in Germany.

They in turn were then followed by Morris's 89th Highlanders: a largely forgotten but interesting unit that deserves to be much better remembered for a variety of reasons. For one thing it was the earliest incarnation of the famous Gordon Highlanders and it was also the very first of the Highland regiments to serve in India, but perhaps its most remarkable claim to fame is the fact that it was also the only Highland regiment ever to be raised and commanded by an American![24]

Staats Long Morris was in fact a young New Yorker who had the great good fortune to marry the Dowager Duchess of Gordon in 1756. Fully twelve years her junior, he was at first regarded by family and friends as an adventurer but, according to her eventual obituary in the *English Chronicle*, he 'conducted himself in this new exaltation with so much moderation, affability and friendship, that the family soon forgot the degradation the Duchess had been guilty of by such a connection, and received her spouse into their perfect favour and esteem'. She for her part was keen to restore the somewhat faded prestige of her house and, like Simon Fraser before her, she saw that offering the Government a regiment was going to be the quickest and surest way of doing it. Her son, the duke, was only sixteen at the time and obviously rather too young for the job. Morris, who was already a serving officer in the 36th Regiment, was ideally suited and an undated memorandum throws some interesting light on how he proposed to go about it:

> Captain Morris, of Lord Robert Manners' Regiment, husband to the Duchess of Gordon, proposes to raise a regiment of Highlanders for foreign service, with the assistance of the Duke of Athol, Lord Findlater, Lord Deskford, Sir Ludovic Grant, and other Highland chief[s]. He asks no levy money and desires no rank for himself or officers till the battalion is completed and approved on a review by the end of April next or sooner.
>
> The undertakers for other Highland corps had three pounds per man levy money, and had their commissions immediately. They did not undertake to raise the men within a limited time. If Captain Morris

succeeds in this attempt he expects to command the corps with the rank of Lieutenant Colonel, like Montgomery and Fraser. The Duke of Gordon will have a company.[25]

The Government was not slow to recognise a bargain when it was offered and both Morris and his step-son, the Duke, had their commissions in the regiment, as lieutenant colonel commandant and captain respectively, dated 13 October 1759. Unfortunately, although Morris (or rather the Duchess), had been promised the support of a number of prominent local families, they were not, with the exception of Sir Ludovick Grant, Highland chiefs as the term is usually understood and their power over their 'people' turned out to be considerably less than they hoped. Moreover, it soon became clear that the most eager of the would-be recruits had already been encouraged by those very same gentlemen to enlist under either Montgomerie or Fraser. Consequently, even within the regiment there was considerable competition for the few young men still willing to 'go for a soldier' and one of the Duchess's neighbours, Lord Moray, went so far as to warn his chamberlain at Inverness that:

> As Mr Dunbar of Duffus his son has gott a commission in Collonel Morris's Battalion, he will immediately sett about recruiting. I am informed that Drumnaglas has got a company in said battalion. I do call upon you and all those under your care who pretend friendship and regard for me and my family to be aiding and assisting to Captain Dunbar; and if any other recruiting party should interfere with him, I desire that my weight be thrown into Captain Dunbar's scale, where the terms are equall, and if I hear (and hear I will) that after you receive this letter any recruits are gone out of the Lordship of Petty and not unto Captain Dunbar's Company, I will not easily forget nor forgive it to those who have had the smallest hand in contributing towards it. You may let my vassals know that they cannot come to me with a stronger claim to my friendship than by giving me proof that they deserve it by giving substantial assistance to Captain Dunbar, notwithstanding the pretext of Drumaglash his company.[26]

On the face of it, the language was pretty similar to that used by Sir Ludovick Grant when he helped raise men for Montgomerie two years before, but it was far less effective – once again this was hardly a levying of the clans and Moray was no Highland chieftain. The Lordship of Petty is very much on the Lowland side of Inverness, both in geography and character, and although Captain William McGillivray of Drumnaglas's elder brother Archibald had himself recruited a company there for the Pretender in 1746 and then died leading Lady Mackintosh's Regiment at Culloden, blind obedience was no longer to be expected from either his people or from Moray's 'vassals'. Instead, given the Gordon family's long-established dominance in the north-east of Scotland, it was probably inevitable that most of the officers and men that eventually joined to the regiment came not from the Highlands proper, or even to any great extent from the hills of Strathdon, Cromar and Deeside, but rather from the low country of Moray and Banffshire, and the broad farming country of Buchan and Formartine, as well as from the Aberdeen area itself. They included John Beverley, 'born in the parish of Old Aberdeen and lately servant to James Christie, horse-hirer in Aberdeen'; John Gordon, a tailor born in the sandy coastal parish of Belhelvie; Alexander McIntosh, a 'labouring servant' from Marnoch in Banffshire; William Young, aged thirty-three, a tinker; nineteen-year-old George Smith, a labourer in the parish of Cairney and John Archibald, a forty-year-old shoemaker – none of whom fit the popular stereotype of Highland clansmen. As it happens we only know about these particular men because they were advertised as deserters in the *Aberdeen Journal*, at various dates between December 1759 and March 1760, but there is no reason at all to suppose that they were untypical of the regiment's recruits. Indeed, nearly all of Morris's soldiers would in the end be raised in districts not normally considered to be part of the Highlands, and from amongst men whose first language was Scots (or more properly north-eastern Doric), not Gaelic.

It was an inevitable trend, which continued and increased almost exponentially when the American Revolution broke out in 1775. Predictably enough, like Loudoun's before them, all of the new Highland regiments, including 2/42nd, had disappeared from the Army List at the end of the Seven Years' War in 1763, leaving the original battalion of the Black Watch as the British Army's sole kilted regiment. It was a distinction that it was not destined to enjoy for long. This time around no fewer than fifteen new battalions would be raised in Scotland during the course of the war – and irrespective of their real origins all but four of them would be designated as Highlanders and dressed in bonnet and plaid.

As it happens, the first of the new regiments to be authorised, the two-battalion-strong 71st Highlanders, was recruited by the very same Simon Fraser– now Major General Simon Fraser MP – who had raised and led the 78th Highlanders in the previous war. Once again he spread his net widely, called in old favours and pledged future ones and by April 1776 had marched no fewer than 2,340 recruits to Glasgow, where they embarked for America and earned a bloody reputation that was second to none. Fraser himself did not accompany them of course, for

1   This miniature is traditionally identified as Major General Simon Fraser, who raised the original 78th and then the 71st Highlanders. However, while there is an undeniable resemblance to Lord Lovat of the 'Forty-Five', the style of the uniform suggests he may actually be the Simon Fraser who raised the short-lived 133rd Highlanders in 1794 and died a lieutenant general in 1807. (Private Collection)

his political duties as one of the members of parliament for Inverness had the first call upon his valuable time, but he had shown what was possible. Unsurprisingly he was once again soon followed by a positive procession of other great and would-be great men of the Highlands, all of them eager to follow his example and restore their own shattered fortunes. All too quickly, however, it soon became obvious, just as in the first time around in 1757, Fraser had already skimmed off the best of the potential heroes, which meant that for those coming after him it would prove to be a frustratingly uphill struggle.

At one point, back in September 1745, when the Pretender's supporters were bidding fair to seize control of Scotland, a Government agent reported how:

> Cameron of Kinlochlyon [sic], Cameron of Blairchierr, Cameron of Blairmachult, Cameron of Glenevis, and Cameron alias MacKalonie of Strone, heads of the several tribes of the name of Cameron, came from Locheil's country and entered Rannoch with a party of servants and followers to the number of about 24 and went from house to house on both sides of Loch Rannoch ... and intimate to all the Camerons, which are pretty numerous on both sides of the loch, that, if they did not forthwith go with them, that they would that instant proceed to burn all their houses and hough their cattle; whereupon they carried off the Rannoch men, about one hundred, mostly of the name of Cameron ...

Thirty years later it was a very different story altogether. No matter how much men such as the Laird of Grant and Mr Dunbar of Duffus might try to exert their old influence, the Highland chiefs, both great and small, now found to their dismay that they had to bargain with their tenants and clansmen rather than command them. Thus, John Cameron of Kinlochleven – the son of the man who had once gone through Rannoch with fire and sword in the Pretender's name – wrote to the young Duke of Gordon in May 1778, offering that:

> If your Grace will give me the farm of Kilmanivag and Brackletter for five years, I will furnish your Grace two handsome men tomorrow. I would be glad to give my assistance to your Grace without those terms, but, as it is not in my power to accommodate the friends of those who go, I am obliged to ask these as I have no lands of my own.

In other words, Kinlochleven knew of two men who were willing to enlist if some proper provision was made for their dependants. Providing the duke would give him a five-year lease on the farm, he would undertake to look after those 'friends' and the duke would get two recruits for his proposed regiment of Northern Fencibles.[27]

Others were slightly more modest in their demands. A man named Donald McBain, for example, unabashedly stated he would enlist in the fencibles simply on condition of being made a sergeant and getting a new lease of his farm, while John Stewart, equally typically, offered his services on condition that the duke gave his father and brother full possession of their farms.

There was little or no romance in this bargaining, no trace of that once-vaunted clan loyalty, and it was all summed up by Robert Macpherson, the minister of Aberarder, in Inverness-shire, who tartly recorded how recruiting for both Fraser's regiment and for the Duke of Gordon's Northern Fencibles in Badenoch was hampered by the fact that:

> The spirit of clanship has absolutely ceased, as to its more important consequences, all over the Highlands, and more especially in this county [Inverness-shire]. The principal heads of families have very much fallen off for these circumstances, and proportionable to that is the decrease of their influence among the common people. These, again, are now happily aiming at emigration, and trust to their own industry and protection of the law more than to the precarious support formerly afforded them by their demagogues or heads of tribes ... the few remaining sparks of clanship had by that time been kindled into a flame, which with their sympathy for Clunie's misfortunes made them enlist with their chieftain in preference to all mankind. But the fit did not last long.[28]

Thanks to that brief 'fit', Duncan MacPherson of Cluny (the son of the Jacobite who defected from Loudoun's 64th in 1745) found enough recruits from amongst his erstwhile clansmen to win him a major's commission in the 71st and, from there, promotion into the Scots Guards, but it was harder work for those officers lacking similar connections. Significantly the Reverend MacPherson also commented that: 'no person appeared in the country for Captain [Hamilton] Maxwell to take upon him the horrid drudgery of drinking whisky and to act the recruiting sergeant among the people.' Fortunately, however, Captain

Maxwell's sister was none other than the new Duchess of Gordon, who would in time prove herself to be an even more formidable recruiter than her mother-in-law. It was she who effectively raised his company for the 71st for him, mustering it at Fochabers and filling it with eighty-nine low-country lads from Elgin, Banffshire and Aberdeenshire, rather than in Badenoch. Consequently its muster roll includes few 'real' Highlanders but was filled instead with farm labourers and tradesmen, and even a stray bricklayer from Lincolnshire! Nevertheless, all of them would wear the kilt when they marched south to Glasgow.[29]

Similarly, when Lord MacLeod raised his 73rd Regiment in 1777, he and his officers eventually found a fairly respectable 840 genuine Highland recruits for it in the far north, where the spirit of clanship was presumably not yet completely extinguished. However even Stewart of Garth admits that they still had to augment them with a further 236 Lowland Scots and 34 English and Irish recruits in order to bring the battalion fully up to strength. It was pretty much the same story with the other regiments. Only half of Colonel John Campbell of Barbreck's 74th Highlanders were raised in Argyllshire: the remainder had to be found in the rather less picturesque streets and ale-houses of Glasgow or elsewhere in the Lowlands. John MacDonnell of Lochgarry's 76th, as might have seemed right and proper, had seven Highland companies, totalling about 750 men, who had been mainly recruited for him with considerable difficulty by Lord MacDonald away out in the Western Isles. However, two other companies came from Lowland Scotland – which in practice usually meant Edinburgh or Glasgow – and Captain Bruce recruited almost his entire company in Ireland! In spite of the pretensions of their commanders to imitate the clan chieftains of old, the inevitable result was at best a steady, and in some cases a quite dramatic, erosion of the original Highland 'distinction' in these regiments.

Even the Black Watch, who were by now very pointedly calling themselves 'the *old* Highland regiment', were not immune from this process. Captain John Peebles's diary provides what is probably the best and most vivid picture of life in the regiment during the eighteenth century, but while the reader is left in absolutely no doubt that Peebles belonged to a Scottish regiment, its Highland character seems rather more elusive. In fairness, Peebles was an Ayrshire man who originally joined Montgomerie's 77th and the force of circumstances saw the regiment serve through most of the American War in trousers rather than kilts, but they were clearly now soldiers not clansmen. When they were inspected in 1768 all of their basket-hilted broadswords, once described during the Rising as the Highlanders' 'darling weapon' were noted to be in storage, and a subsequent inspection report in 1775 produced the interesting explanation that: 'Lieutenant Colonel [Thomas] Stirling says that the Highlanders on several occasions declined using broadswords in America, that they all prefer bayonets, and that swords for Battalion men, though part of their dress and establishment, are incumbrances.'[30] There was justification enough in that particular complaint, for as regular British soldiers their primary weapon was the .75-calibre Land Pattern musket: the famous 'Brown Bess'. Even if the circumstances demanded that instead of shooting at the king's enemies, they should charge straight at them – a tactic now employed by most British soldiers in place of the old platoon-firing, and one which proved extraordinarily effective against the American rebels – then seventeen inches of wickedly sharp bayonet slotted onto the end of the musket was going to be every bit as intimidating as a broadsword.[31] A bayonet was also going to be a whole lot lighter and handier. Mindful no doubt of the truth of the old joke that a soldier is first and foremost something to hang things on, Stirling's men clearly no longer regarded their broadswords as the status symbol that once proved so enticing to Garth's elegant Highland gentlemen. Instead, they saw them as just one more bit of useless weight they would rather not hang on their overloaded shoulders if they could help it.

Perhaps the truth of the matter was that the rank and file were no longer Highland gentlemen by the strict definition of the term. The gentlemen were now the officers and the ranks were filled with commoners: the 'scrubs' who were unfairly blamed for the Black Watch mutiny. To Garth and the other traditionalists this was a sad alteration from the days of the old Highland Watch when the 'privilege of bearing arms' was one of the major perks of the job, but at least the 42nd and the other Highland Regiments still officially wore the kilt. In the years that followed there would sometimes be occasions when Highlanders protested at having to wear breeches or trousers – though less frequently than is sometimes claimed – but never did any of the Lowland recruits, even those from Ayrshire, protest at being ordered to wear a kilt.

Already, in Scotland itself as elsewhere, 'Scotchmen and Highlanders were regarded as synonymous words' and wearing Highland dress was consequently coming to be seen as the distinctive mark of a Scotsman. Thus, as a still greater expansion of the British Army dawned in the last decade of the eighteenth century, the Highland regiments, whether they were recruited in Eriskay or Edinburgh, truly came into their own.

~ 2 ~

The Black Watch and Mr Pitt's Army

According to what is now a well-established regimental legend, it was almost exactly half a century after its original baptism of fire at Fontenoy before the Black Watch earned its famous red hackle, in what was an otherwise eminently forgettable little action just outside the Dutch village of Geldermalsen in January 1795.

Inevitably, Britain was once again at war with France at the time, and after what had been quite a promising start, was also very much on the losing side of that war. The bright hopes of early victory when the Allied armies invaded France in early 1793 soon faded as the grand advance ground to an ignominious halt against the French barrier fortresses and then stalled completely in a welter of indecision and mutual distrust. Soon the rag-tag French Revolutionary armies seized the initiative once more and pushed north through Flanders and into Holland. Both the Prussians and the Austrians, who had hitherto provided the bulk of the coalition forces, faded from the picture and by December 1794 the British Army and its few remaining allies were reduced to holding a rather tenuous position stretching along a front of nearly ninety miles behind the River Waal. Ordinarily the broad river should have opposed a formidable barrier to any further advance by the French, but instead that particular winter turned out to be one of the coldest of the century and when the rivers froze the French abandoned convention and renewed the offensive just as soon as the mud and ice were hard enough to bear the weight of their guns.

On 27 December a French detachment boldly pushed across the Waal itself by way of the fortified, but slackly defended, island of Bommel; they took another outpost at nearby Tiel without any resistance, and then got as far north as Meteren before some stray Hessian troops stopped them. At that point Major General David Dundas was hastily sent to nearby Geldermalsen with ten British battalions and orders to mount an immediate counter-attack. Despite being delayed by the inevitable bad roads this operation duly got underway early on the morning of the 30th and successfully tumbled the French back across the river without too much difficulty. So far so good, but Dundas soon realised he had only won a temporary respite and the French, having called up reinforcements of their own, launched a renewed attack at noon on 4 January. Once again the Dutch incontinently abandoned Bommel and Tiel without fighting; next day, realising that he was now facing a major offensive all on his own, Dundas prudently decided to withdraw.

To give all his transport and heavy guns time to get clear, one of his infantry brigades, comprising the 33rd, 42nd and 78th Regiments of Foot, was deployed as a rearguard just to the south of Geldermalsen itself. Convention decreed that as the senior battalion, the 33rd (then commanded by none other than a certain Lieutenant Colonel Arthur Wesley) should stand on the right of the line, the Black Watch on the left and the junior 78th Highlanders in the centre, with the light companies of all three battalions deployed well forward in a picket line.

They did not have long to wait. Soon the first French scouts and skirmishers turned up, cautiously feeling their way forward. There should have been no real cause for concern at this point, but all at once things suddenly started to go wrong. The leading regiment of French cavalry wore a uniform very similar to that of the Choiseul Hussars, a unit of French Royalist émigrés serving in the British Army. Predictably, a degree of uncertainty as to their identity meant that they were allowed to come far too close without being challenged, just as had happened in a remarkably similar incident a few weeks before.[32] By then it was far too late to stop them and they charged straight in amongst the outer line of pickets, who promptly bolted for the village. The French, naturally enough, followed hard on the fugitives' heels, cutting them down with some enthusiasm and were only halted when they came up against the thin line of redcoats standing in the snow just below Geldermalsen. A brief, but no doubt exciting, fight then followed in which the cavalrymen were repulsed and a number of them were taken prisoner. In all the haste, confusion and excitement, however, a pair of small cannon, which had been placed well forward of the main battle-line for the express purpose of supporting and covering the pickets, had also been overrun and as the French fell back again, they quite naturally tried to take the captured guns with them. Determined to prevent this, a staff officer named Major John Rose[33] quickly rode up to the Black Watch, who were standing on the left of the brigade, and ordered them to charge at once. This was something the Highlanders understood, and, led by Major George Dalrymple[34] of the 42nd, the assault was immediately delivered in fine style. The cavalrymen, who were still in some confusion, promptly bolted rather than wait for the Highlanders' bayonets, thus leaving the errant guns to be recovered and quickly manhandled back to the village. Effectively that marked the end of the battle, for by the time the French infantry eventually arrived the winter light was fading and as neither side was too keen on fighting in the dark for no real purpose, Dundas was able to disengage and pull back without further molestation.

It had certainly been a very neat little action – when the regiment returned to England some months later it was rumoured within the ranks that the 42nd was to get some kind of distinctive badge for its gallant conduct in retaking the guns. This proved to be the case when they were paraded at Royston in Hertfordshire, on 4 June 1795, to fire the customary three volleys in honour of the King's birthday: afterwards, the men were surprised and delighted when a large box was brought onto the field and a red hackle distributed to each soldier in commemoration of the action.

Such at any rate is the substance of the legend, and January 5, the anniversary of that fight at Geldermalsen, is still gloriously celebrated by the regiment as 'Red Hackle Day'. Nevertheless, there is something rather curious about the whole business, for there is in fact no evidence at all that those who were actually involved in the affair ever regarded it as having been anything special, far less a feat deserving of such signal notice. It was merely just one very minor incident at the commencement of an inglorious retreat that would end with the frozen and half-starved remnants of the army being evacuated through Bremen some months later. That brief little skirmish in the snow, along with the handful of other stumbling, mismanaged fights that punctuated the wintry anabasis, were certainly not to be compared with some of the other service the Black Watch had seen before – such as its bloody debut at the great set-piece battle of Fontenoy in 1745. Or, more notably still, that even greater bloodbath at Ticonderoga in 1758, where it lost a staggering 8 officers, 9 sergeants and 297 men killed, and another 17 officers, 10 sergeants and 306 soldiers wounded, while vainly trying to storm an impregnable line of fortifications manned by the cream of the French army. Outside Geldermalsen by contrast the regiment had lost just one man killed and eight others wounded. Even then the chances are that some or all of them went down when the French cavalry first collided with the battle-line, or even afterwards when their infantry came up in the closing stages of the battle, rather than in that dramatic but almost certainly bloodless rush for the guns.

Indeed, and entirely damningly, David Stewart of Garth, who was himself serving as a lieutenant in the regiment at the time, barely skims over the action in his affectionate history of the Highland regiments. In contrast to the detailed anecdotes provided about similar fights, he contented himself with offhandedly remarking that:

> ...they [the French] attacked General Dundas at Gildermalsen, but were received with great firmness, and repulsed with the loss of 200 men. The British lost 3 privates killed, and 1 general officer (Sir Robert Lawrie) 2 captains, 1 subaltern, and 54 privates, wounded; the loss of the 42nd being 1 private killed, and Lieutenant Coll Lamont, and 7 privates wounded.

Nothing in there you see about a gallant charge to take the guns, and certainly nothing at all about the regiment being afterwards granted its famous red hackle or for that matter any other mark of distinction as a reward in recognition of its conduct – an omission that is all the more significant given the eagerness with which Garth hastened to meticulously record the regiment's other triumphs great and small.[35]

Mindful of this curious silence, it has plausibly (if perhaps not entirely convincingly) been suggested by some historians in more recent times that instead the hackle might perhaps have been granted in recognition of the Black Watch's long service in North America.

Once again, however, although this particular theory is in some ways a rather more attractive one than the Geldermalsen story, the facts do not really support this interpretation either. Some units serving in the American War – including Simon Fraser's 71st Highlanders – did apparently adopt red tufts or hackles at the time to mark themselves out as elite regiments, but as far as is known the Black Watch was not one of them. In any case, although the regiment did spend a very considerable part of its early existence in North America, it had been at home for nearly seven years before the hackle was adopted without any fanfare or official announcement – in the middle of a quite different war.

Hackles, in point of fact, were not worn by *any* of the Highland regiments before 1795, the only adornment to the bonnet before that date being the obligatory black cockade above the left ear and a spray of black ostrich feathers, or sometimes worsted ones in imitation. At some time during that year, however – and traditionally the annual issue of new clothing was worn for the first time on the King's birthday parade – all of the Highland regiments adopted cut feather hackles that were colour-coded to distinguish between the different companies and specialists within the battalion: plain white hackles for grenadiers, green hackles for light infantrymen, blue for pipers, yellow for drummers and white over red hackles for everybody else. Exactly the same system was already being used by ordinary regiments of the line, except that it was more commonly a coloured woollen tuft that was placed on the hat, rather than feathers. It was not therefore the adoption of the hackle itself at this particular moment in its history that was unique to the Black Watch, but the fact that the regiment chose to flout established convention by opting to wear a distinctive plain red one for all ranks. There is no reason whatsoever to doubt that the new hackles were indeed served out to the men during that particular birthday parade, but while Geldermalsen might have provided the excuse, the choice of red ones was made not to commemorate an obscure little skirmish but rather to reaffirm the Watch's status as the 'Old Highland Regiment', amidst a veritable explosion of newer battalions.

Just as in the last war the very first new regiment to be raised was a Highland one: Francis Humberston Mackenzie's 78th (Ross-shire Buffs), and it was followed within a matter of months by Allan Cameron of Erracht's 79th Highlanders. Both battalions served alongside the

Black Watch in Flanders and the Ross-shire Buffs actually fought shoulder to shoulder with them at Geldermalsen, although obviously not with sufficient distinction to share that red hackle. As it happens, both they and the Camerons had each adopted distinctive tartans when they were first raised. The Ross-shire Buffs took the Army's usual dark blue and green sett, (officially referred to as 42nd) with the addition of red and white overstripes; while the Camerons – or Cameronian Highlanders as they were then erroneously designated in official circles – had a complicated and quite unique sett, supposedly devised by the colonel's mother.

At first sight the embracing of idiosyncratic regimental tartans by both of the new regiments would appear to be unexceptionable and indeed entirely sensible. Indeed, for many years previously, the original blue and green army tartan worn by the 42nd itself, now variously known as the Government sett or simply as Black Watch tartan, had itself featured a red overstripe. Since this red line appeared on both an illustration of a grenadier painted for the Duke of Cumberland by David Morier in 1748 and on a later one of another grenadier by Charles Hamilton Smith in 1812, it was once thought by uniform historians to be a distinction reserved for the elite grenadier company. Instead, however, the pattern books kept by William Wilson of Bannockburn – the principal supplier of tartans to the early Highland regiments – show that in the early 1800s this particular variant of the army sett with a single red line was simply known as '42nd kilt pattern', clearly indicating that it was being worn by the rank and file of the whole regiment.

Our friend Stewart of Garth recalled having been told when he joined the regiment in 1792 that this red line or overstripe was introduced when Lord John Murray became the regiment's colonel back in 1745 –which is why the same tartan is now also called Murray of Atholl. There seems no reason to doubt Murray's involvement in its adoption, and the timing is doubly significant, for 1745 was also the year in which the second Highland regiment – Loudoun's short-lived 64th – was raised. It was also of course the year when the last Jacobite Rising began and part of the Government's response to that Rising, as we have seen in the previous chapter, was the raising of a whole host of Highland independent companies, and all of *them* were eventually dressed in short red jackets and the army's blue and green tartan. Thus the start of Murray's colonelcy coincided with the appearance of two new Highland units, both dressed very similarly to his own, albeit Loudoun's had white facings and the independent companies yellow ones. They may well have been altogether too similar in appearance, for it is very hard to avoid the suspicion that Murray added the red overstripe to the original rather plain tartan in order to distinguish his 'Old Highland Regiment' from these new levies.

Not just two rivals, but a whole host of new Highland regiments were now being raised. Rather than accept the plain and quite unassuming army sett, many of them were also adopting quite distinctive tartans with a bewildering variety of single and multi-coloured overstripes. Some regiments, following the Camerons' lead, scorned the army tartan entirely and instead decided to adopt unique setts of their own, such as the red Fraser tartan, worn, inevitably, by the Fraser Fencibles, the Baillie tartan of the Loyal Inverness Fencibles and the Mackay tartan of the Reay Fencibles. The majority, however, went for variations on the old theme – the Duke of Gordon's Northern Fencibles and the 100th/92nd Gordon Highlanders that followed them, as well as Sir John Sinclair's Rothesay and Caithness Fencibles all adopted the army tartan with the addition of a single yellow stripe, while the Breadalbane Fencibles wore the same but with a double yellow stripe. Out in India, when the heat allowed, the 71st Highlanders also occasionally wore what is now called the Mackenzie sett, which was the old army tartan, but this time with red and white stripes (it is still a matter of contention as to whether they or the 78th adopted it first).[36] Worst of all, from the Black Watch's point of view, Sir James Grant of Grant settled upon the army sett with a single red stripe – the '42nd kilt pattern' – for both his Strathspey Fencibles and 97th (Inverness-shire) Regiment, as did the 3rd Battalion of the Breadalbane Fencibles, and the Ross and Cromarty Rangers, and there may well have been others as well, now forgotten.

Amidst all this colourful display Lord John Murray's simple red overstripe was no longer the unique distinction he had once intended it to be and although it would continue to be worn by the Black Watch at least until the end of the war, it was clear that something else, besides the dark blue facings of a royal regiment, was needed to set the 'Old Highland Regiment' apart from all the upstart newcomers. The Geldermalsen affair, far from meriting any particular commemoration, merely provided a very timely and convenient excuse for the adoption of that all-important mark of distinction that could not be usurped by others this time – the red hackle. As such it proved an immediate success and after the war a Horse Guards circular, dated 20 August 1822, would very firmly remind the commanding officers of Highland regiments that: 'The red vulture feather prescribed by the recent regulations for Highland regiments is intended to be used exclusively by the Forty-Second Regiment: other Highland corps will be allowed to continue to wear the same description of feather that may have been hitherto in use.'

To properly understand why this unique regimental distinction suddenly became so important, and to learn something of the background to the raising of a quite unprecedented number of new Highland battalions at this time, it is necessary to digress a little and to go back to the early months of the war, when the whole British Army suddenly expanded at breakneck speed – on a scale that would not be matched again until the late summer of 1914: the beginning of the 'War to End all Wars' and the creation of the 'Kitchener Armies'.

To all appearances, in February 1793 Revolutionary France had committed suicide. Four years earlier the storming of the Bastille and the proclamation of the Republic supposedly signalled the beginning of a new and exciting era of political reform, popular democracy and prosperity in France. Alas it proved to be altogether rather too exciting, and as with all-too-many revolutionary movements, the *Liberté, Egalité et Fraternité* that it promised soon gave way to an increasingly bloody and destructive spiral of violence and instability. Bankrupt after four years of worsening political turmoil, beset by economic collapse and famine both at home and abroad, threatened both by factional infighting played out in the streets of Paris and pro-Royalist revolts in the provinces, and already at war with Austria, Prussia and Spain as well as with a number of smaller states, France's beleaguered Government executed King Louis and declared war on all the remaining powers of Europe on 1 February 1793. This seemingly insane declaration of war might not have been altogether unexpected or even unwelcome to His Britannic Majesty's Government, whose initial benign indifference to the events of 1789 had long since cooled into suspicion and scarcely veiled hostility. Nevertheless, although the Government may not have been particularly surprised to find itself at war at that moment, it had done little or nothing to prepare for one and the army in particular was far from ready for the scale of the conflict that now lay ahead.

In spite of this, it would be a mistake to casually accept the view so trenchantly advanced by the noted historian, Sir John Fortescue, that in 1793 the army was in a parlous state of decay and suffering from near-criminal neglect. Arguably, if anything the reverse was probably the case. The army had certainly come home from the American War ten years earlier in a near-shattered condition, but contrary to popular legend, while it was over there it had actually acquitted itself surprisingly well against the rebellious colonists on the battlefield. Far from blundering around helplessly while eagle-eyed American riflemen fired on them from the bushes with impunity, both officers and men proved to be tough and adaptable, and attained a high degree of professional skill. This stood them in great stead when the French intervened on the side of the colonists and the scope of the war widened to encompass the West Indies. Unfortunately, tactical success on the battlefield, no matter how frequently or how handsomely won, had rarely bought corresponding political gains. Quite remarkably, George Washington contrived to lose virtually every battle he ever fought, but the surrender of Lord Cornwallis to a Franco-American army at Yorktown in 1781 at last compelled the British Government to acknowledge that a rebellion on the far side of an ocean could not be subjugated by military force alone. Peace was signed in 1783, American independence was grudgingly acknowledged and, as usual, the size of the army was cut back savagely to reduce the burden on a nearly bankrupt exchequer.

Other than three Highland regiments, which just happened to be serving in India at the time, every one of the many battalions raised in Scotland, England, Ireland and in North America itself since the outbreak of the war in 1775 was 'reduced' and its officers retired on to half-pay. Even those older units which did escape reduction were all hopelessly under-strength and badly in need of rest and rebuilding. And that was exactly what they got. As it happens, it did require nearly a whole decade for the army to fully recover from the effects of the American War, but by the end of that period the annual inspection reports submitted to headquarters were all painting a consistent picture of efficient, properly trained and well-led units. Even reading between the (sometimes creatively written) lines it is apparent that far from being in a sorry state of decay the army's regiments were indeed officially reckoned to be 'fit for service'.

Unfortunately, thanks to an ever parsimonious Treasury, that comforting official assessment was only true up to a point and was more than a touch misleading: although there is no doubt that the regiments were again perfectly formed, they were also rather too small – and too few in number.

Anticipating Kaiser Bill's unfortunate remark of just over a century later, the British Army of 1793, whatever its true condition, was indeed a 'contemptible little army', which, like its later counterpart, was mainly organised for colonial defence rather than for fighting a major European war. Apart from the cavalry and the Footguards, (and of course the Royal Artillery, who were always administered and accounted separately) the disposable strength of the fifty-thousand-strong army at the outbreak of war theoretically amounted to just seventy-seven regiments of foot, of which the 1st (Royal) Regiment boasted two battalions and the 60th (Royal Americans) four, to make a total of eighty-one battalions of the line. On paper that might appear to be more than adequate for most contingencies, but the problem facing the British Government in February 1793 was that almost none of those battalions were immediately available for operational service. All in all, a total of nineteen battalions were then serving out in the West Indies; twenty-five more were scattered between fixed garrisons in Ireland, Gibraltar, Nova Scotia and the Canadas, and a further nine were half a world away in India. That left only twenty-eight infantry battalions stationed in mainland Great Britain and the Channel Islands, and even they, for the most part, could not be released for operations at short notice. Some, obviously enough, were still in the ordinary course of rebuilding and retraining after a turn of duty overseas and were in no condition to be sent anywhere in a hurry. As for the others, until the county militias could be mobilised and deployed, most were going to be needed for the ordinary defence of the realm: for the guarding of fortresses, dockyards and other key points, and inevitably as and when necessary for maintaining public order in a country lacking a civil police force.

When political imperatives – and an unexpected French offensive against the Channel ports – forced the Government to respond within days of the outbreak of hostilities by sending a small expeditionary force to Flanders, just three ad hoc battalions of Footguards were initially assigned to the task. This was not because they were the very best Britain had to offer – in fact they were all shockingly drunk when they embarked – but simply because they were the *only* troops that could be released there and then. More battalions trickled after them as soon as they could be brought up to strength by drafting raw recruits from the new independent companies, but almost at once there were other equally urgent commitments arising in the West Indies and in the Mediterranean and soon there was a rising clamour on every side for men – not just men, but whole battalions.

Even at the very outset of the war, thousands of new recruits were desperately required just to fill out the ranks of the existing regiments, let alone to increase the operational size of the army. In a typical example, when 1/1st (Royal) Regiment, otherwise known as the First Battalion of the Royal Scots, embarked from Cork for a routine spell of garrison duty on Jamaica in 1790 it was fully recruited up to its authorised peacetime establishment of 370 rank and file. Despite the relatively high turnover in personnel usually associated with a Caribbean posting, it was still mustering a very creditable 355 men on 1 January 1794: only fifteen men short of its original total, although a worryingly high number of them were noted to be in hospital.[37] Meanwhile, war had broken out with France, and as an immediate result the establishment of all marching regiments of foot was officially raised from 370 to 850 rank and file. Suddenly, literally at the stroke of a bureaucratic pen, this particular battalion was deemed to be under-strength by some five hundred men – a deficiency that was impossible to remedy until it could eventually be brought home again in 1797. Nor was this problem confined to those units serving overseas – even regiments that were actually stationed in the British Isles at the outbreak of war found it difficult to fill their depleted ranks in the face of unprecedentedly fierce competition, as the biggest and most frantic recruiting boom of the eighteenth century got underway.

Unsurprisingly the scale of the army's expansion inevitably resulted in enormous problems. Sheer inexperience, as well as political interference, well meaning or otherwise, meant that for those first three years of the war inefficiency, ineptitude and corruption – although by no means universal – ran virtually unchecked.

In describing the ensuing debacle in the fourth volume of his magisterial *History of the British Army*, published in 1906, Sir John Fortescue was in his element:

> ... the Government could think of no better plan for augmenting the Army than to encourage young men of means to raise men for rank, or in other words to offer them rank in the Army in proportion to the number of recruits that they could produce. This was an old system which hitherto had been confined chiefly to the raising of independent companies, and had therefore led to no higher rank than that of Captain. Even then it had been vicious and had been repeatedly condemned; and it was no good sign that in 1793 a Lieutenant had advertised in the London papers, offering two thousand guineas to anyone who could raise him one hundred recruits in six weeks, and get them passed at Chatham. But it was now extended to the raising of a multitude of battalions which, for the most part, were no sooner formed than they were disbanded, and drafted into other corps ... There was instantly a rush to obtain letters of service; and commissions became a drug in the market. It was said that over one hundred commissions were signed in a single day, while the Gazette could not keep pace with the incessant promotions. The Army-brokers, who in the days of purchase negotiated for officers the sale of commissions, exchanges and the like, carried on openly a most scandalous traffic. "In a few weeks," to use the indignant language of an officer of the Guards, "they would dance any beardless youth, who would come up to their price, from one newly raised corps to another, and for a greater douceur, by an exchange into an old regiment would procure him a permanent situation in the standing Army." The evils that flowed from this system were incredible. Officers who had been driven to sell out of the Army by their debts or their misconduct were able after a lucky turn at play to purchase reinstatement for themselves with the rank of Lieutenant-Colonel. Undesirable characters, such as keepers of gambling houses, contrived to buy for their sons the command of regiments; and mere children were exalted in the course of a few weeks to the dignity of field officers. One proud parent, indeed, requested leave of absence for one of these infant Lieutenant-Colonels on the ground that he was not yet fit to be taken from school. It must be noted, too, that, thanks to

the Army-brokers, these evils were not confined to the new regiments, but were spread, by means of exchange, all over the Army; and, since the great majority of the regiments were abroad on active service, the old officers, who were daily facing danger and death, suddenly found themselves inferior in rank to men undistinguished by birth or intellect, and without the smallest pretension to military ability.[38]

It is an eloquent indictment, and therefore an eminently quotable one, which still unduly influences more modern histories. However, although justified up to a point, it also owes far more to hyperbole than dry facts – there were *very* few infant officers, for instance – and in any case it takes no account of the genuine difficulties involved in such a massive expansion of the army at such short notice. It is also very significant that Sir John's critique was written sometime before 1906, for less than a decade later he would have found a worthy comparison in the raising of Kitchener's 'New Armies' in 1914 and 1915: for that mighty effort threw up exactly the same problems in organising, equipping, training – and competently officering – all those additional battalions. It would also be very difficult for him or anyone else to assert that the authorities in 1914 coped with those problems with any markedly better success than their predecessors in 1794.

When viewed objectively, the immediate steps taken by the War Office in 1793 to address the urgent demand for men were actually sensible enough. In recognition of the likely scale of the problem, a whole clutch of independent companies were authorised during the first six months of the war, with no other purpose in mind than to be a vehicle for recruiting. Far from being intended for any kind of actual service, once each company was completed it was to be immediately drafted into the ranks of those veteran battalions deemed to be in most urgent need of men. It was an experiment that had been tried with some mixed success in previous conflicts and more recently during the so-called 'Spanish re-armament' a couple of years before. As Fortescue rightly noted, the quality of the recruits thus produced had generally left something to be desired since the officers had no incentive to do more than deliver the requisite number of bodies, whatever their condition. On the other hand, the speed with which they had been gathered in had dramatically out-performed more conventional regimental recruiting parties, which is why there was no real alternative to employing what was in reality a tried and tested procedure.

Nevertheless, although these independent companies might ease some of the immediate recruiting problems, they could not increase the operational size of the army. No matter how much contemporary critics such as Henry Bunbury or later historians such as Sir John Fortescue might deplore the fact, it was inevitable that the massive expansion of the army needed to meet its burgeoning overseas commitments could only be accomplished by creating entirely new battalions – which were in turn led for the most part by new officers, who were learning the job as they went along. Neither the battalions nor the trained officers to lead them could be conjured out of thin air – and here the parallels with 1914 are compelling. The task presently before the government, led by William Pitt the Younger and managed by Henry Dundas, was not merely to bring the existing contemptibly small army onto a proper war footing, but in effect was also to anticipate Field Marshal Kitchener a hundred years later by recruiting a completely new army to meet the demands of a conflict that was rapidly spiralling out of control. To their unacknowledged credit, they managed to stave off doing so for those vital first six months, while men were sought for the 'old' regiments, partly through their own efforts and largely by drafting from the new independent companies. However, by August the pressure was too great to hold back any longer and the raising of the new regiments began.

Over the course of the next three years a total of more than eighty additional battalions and at least ninety-two independent companies (the exact number is uncertain) would be raised or at least authorised for the regular army. In reality the equivalent of far more would actually be recruited, drafted and then recruited afresh – often more than once.

In itself, this massive and continuing increase in manpower – which was achieved in the face of direct competition with an equally voracious Royal Navy – was impressive enough, but there was more. With most of the new regular battalions being required for service overseas as soon as their ranks were filled, let alone trained or even properly equipped, the Government also authorised the raising of an intitial seven, and then ultimately sixty, fencible battalions. Originally formed in Scotland as a substitute for the militia, fencibles were similar to regulars, but differed from them in one crucial respect. While ordinary regiments of the line could be sent to serve anywhere in the world, fencibles, like the original Territorial Army of 1908, were intended from the outset to be home defence units only. In fact those first seven regiments, as we shall discover, were limited to service inside Scotland itself, until and unless the French actually landed on British soil. Gradually, as more fencible units were raised, not only in Scotland but eventually in England and Ireland as well, the terms of service for each succeeding levy were progressively extended until some of the very last battalions to be authorised could, if required, be sent anywhere in Europe. Many fencibles would therefore play a crucial role in defeating the Irish Rebellion of 1798, where they far exceeded the number of regulars involved, and others later found themselves doing garrison duty in Portugal and in the Mediterranean. One Irish fencible unit even ended up in Egypt, which was definitely stretching things a little.

The problems for the army and the government did not end, or even begin, with finding sufficient men to fill the ranks of these new regiments, whether regulars or fencibles – for a whole host of additional officers were also required to lead them. On paper and without taking into account the ordinary wastage expected of any organisation, the new infantry battalions created between the summers of 1793 and 1795 alone required over four thousand additional officers at every level from ensign up to colonel. This was quite apart from those new entrants wanted to maintain and expand the existing battalions, and those needed for the new independent companies (albeit many transferred with their recruits into the battalions they were intended to feed), and all of those wanted for the cavalry, the artillery and engineers, the fencibles – and, of course, the navy and the marines, who were also undergoing a similar expansion.

Many, it was piously expected, might be drawn from the ranks of the half-pay, or promoted from 'old' corps. There was certainly no difficulty in finding the latter (who of course immediately needed to be replaced in their turn), but the Government invariably overestimated the number of 'dug-outs' willing to return to the army some ten years or more after their old regiments had been disbanded – particularly as those men who were genuinely willing (and able) to serve, and had any ability or aptitude for the job, had already exchanged back onto full pay long ago. In short it was patently impossible for the army to find all the officers it needed from within the existing regiments. Faced with exactly the same problem in 1914, the War Office was reduced to commissioning new officers using no better criterion than their having attended a public school! It is little wonder then that some of this new intake, both in 1794 and in 1914, would turn out to be unsuitable – sometimes spectacularly so –particularly if drawn directly from civilian life and promoted far too rapidly.

Furthermore, the process of raising for rank so heartily condemned by Fortescue was by no means the innovation that he claimed or confined to independent companies. As we have already seen, the earlier Highland regiments, and indeed all new regiments added to the Army List, were created by this means, which was itself inextricably linked to the prevailing purchase system. At first sight the notion that officers could buy promotion all the way up to command of their very own regiment seems iniquitous to modern eyes and, as a system, purchase has undoubtedly been more frequently criticised than understood. However, in the context of its time it actually worked surprisingly well and was in reality no different from buying into any other profession of the time, such as a medical or legal practice. Arguably, therefore, it produced a rather more cosmopolitan, culturally diverse, and even (on the whole) a far more able group of officers than the rather more ossified 'officer class', which was drawn almost entirely from the landed gentry that dominated the late Victorian army. Moreover a surprisingly high proportion of promotions in this period were gained not through purchase but by seniority, and often through sheer merit as well. While the rich (i.e. the nobility and landed gentry) were obviously best placed to take advantage of the system, long-term business or personal loans were often a rather more significant factor than inherited wealth in producing the necessary funds and it is no coincidence that some of the more prominent army agencies, such as Cox and Greenwood, actually evolved into banks.[39] Raising for rank was simply a means of paying for promotion in kind rather than with hard cash, whether borrowed or otherwise.

The basic principle behind it was straightforward enough. A would-be commanding officer would first obtain letters of service from the Crown, which were in effect a contract authorising him to raise an independent company or even a whole regiment. He in turn then nominated his officers who were actually to go out and do the recruiting for him. The size of the quotas attached to each rank could vary: typically, for a regiment a lieutenant colonel was personally expected to find seventy-five recruits for his own company, while his second-in-command, the major, had to find forty-five men. Each of the battalion's seven captains had to recruit thirty men apiece for their companies, while their lieutenants had to find another twenty and the ensigns (the lowest commissioned rank in each company) each needed to find ten more in order to obtain their commissions. In principle, it is hard in some ways to see why the practice should have been considered so objectionable: if a would-be officer could not persuade men to enlist under his own banner, he was hardly likely to inspire them or anyone else to follow him in battle.

In practice, of course, it rarely proved to be quite so straightforward, especially when they were competing with a host of other recruiting officers, and were under severe pressure to find their men within a very limited time. The official cash bounty held out as an inducement to enlistment was routinely augmented, sometimes from the colonel's own pocket, or from his captains' pockets if they were keen enough, and sometimes – surprisingly frequently in the early days – by a patriotically minded city corporation or other sponsor. Once again the close parallels between the raising of local units – such as the Aberdeenshire Regiment or the Royal Glasgow Regiment, for example – in 1794 and the 'city' battalions of 1914 are unmistakeable. If the timing was right, this additional bounty money might prove decisive, but unless it was accompanied by civic enthusiasm, and a positive determination to create a 'local' regiment, simply topping up the bounty all too often led to the relatively limited pool of potential heroes holding out for the highest bidders amongst the recruiters – sometimes quite literally.

It was reported for example in the *Morning Chronicle* of 29 April 1794 that in Edinburgh's Grassmarket, 'A stout young countryman, being determined to enlist, collected the recruiting parties together, and fairly set himself up for public auction, but he would not admit of any offer less than a guinea. The bidders were many; and he was at last knocked down at twenty guineas.'

Inevitably then, many aspiring officers, lacking the enthusiastic assistance of the provost or mayor and corporation, turned to crimps: this universally despised method of finding recruits was in fact illegal and simply amounted to their avoiding the drudgery of recruiting by buying the required number of men from a middleman. Moreover, as the compatriots of that 'stout young countryman' were generally well able to fend for themselves when it came to enlistment, those men being offered by the crimps were pretty much the left-over rubbish that no experienced recruiting sergeant would touch. Even without the involvement of crimps the system of raising for rank was potentially wide open to such abuses and not surprisingly complaints abounded about the poor quality of the men recruited in this way. Major General Banastre Tarleton, once a rather too-dashing hero of the American War – and widely considered quite unfit to command a quarter guard – wittily remarked in Parliament that the army's ranks were being filled with 'infancy and dotage', while one newly raised Irish regiment was equally damningly described by its local MP as being 'filled up with decrepit men from seventy to eighty years, and of boys little more than twelve.' These claims, enthusiastically recounted by Fortescue, were no doubt something of an exaggeration, but nevertheless the apparent prevalence of old men and young boys amongst the new levies was a very common theme of complaint both at home and abroad.

Ordinarily the army in fact had very firm views about the sort of men it wanted – and more importantly those it didn't want. For obvious reasons it preferred young men, and in fact all but seven of those raised by the Duchess of Gordon for Captain Maxwell's company at the outset of the American War were under thirty years of age, with the majority falling into the comparatively narrow sixteen–twenty age band. Equally predictably, sturdy countrymen were also preferred and recruiting parties working country markets and hiring fairs were regularly instructed only to take such men 'as were born in the Neighbourhood of the place where they are Inlisted in & of whom you can get and give a good account.'[40] This was perhaps being a little too optimistic considering the circumstances, but the ranks were certainly not being filled with the sweepings of the jails, or with men who had been given the stark choice of enlistment or the gallows, as popular legend would have it. Occasionally in wartime, as we shall see, some less-than-desirable characters were indeed swept up by various 'impressment' or 'comprehending' Acts, designed by the fertile genius of politicians to force the idle poor into the army. But even when they worked, that was a very different matter from simply decanting the prison population into the ranks. Men running away from pregnant girlfriends were one thing, but fugitives from the law, whether in the form of condemned criminals or even runaway apprentices, were quite another as far as the army itself was concerned, and recruiters were routinely enjoined to avoid taking on 'Strollers, Vagabonds, Tinkers, Chimney Sweepers, Colliers or Saylors.'[41] Unsurprisingly, however, the sheer demand for men meant that these standards were lowered, if not actually abandoned, in wartime – not just because the recruiters were necessarily less choosy, but simply because at peak periods rural recruiting had to give way to a much more cost-effective concentration of effort on large towns. This in turn inescapably resulted in an influx of the urban poor and desperate: the sickly and malnourished products of the slums, the old men and young boys who would horrify the officers receiving them in 1794 and 1914 alike.

Highland regiments on the other hand were still widely considered, with good reason, to be something apart. Although a certain amount of recruiting for them always took place in Edinburgh and Glasgow, it was normally by way of 'topping up' the numbers after the majority of the men had already been enlisted in rural areas. Leaving aside for the moment any notion of them being romantically characterised as a martial race, the sturdy countrymen joining Highland regiments were often perceived as being, at the very least, equal to the physical (and moral) standards once expected of all pre-war recruits – a perception helpfully reinforced by the fact that the very first regiments to be raised from the pick of the available recruits at the outset of both the American War and the present French War were Highland ones. What was more, and increasingly importantly, not only was it still believed that their martial qualities included an absolute devotion to their leaders– at the same time, it was fondly supposed that the natural sense of loyalty and political innocence that had once blindly led them into Jacobitism, also meant that they were immune (or at least far less susceptible) to the democratic creed of *Jacobinism* now supposedly infecting the urban mobs.

Mistaken and even risible though some of these notions may have been, they provided yet more encouragement, were any needed, for the sanctioning of one Highland battalion after another. The great Highland Proprietors – as the former clan chieftains were now rather genteelly starting to call themselves – had once again seen an opportunity to serve both their king and their own interests, and seized it with both hands. Thus the unprecedented recruiting boom of the mid-1790s inevitably led to the creation of a whole host of new Highland battalions, and even some quasi-Highland ones such as Andrew Hay's Aberdeenshire Regiment and Hugh Montgomerie's Royal Glasgow Regiment. By the summer of 1795 there were no fewer than fifteen new regular Highland regiments in the Army List, either complete or in the process of being recruited, with a similar number of Highland fencible battalions – all of them wearing kilts or trews, or at least some semblance of Highland dress. Little wonder then that the Black Watch should feel the need to adopt that red hackle to distinguish themselves from the upstart newcomers.

As it happens a reckoning was coming and not all of the brave new regiments would last the year out. At least three of them would be drafted as reinforcements into the ranks of the 42nd, but before that happened, however, the recruitment of those regiments would re-open old feuds in the Highlands and strain ancient loyalties as never before.

~ 3 ~

The Highland War Begins: The Cameron Highlanders

When Sir John Fortescue so stridently denounced the flock of irresponsible and disreputable adventurers who seemingly rose quite effortlessly to the command of regiments in the early days of the French War, one of those he certainly had in mind, and indeed specifically mentioned, was a Highland gentleman named Allan Cameron of Erracht, who 'after much importunity' was rather grudgingly permitted to try his hand at raising a regiment, which would eventually become famous as the 'Cameron Highlanders'.

Just a month after the outbreak of war with France, the very first of the new battalions to be authorised, on 7 March 1793, was the 78th (Highland) Regiment, raised and led with the rank of lieutenant colonel commandant, by the entirely respectable Francis Humberston Mackenzie of Seaforth. Erracht, who followed in his footsteps six months later by recruiting the 79th Highlanders, was altogether a very different character, and the term 'adventurer' is truly the only word that can adequately describe him. Born in 1750 into a prominent Lochaber family, he found it necessary to flee abroad at the age of twenty-two, after killing a kinsman in a duel – first to Jamaica and then on to South Carolina. There he worked for a time for the Southern Indian Department, charged with smoothing relations between the indigenous tribes and the ever-encroaching white settlers. Whether he regarded this as anything more than a sinecure is unknown, but when the American Revolution began he promptly accepted a lieutenant's commission in a proposed Loyalist volunteer regiment. The grandly titled Queen's Royal Regiment of Rangers[42] was optimistically intended to be raised not in South Carolina but from amongst the settlers of the north-west, in the semi-wilderness area up around Detroit. Unfortunately, long before Erracht and his would-be commanding officer, John Connolly, got there, they were arrested by suspicious Patriots and flung into a Philadelphia jail. Not until January 1778 was Erracht released, and by that time both of his ankles had been badly shattered after falling from a high roof in a failed escape attempt. Without having heard a shot fired in anger he therefore sailed to England for 'the Advantage of Surgical Advice' with nothing to show for his very real sufferings but the empty title of lieutenant and a pension of just £100 a year.

Nothing daunted, once in London he immediately set about wooing and marrying Ann Phillips, the thirteen-year-old daughter of a wealthy plantation owner, who was very conveniently away in Jamaica at the time! Once an understandably upset Mr Phillips had been placated by the arrival of the first of his grandchildren, Erracht's not-inconsiderable financial problems were taken care of and he set about obtaining a promotion commensurate with his new social position. Strictly speaking he was not really an officer at all. The only commission he held at this time was a provincial one granted by the *soi-disant* royal governor of Virginia, Lord Dunmore, which conferred no permanent rank in the regular army. (Indeed Erracht's name was not to appear in the official Army List in any capacity until 1795!) Nevertheless, in a remarkably worded memorandum dated 27 February 1784, Erracht boldly proceeded to address his claim for something better to the Commissioners for American Loyalist Claims at the Audit Office. Asserting that although he had only been made a lieutenant by Dunmore, he had been promised a captaincy once the regiment was raised, and therefore, he continued with astonishing effrontery,

> ... I should in point of justice have been the eldest Captain in the above Regiment (nay, have had the rank of a Major) in the beginning of the year 1777 ... Having never resigned the Service, but compelled as I was to come to England for the Advantage of Surgical Advice, I am not without a confident hope that my Claims to the half-pay and Rank of a Major in America will be judged no impertinent or unjust request ...[43]

In other words, despite having only been commissioned as a temporary lieutenant in a proposed provincial regiment that never amounted to more than three men – its would-be commanding officer, himself and one other putative subaltern – Erracht was now boldly arguing that if it *had* actually been raised he would have become its most senior captain and consequently was likely to have been promoted to the rank of major by the beginning of 1777. Therefore, in his own mind at least, he was morally entitled to be actually awarded the rank of major and of course a suitable pension to go with it! Just what the honourable commissioners made of this rather audacious fantasy is not entirely clear, but Erracht had evidently convinced himself, for from this point onwards he quite unilaterally began calling himself 'Major' Cameron.

In fact it took two years for his ingenious claim to even be considered amidst the plethora of other more worthy supplications for assistance. In a quite unrelated development, in 1787 four new regiments – two of them Highland ones – were authorised by the government for service in India, and Erracht immediately grasped at the opportunity to justify his self-appointed rank. This time he quickly convinced himself that, given enough money by his wealthy father-in-law, he could easily find enough recruits to earn a senior position in one of the new regiments. Accordingly he wrote with his customary boldness to the East India Company on 24 March 1788, assuring its directors that he was willing 'to raise within two Months, or even Six weeks, if absolutely necessary, from 150 to 200 unexceptional Men,' if only he could have 'the Majority of either the 74th or any of the other three Regiments in question'. He also copied Henry Dundas into the correspondence. Besides being a prominent member of the Government's Board of Control, which oversaw the company, Dundas was a political heavyweight who ran Scotland, and most of the Government besides, for Billy Pitt, so trying to enlist his support at this stage was only prudent. All the same, the would-be major might perhaps have been overdoing it when he grovellingly assured Dundas that:

> Should I fail in all my Applications upon the above subject, I would, even in that Case, reckon myself highly <u>gratified</u> & very <u>thankful</u>, if His <u>Majesty</u> could be moved to be <u>graciously</u> pleased to Honor me in the mean time, with <u>Brevet</u> Rank, in Hopes I may upon some future

Occasion have it in my power to <u>shew</u> my Attachment to <u>His</u> Crown & Government in the <u>line</u> I so much solicit.[44]

Once again, perhaps not altogether surprisingly, nothing came of this bombastic appeal. The major's job in the 74th went instead to Francis Skelly, a genuine veteran of the American War, who had once been the lieutenant of Captain Hamilton Maxwell's company of the old 71st Highlanders. Far from coincidentally, Maxwell himself was now the lieutenant colonel and de facto commanding officer of the new regiment and both of them, seemingly, were there because one was the brother of the Duchess of Gordon and the other, Skelly, was a first cousin to the duke himself. The Gordon family might no longer command the absolute obedience of their own immediate tenants, but the raising of the 89th Highlanders back in 1759 had enabled the Duke of Gordon – and, perhaps just as importantly, the Gordon women – to establish a powerful network of influence both inside the army and, to a lesser extent, within the East India Company as well. In the circumstances Erracht never stood a chance of being appointed and the likelihood is that, despite trying to enlist Dundas' support, he was never even considered as a possible candidate for the 74th.

This would only be the first of a succession of bruising encounters in which his ambitions would time and again fall foul of the Gordons, but in the meantime he continued to cultivate Dundas and anyone else possessed or believed to possess any influence; he even persuaded him to be Godfather to one of his children. Far from being cast down by his failures, Erracht's ambitions grew and having seen the apparent ease with which the 'Indian' regiments were raised, it was a complete regiment of his own that was now spoken of. Offers to raise one in 1790 and again in 1791 were equally unavailing, but at last, with the coming of the French War in 1793, his persistence paid off and he finally obtained his heart's desire in the shape of those long-hoped-for letters of service. After authorising the raising of Seaforth's 78th, the Government had allowed the existing regiments of the line five months in which to find the additional men they needed to bring themselves up to their full wartime establishment. By August, however, with military commitments spiralling out of control, there was no alternative but to give the go-ahead for the new regiments – when that happened Erracht found himself the first in line, and a whole month ahead of the next applicant, Lord Paget.

Oddly enough, although the letters of service for the raising of the 79th (Cameronian) Regiment were grudgingly signed on 17 August 1793 by the Secretary at War, Sir George Yonge, Erracht's own commission, dated ten days earlier, was signed by Henry Dundas himself. In due course Dundas was shortly to become Secretary at War, in addition to his multitude of other roles, both official and unofficial: including home secretary, president of the East India Board of Control, treasurer of the navy (a nominal post) and a number of other less public jobs. At that point in time, however, he did not yet have any official standing in the regular army or its political administration. His authority to sign Erracht's commission is therefore extremely questionable and doubtless explains why his client was given no levy money in advance and was only allowed the temporary rank of major commandant, rather than the more customary commission as lieutenant colonel commandant, which had earlier been conferred on Seaforth – and which would very shortly be granted to Paget for raising *his* regiment. Notwithstanding Dundas's patronage, it is obvious both from these circumstances and from what followed that Yonge and everyone else at the War Office was decidedly leery of the Highland adventurer.

It was just as well, therefore, that Erracht had already secured the all-important financial backing both from his father-in-law and from the City banking house of Hibbert, Fuhr and Hibbert. Raising a regiment in this era was very much a commercial venture and while the government would, in the very fullness of time, settle up an agreed level of costs, it was essential that any would-be commanding officer had immediate access to sufficient ready money to raise and maintain the regiment by himself until such time as it was inspected and accepted onto the official establishment. Conversely, no matter how meritorious or enterprising he might be, an officer who was unable to demonstrate that he enjoyed the requisite financial backing had little or no chance of being granted the opportunity to raise a regiment.

In short Erracht owed his speedy grant of letters of service, ahead of Lord Paget and a score of others, not just to his weighty social and political connections, essential though they were, or even to any naïve belief in his ability to readily muster hundreds of Highland clansmen, but simply to the patronage of Dundas and to his City backers and the money they were prepared to invest in him. However, while that borrowed money was now about to go a long way towards meeting the considerable costs of actually raising the regiment, Erracht was to find himself very much on his own once he crossed the border. Political influence in London or even in Edinburgh counted for nothing in Lochaber.

Unlike the majority of those who had raised Highland regiments in the past, such as Fraser and Seaforth, he was of course neither the head of his clan nor the possessor of broad acres of land – and with them a numerous tenantry capable of being cajoled or coerced into following his banner. Erracht moreover was also a London-based absentee. No matter how much his supporters might then (and afterwards) dwell upon his supposed popularity in the area, all of this placed him at a serious disadvantage from the very outset. Even the great men of the Highlands were finding to their discomfort and occasional distress that as landed proprietors rather than chieftains they no longer enjoyed the power once wielded by their ancestors over their former clansmen.

In Lochaber this decline in influence was compounded by the fact that the present Donald Cameron of Locheil, the grandson of the 'Gentle Locheil' who led the clan to disaster at Culloden, was an amiable but weak and financially embarrassed young man, still very much under the influence of his former tutor, or guardian, Ewen Cameron of Fassfern.[45]

Handled more carefully, this weakness might have worked to Erracht's advantage, but three years earlier, while the chief was still a minor and under Fassfern's guardianship, the major had tried to improve his local standing by using the ever-accommodating Mr Phillips's money to purchase the freehold of the lands of Erracht and Inveruiskvuillin from the young man. There seems no reason to doubt that, at the time, the cash-strapped Lochiel may have entered into the transaction freely and even eagerly, but legally, as a minor, he was incompetent to do so and Fassfern and the other trustees immediately commenced legal proceedings to recover the lands. As is always the way of such lawsuits the legal arguments dragged on until January of 1795 before the case was eventually decided in favour of the trustees. In the meantime, naturally enough, it contributed to thoroughly poisoning the atmosphere in Lochaber, and is no doubt at least part of the reason why

Erracht would shortly come to speak of 'appealing to ... forgiveness of byegone events'.

In the meantime, therefore, the major (as he could at last legitimately call himself) at first ventured no further north than Stirling, and if the authorities had been anticipating that he would direct his recruiting activities to the far reaches of the Highlands rather than compete nearer at hand with those officers still struggling to find men for the old regiments, they were to be sadly disappointed. Instead he began by picking them up from the streets of Paisley, Dumbarton, Glasgow and nearby Dunblane, rather than taking them from the hills and glens of the north and west, as might have been thought proper for a real Highland regiment.

Perhaps for the sake of appearances, he did manage to send a number of his officers into Lochaber in search of men: Ensign Gordon Cameron of Letterfinley, for example; with Archibald Campbell of Bragleen, and other young men from Drimnin and Achnacone, all of them eager to earn their subalterns' commissions by enlisting the requisite number of recruits from amongst their fathers' tenants. But only two captains went to supervise their efforts and Erracht himself delayed showing his face in Lochaber for as long as possible. Eventually, however, there was no avoiding it, and he decided he would go to Fort William for the Martinmas Fair, for as he wrote to his brother, Ewen Mor, 'Having been favoured with the honour of embodying a Highland Regiment for His Majesty's service, where could I go but to my own native Lochaber, and with that desire I have decided on appealing to their forgiveness of byegone events and their loyalty to the Sovereign in his present exigencies.'

Nevertheless, his continuing reluctance to go there in person is plain from the extraordinary lateness of the visit: Martinmas falls on 11 November and his letters of service, as was customary, required him to have completed his regiment within three months. By then he had just a week in hand, but to all appearances he duly got his men. However, the accounts of the time are tolerably vague as to just how many of them were actually enlisted there and then, and although £12 8s 3d was spent on sixty-six gallons of whisky while Erracht was making a brave show of himself at Fort William, the likelihood is that most of the recruits had already been found for him by Letterfinley and Bragleen and the other young subalterns long before his arrival. In the end it was really no more than a hurried and, as it turned out, nearly disastrous exercise in bravado. As Dr Clerk, the minister of Kilmallie, observed in a letter written long years afterwards, in 1877:

> ...It was late in the day when he [Erracht] entered the field, & being on the worst possible terms with Locheil had not much chance of getting up men in Lochaber. But 1st he had plenty of money through a Miss Philip a Welsh heiress of great property having fancied and married him. 2nd He was a very cool clever fellow & knowing the value of a Highland regiment – he set up his Camp in Fort William on the Parade Ground between the Fort and the Village, had a couple of Pipers playing all day, & some Soldiers in Cameron tartan swaggering about. Meantime he sent many agents to the towns in the South, Glasgow, Paisley etc, and some to the North of Ireland to get up recruits by every possible means, giving them a handsome Bounty out of his Wife's money. – Batch after Batch of these recruits was marched up to Fort William where drill serjeants were ready for them & there the '79th Highlanders' was soon got up – I do not suppose that of the 650 men that went to form the Regiment at its first getting up there were six score Highlanders. But what of that! Allan Mor was richly rewarded and knighted, & they made good enough soldiers.
>
> 'I know this story is true, old men are still living who saw the thing done. One man, Ewen Cameron, a 92nd man – between 80 and 90 years old – often told it to me – but there is no public proof of it – consequently there is no good whatever in publishing it; but that is the true account of the Highland 79th.[46]

Dr Clerk was obviously mistaken in placing Fort William rather than Stirling at the centre of Erracht's recruiting efforts, but otherwise the story rings true enough, both in describing how he was on bad terms with Locheil and in stressing how so many of his men actually came from Glasgow and Paisley and other places far removed from Lochaber. But there was more. Clerk's other comment that Erracht 'came late in the day' is in its way even more significant, for young Locheil himself had already been busily engaged in recruiting all the Lochaber men he could persuade to follow him – and for a quite different regiment.

On 1 March 1793, long before Erracht's efforts to secure a regiment bore fruit, the Duke of Gordon was granted letters of service for a new fencible battalion. So too, as it happened, was his neighbour, Sir James Grant of Grant, and five other noble gentlemen, including the Earl of Breadalbane. Competition for men in the north of Scotland was obviously going to be fierce and with that very thought in mind, when the prospect of raising the regiments was first mooted, Sir James – 'The Good Sir James', as he was known – immediately wrote to his neighbour, declaring that:

> As your Grace and I have both offered for Fencible Regiments Mr Dundas wishes us to understand one another so that there may be no inconvenient Interference – Supposing us to have so large a district as from Aberdeen to the west Sea besides any aid we may get otherwise I do not see there can be any difficulty for us to make out the Twelve Hundred men that is Six Hundred for each Regiment neither interfering by themselves or their parties with the others property.

The duke, naturally, responded with equal courtesy and Sir James accordingly informed Dundas – whose remit as home secretary legitimately included the fencible regiments, if not the regulars at that stage – that they had been 'Communing' and understood each other perfectly.[47]

That understanding, however, did not neatly divide the countryside as it might have been expected to do – giving, say, the duke a free hand from the mouth of the Spey eastwards to Aberdeen, while Grant similarly enjoyed unfettered access to the Highlands from the Spey west to the Minch. On the contrary, they were agreed only in not trespassing upon each other's freehold lands and tenants. Thus, although Sir James immediately wrote to his factor instructing him to 'lose no time in acquainting the Gentlemen upon Sir James's Estate of Strathspey that he hoped that they would not engage to assist others untill they heard further from him,' it was clearly understood by both noblemen that it was open season on the inhabitants of any lands not in the actual ownership of the other. Significantly, the Duke of Gordon's own instructions from Yonge contained a curious note that:

> The beating order to authorise this levy, being made out in the usual form, allows recruiting to be carried on in any part of Great Britain. It is meant, notwithstanding, to be confined, according to your Grace's proposal, to

the counties of Inverness and to such other counties wherein your Grace's estates and superiorities are, and to the neighbourhood hereof.[48]

Thus it was that the Duke turned his eyes beyond Grant's Strathspey and Urquhart to the far reaches of Inverness-shire and in particular to the wild country of Lochaber, which was one of those feudal 'superiorities' referred to by Yonge. So far, this notional overlordship, granted long ago by the old Scottish kings in a vain attempt to impose some law and order on the area, had largely been ignored by the Camerons and everybody else, but now young Locheil eagerly accepted a captain's commission in the Duke's Northern Fencibles, along with the opportunity it offered him to behave like a Highland chieftain of old.

Another of the Duke's officers, Pryse Lockhart Gordon, was unimpressed by the play-acting this entailed and in his engaging memoirs penned a remarkable portrait of his brother officer:

> He had been bred, if not born in France, owing to the misfortunes of his family, who had been obliged to emigrate, and did not see his mountains until he was an adult. His father had been very popular, and the return of his representative was hailed with joy. Many of the old Jacobites were still living, and they puffed up the stripling with ideas of chieftainship and power which no longer existed ... Unfortunately, the young chief had imbibed false notions of his own consequence and of the altered state of the Highlands, and his education had been neglected; he took but little pains to make himself acquainted with the statistics of his own country; he had quite the air and manners of the Frenchman ... Nothing could be more unlike a Highland chief; in his exterior he would have better graced a levee at Holyrood than the head of a regiment in the field: he was tall and elegantly formed, and extremely graceful – more of Adonis than Mars, and quite unlike a native of Lochaber. Such was the hero who called out his clan on the commencement of the French Revolution to join the standard of the Cock of the North.[49]

Lockhart Gordon was a talented raconteur and more than once he engagingly related anecdotes pointing out the absurdity of young Lochiel's behaviour. Some of them no doubt improved considerably in the telling, but the insight that his stories, and other more official correspondence, provide into Locheil's character is significant. He was all too evidently an immature and rather insecure young man, much too anxious to assert himself after those long years under the close supervision of his guardians and, as Lockhart Gordon emphasises, altogether far too eager to assume all the fashionable trappings of a Highland chieftain of old. Whether or not he bore any genuine animosity towards Erracht over the land business, there was no doubting the sincerity of his belief that the inhabitants of Lochaber were indeed his hereditary clansmen and therefore his and his alone to command – or to enlist – then or at any time in the future.

Adding considerably to his sensitivities on this score was the fact that the Erracht branch had for centuries considered that they were the rightful chiefs of Clan Cameron, for the present line of Locheil was descended from an illegitimate son of an early chief, whilst the Erracht line descended from a younger but unquestionably legitimate son. From the outset, therefore, both Locheil and Fassfern were suspicious of Erracht's real motives. His 'beating up' for men in Lochaber in open competition with his chief was a dangerous affront in itself, but to then have those men swaggering around Fort William in his own personally designed 'Cameron' tartan rather than in the familiar but quite anonymous army tartan, was not merely provocative, but a brazen challenge to Locheil's leadership of the clan.

Consequently, far from being generally welcomed, Erracht was seen as an unwelcome and even a dangerous interloper in Lochaber; first and most obviously by Locheil and Fassfern, but also by the Duke of Gordon. Both of them must have combed its glens once already for men, but Locheil's thoughts were even now turning to the raising of a whole fencible regiment of his very own; while the Duke similarly had plans to second his fencible regiment with a regular battalion of the line – and Fassfern's eldest son John was already being promised a captain's commission in the proposed Gordon regiment. To all three, therefore, Lochaber – or rather its young men – figured prominently in their calculations. The last thing they wanted to see was Erracht filling up his ranks at their expense and so they and their friends would do everything in their power to impede his progress, and even attempt to encompass the destruction of his regiment.

In the meantime the major had the far more pressing matter of time to worry about, and having gathered in his recruits he hurried back over the hills to reach Stirling again before the 18 November deadline.

Happily he arrived there with a few days to spare, but any euphoria he might have enjoyed over his apparent success was immediately dispelled by an unexpected and near-fatal setback. In spite of a general prohibition against enlisting any men already serving in the militia – or in Scotland in the fencibles – he had quietly obtained some seventy or eighty men from the Breadalbane Fencibles (at ten guineas apiece) to make up the required numbers ahead of the deadline. However, no sooner was he arrived back at Stirling than he received '... an Official Mandate couched in harsh terms, desiring him instantly to return the men to the corps from which they had volunteered and threatening to bring Lord Breadalbane, Lieutenant Colonel Maclean of Coll, the immediate Commanding Officer, as well as himself to a general Court Martial'.[50]

Notwithstanding this furious bluster, there is no getting around the fact that what Erracht had tried to do was simply illegal and he was indeed lucky to avoid that threatened court martial. The men had to be returned and he had no alternative but to send his recruiting parties out all over again – and this time in the face of fierce competition from a whole slew of other new regiments that had been authorised in the interim.

His bankers were evidently appalled at the spiralling costs, for on 13 December he wrote from Stirling to George Hibbert, acknowledging that:

> ... you must think I exceed in money Matters, but while I can boast of more than any in Britain by having Levied and Subsisted within the last 3 months upward of 700 men upon the Strength of a Private Purse without drawing a single penny on acct ... be not afraid that I shall land ultimately so very unpleasantly in point of expence as you may at first view imagine ... I have very little reason to expect any indulgence from his Lordship [Lord Adam Gordon] who & his connections have shown a very ungenerous & marked opposition to me since I began recruiting. And Altho the Dutches [of Gordon] is open Mouthed against me on acct of the Disappointments, and wrote forbidding the Duke's tenants or their connection to enlist, the chief part of my Corps is composed of Highlanders. And there may be occasion for an explanation of the Motives that actuated them. But in spite of all they could secretly & otherwise to oppose me, I have carried my point, which, with the above

exception, seems to give general satisfaction – indeed, my Success excites astonishment under all the circumstances of the undertaking, nor did my most sanguine friends believe till now that I could accomplish it.

It is hard to imagine this incoherent diatribe being in any way reassuring, particularly when the 'Private Purse' in question was actually Hibbert's, but by the end of December Erracht was boasting to Lord Amherst, the all-but-senile commander-in-chief at Horse Guards, that his battalion was at last complete and that he had not 'raised a Single man by Aid of Crimps – or South of Edinr. – or in Ireland'. It was accordingly inspected and accepted onto the establishment by General Leslie on 3 January 1794 – too late for Erracht and his officers to be entered in the Army List for that year.[51] Nevertheless, Erracht was quick to inform his father-in-law that 'but for the <u>resentful</u> conduct of Lord Adam Gordon, I would have got through the Undertaking with more real éclat and ease than any man that ever Attempted to raise a Corps' and went on to crow that, '. . . the Victory (Over one of the most powerful families in the North) is so very complete as to Mortify the whole connection.'

Little did he know, his troubles from that particular quarter had only just begun. Much as Erracht might smugly congratulate himself on having apparently overcome the opposition of the Gordons, it can have been no coincidence that no sooner was the regiment accepted onto the official establishment than it was ordered across to Belfast and out of Scotland barely a month ahead of letters of service being granted to the duke's eldest son and heir, the Marquis of Huntly, on 10 February 1794. It was no doubt some consolation to Erracht that on the same day he himself was unexpectedly gazetted lieutenant colonel commandant of the 79th, thus at last enjoying the same rank, if not the same seniority, as his fellow commanding officers. However, in his joy he overlooked the fact that the commission was still only a temporary one; moreover, if Erracht considered his regiment's hasty posting to Ireland as a fortunate escape from the baleful influence of the Gordons, he had again overlooked Locheil, who was shortly to make his resentment felt from a quite unexpected direction.

In August the regiment was unexpectedly ordered to Flanders, and the haste, urgency and lack of preparation with which this move took place may be judged from the fact that it landed at Flushing (Vlissingen) with only one officer to a company and just eight rounds of ball ammunition per man.[52] The other regiments, both old and new, which were being shipped over at the same time may well have been in a similarly parlous state, but clearly, no matter how Erracht defended it, the regiment was still by no means complete. Nor, by any stretch of the imagination, were its officers and men properly fit for service, which makes it all the more unfortunate that it immediately came under the command of Sir Ralph Abercromby.

Opinion is somewhat divided on Abercromby. Popularly, he is closely associated with the Duke of York in bringing about the renaissance of the British Army after the chaos and setbacks of the early war years. While the duke is credited with reforming the administration of the army, to Abercromby goes the apparent honour of leading it to its first real victory in Egypt in 1801. Very conveniently for his posthumous reputation, however, he was to be fatally wounded in the very moment of

2   Erracht's nemesis, Sir Ralph Abercromby (1734–1801)

victory and so carried off to eternal glory before he had the opportunity to mar his triumph by committing any blunders.

As it happens, Abercromby's real failings probably did not lie in any sort of propensity for blundering, but in being rather too careful to avoid making blunders by avoiding doing anything at all. One of the more notable things he had avoided doing, seemingly as a matter of conscience, was to see any service in the American War. Whether this may in itself have been a cause for friction between the two men is unclear, but it seems likely. Erracht's own service in America had been as brief as it was inglorious, but he had thus far been in the habit of milking it for all it was worth and may have been tactless enough to do so now in Abercromby's hearing. A little reflection would also suggest that Abercromby, a stolid professional soldier who had taken a quite unexceptional seventeen years to rise from a cornet of dragoons to lieutenant colonel, might quite naturally despise a man who had achieved that rank overnight without having done a day's soldiering in his life. Furthermore, Sir Ralph was also a firm adherent of the 'Prussian' school of tactics, which was being promulgated throughout the army by his colleague David Dundas, and disdainful of the important tactical innovations learned through bitter experience in America. Like Dundas he was obsessed with the importance of close-order drill and a slavish obedience to the drill-book – the effect of the arrival of a half-trained, poorly officered rabble of recruits led by a strong-minded political appointee with no proper military experience may therefore be imagined.

Whether this unfavourable impression contributed to Abercromby's failure to get into action against the French at Boxtel on 15 September 1794 is a moot point, but it would not be the first time or the last that a professional soldier declined to fight because he lacked confidence in his men. The previous day the post had been captured by the French and Abercromby was sent with ten battalions, including the 79th, to retake it. In the event he advanced cautiously, skirmished half-heartedly and withdrew rapidly. Whether he was justified in doing so is debatable: the official story is that he realised just in the nick of time that he was up against not just a detachment, but the whole French Army, and therefore skilfully extricated himself at just the right moment. On the other hand the general opinion at the time was that he had deliberately

3   General David Dundas (1735–1820)

misinterpreted the discretionary clauses of his orders to avoid fighting at all. At any rate the result was that the 79th fired not a shot and lost not a man, but by the time the whole sorry campaign was over some two hundred of its men had succumbed to 'the severity of the season and the want of necessary supplies of food and clothing'. Nevertheless they may have done better than many, for as our friend Stewart of Garth commented: 'In the march through Holland and Westphalia in 1794 and 1795, when the cold was so intense that brandy froze in the bottles, the Highlanders, consisting of the 78th, 79th and the new recruits of the 42nd (very young soldiers) wore their kilts and yet the loss was out of comparison less than that sustained by some other corps.'[53]

Be that as it may, the suffering on the retreat that followed the Black Watch's successful rearguard action at Geldermalsen on 5 January was unprecedented in its horrors. Late on 15 January the 79th elected to march through the night simply because the wind-chill was so severe that if they had halted, all or most of them would have been dead by morning. Others were less fortunate:

Far as the eye could read over the whitened plain were scattered gun limbers, wagons full of baggage, stores or sick men, sutlers' carts and private carriages. Beside them lay the horses, dead; and then scores and hundreds of soldiers, dead; here a straggler who had staggered on to the bivouac and dropped to sleep in the arms of the frost; there a group of British and Germans round an empty rum cask; here forty English Guardsmen huddled together about a plundered wagon; there a pack-horse with a woman lying alongside it, and a baby swaddled in rags, peeping out of the pack, with its mother's milk turned to ice upon its lips – one and all stark, frozen, dead.[54]

That seemingly was the worst day; from the bleak frost and snow of Holland, the 79th were next ordered to the balmier climes of the Isle of Wight, the traditional staging post for units destined to serve in India. However, any equanimity at this prospect was abruptly disturbed by the arrival of quite different orders. On 1 July 1795 Erracht was advised that his regiment was:

> to be forthwith draughted into 3 Regts (40th, 54th and 59th) which are order'd to embark for the West Indies, in a few Days; but you are to keep all your Offrs. & Non-comd. Offrs. and those Men, who are real Highlanders to enable you to proceed in raising your Regt. afresh. – M.Genl Hunter recd HRH Orders by yesterday's Post, to communicate to you H:Majesty's pleasure on this occasion, & begin the Draughting of the 79th Regt. accordingly without loss of Time.

On furiously protesting to General Hunter, who was then in command of all the troops on the island, Erracht was assured there was nothing sinister in these orders and no threat to the continued existence of the regiment, other than that pointed concession that he might retain any of the rank and file who were *real* Highlanders – which very clearly implied that most were nothing of the sort. Nevertheless, in the prevailing circumstances, raising the regiment all over again was going to be well nigh impossible and so Erracht forcefully seized upon the undertaking in his letters of service that the regiment was 'not to be draughted'.

Unfortunately we only have his own very highly coloured account of what happened – or might have happened – next. Erracht immediately obtained leave from Hunter to proceed to London and try to have the orders rescinded. Quite coincidentally, when he stepped off the ferry at Portsmouth he learned that the Duke of York was in fact due there himself the very next day. At first the resulting interview did not go as Erracht hoped, for the duke was about to preside over a wholesale drafting – not just of the 79th, but of nearly all the new battalions – and was consequently unmoved by the existence of the undertaking. Thus far the story is straightforward enough, but then, said Erracht, the duke 'held out the <u>threat</u> of sending Us all to the <u>West Indies</u>'. At this, puffed Erracht afterwards, he immediately retorted to the duke that: 'You may tell the king your father from me, that he may send us to the hottest spot in his dominions – to hell if he likes – and I'll go at the head of them. But he dare not draft us.' Apparently wilting under the colonel's fury, the duke – far from having Erracht cashiered on the spot – agreed to cross to the island and inspect the regiment for himself,. On seeing the men, the duke showered Erracht with compliments and declared himself to have been deceived 'with regard to the <u>state</u> of the Corps & their *Country*'.[55] A more unlikely story is hard to imagine, even from Erracht's floridly inventive pen, and the reality is that despite his battalion still being badly under-strength, it must have been the colonel who persuaded the duke to allow it to go out entire to the West Indies as an alternative to drafting it out of existence.

The Caribbean was to be the most notorious and least understood theatre of war in the 1790s. The wealth produced each year by the sugar islands was staggering and in consequence the West India merchants, amongst whom of course was Erracht's father-in-law Mr Phillips, enjoyed a political influence out of all proportion to their numbers. That wealth and influence also meant that in times past warfare in the region had followed a fairly straightforward set of rules. First one side or the other would send out a fleet, establish a temporary naval superiority in the area, and then use it to land troops on one or more of the islands. The local garrison – invariably comprised of regular troops – would then retire into a convenient fortress and hope that either disease would decimate the attackers, or the arrival of a friendly fleet would reverse the balance of power and bring a relief force before the otherwise inevitable surrender. There was no question of any serious fighting in the interior of the islands, far less devastating the countryside, for the primary object was to secure the wealth of the plantations, not to destroy them.

All that changed with the French Revolution and its dangerous doctrines of equality and the 'Rights of Man'. The huge slave populations on the islands were no longer to be passive witnesses to the ever shifting balance of power, but active participants in the campaigns. Now it was no longer sufficient to capture the principal ports of the colonies: whole islands needed to be subjugated and strongly garrisoned, both against regular troops and the infinitely more terrifying nightmare of a slave insurrection – a nightmare made all too real on the French island of San Domingo, which was currently in the process of becoming the Black Empire of Haiti.

This then was the reason why so many thousands of British soldiers would be sent to the islands rather than to Continental Europe, just at the very time the Caribbean was being gripped by a Yellow Fever pandemic. No-one knows just how many British soldiers died in this apparent holocaust. Fortescue, abandoning any pretence of objectivity in favour of hyperbole and prejudice, declared that official documents must have been falsified or purposefully destroyed, and proposed a quite incredible figure of a hundred thousand dead in the early years alone. In reality the figure was much lower with perhaps twenty-five thousand dead by 1797, but this was still justification enough for the fear and dread inspired by a posting to the Caribbean at that time – which makes it all the more extraordinary that Erracht should voluntarily offer to take the 79th there, when it was already about five hundred men below its proper establishment.[56]

As it happens, heat, disease, boredom and an overabundant supply of alcohol were at first all that the 79th had to contend with – except on San Domingo itself, there was very little military activity in progress by the time the regiment arrived and instead it found itself doing garrison duty on the former French island of Martinique. Nevertheless, if little hostility was to be expected from the former owners, there was, if Erracht is to be believed, a very great deal of hostility emanating from his commander-in-chief, who was none other than Sir Ralph Abercromby. In his mind that enmity arose not from their previous association in Holland, but from the fact that Abercromby's eldest daughter, Anne, had married Donald Cameron of Locheil in June 1795. Once again his bitterness poured out in his autobiography:

[Abercromby's] illiberal and implacable enmity . . . could emanate only from the circumstance of his Daughter having been married to a certain young man . . . with whom Colonel Cameron was openly at variance. That variance regarded local transactions founded upon legitimate ancient feudal rights: in asserting and maintaining which Colonel Cameron was bitterly and powerfully opposed by a <u>ramified junto</u>, whose hostile influence he has good reason to believe is still smouldering behind the political Curtain ready to blaze forth upon every occasion against him . . . How he was surreptitiously stript of his Rank after he had fairly attained, and he thought earned it, has been already shewn. How his Regiment, raised at his sole expense and guaranteed to him by His Majesty's Letter of Service as not liable to be drafted, <u>was in little more than three short years drafted notwithstanding</u>, upon his again unhappily falling under the command of the General Officer above alluded to, upon a station where, being without a superior, he was despotic, shall sortly be shewn. But so it is whenever private resentments are suffered to mix themselves with Public duties, the fruit of so foul an union will generally be some monstrous deformity of injustice.

And now all being quiet, and his plans matured, his splenetic design to strip Colonel Cameron of his Clan Regiment, and of all his military consequence, unfolded itself. The rapid raising by the Colonel of the Cameron Highlanders at a momentous and difficult period . . . so irrefragably manifested his popularity, more especially in the District where his feudal rights and claims lay, that, as his success could have found no favour in the Eyes of that hostile or rival branch of the Camerons with whom, as already observed, Sir Ralph was so closely allied.[57]

His tortured complaint is as revealing as it is disingenuous. The regiment had landed on Martinique in September 1795 with 25 officers, 35 sergeants, 19 drummers and 479 rank and file. By June of the following year 'upward of 100 men' had been lost, and then in August Yellow Fever struck in earnest. Another twenty-six men died within a week and more followed in quick succession. The worst of the epidemic seems to have been over by November, but Abercromby not unreasonably considered that with little more than three hundred rank and file remaining (and even that only on paper) the battalion was no longer fit for service. He began to talk therefore of having it drafted, a common procedure at the time whereby the fit men would be transferred to other units still remaining in theatre while a cadre returned home to rebuild the regiment.

Erracht, as ever, over-reacted, leaping instantly to the conclusion that he was being punished for challenging Locheil – whom he revealingly referred to not as the chief of the Camerons but as a 'rival branch' – by stripping him of his 'Clan regiment'.[58] Once again he tried an appeal to the Duke of York, but this was a forlorn hope and on 11 June 1797 formal orders were received to parade the regiment for the last time and explain to the remaining men that 'from the Reduced State of the Regt. it is impossible to keep it any longer on Foot.' The officers, sergeants and drummers were to go home and try to recruit the regiment anew, while the rank and file were to be offered the opportunity to transfer to a detachment of the 42nd in return for the usual bounty or – in a rather transparent threat – if they declined to do so, they would be formed into independent companies without a bounty.

Thus the original 79th was drafted out of existence after all. By a curious irony the 42nd detachment accompanied the cadre home and on their arrival in England, Erracht lobbied hard to have his men returned to him. On the face of it, taking them to fill up a regiment that was itself returning home does indeed seem unjust, but in fact the Black Watch men were not returning home at all but were only in transit to rejoin the rest of their battalion at Gibraltar. Their need for the 79th men was therefore quite genuine, but a thoroughly paranoid Alan Cameron of Erracht preferred to regard the taking of the draft as yet another act of malice and bitterly complained that 'the stripping him of that regiment . . . could not fail . . . to be regarded [by Locheil and his supporters] as a Family Triumph throughout its Highland and powerful lowland ramifications . . .' Perhaps it was, but Erracht was by no means beaten.

~ 4 ~

High Jinks and Whisky: The Gordons

Conventionally, the history of the Gordon Highlanders begins in late January of 1794 with the arrival at Gordon Castle of a flattering and, to all appearances, quite unsolicited letter from the commander-in-chief, Lord Amherst, inviting the Duke of Gordon to raise a new regiment of the line:

> The King having been pleased to approve of the raising of some regiments in N. Britain, agreeable to the plan of Lord Seaforth's in the last war, I beg the favour to know if it will be agreeable to your Grace to raise a regiment of 1000 men, the regiment having a Lieut. Colonel Commandant and two Majors, the two Majors appointed by the King, and leaving to Your Grace the recommendation of the other officers. The plan of the particulars shall be transmitted immediately to Your Grace if it meets with your accepting the offer.[59]

The invitation was indeed extremely agreeable to the duke – not only did he dash off his enthusiastic acceptance within just twenty-four hours of its receipt, but even that breathless reply was accompanied by an anxious explanation that his response would have been even prompter still had not the mail been delayed 'owing to the great fall of snow which retarded the course of the post for several days'. In short he bit Amherst's hand off, because, far from coming out of the blue, the letter had in fact been anxiously awaited at Gordon Castle for some months. In anticipation of the letter, all manner of careful, but of course entirely unofficial, preparations for raising the regiment were already underway.

As we have seen, almost exactly a year earlier, within a matter of just days of the outbreak of war, Gordon and six other Scottish proprietors – Sir James Grant of Grant, the Earls of Breadalbane, Hopetoun, Sutherland, the Marquis of Lorne and the Honourable Hugh Montgomerie of Coilsfield – were all granted letters of service to raise fencible battalions 'for the internal protection of North Britain'. Getting into the game early was always a good thing and filling the ranks was also eased by the fact that these particular battalions initially had an establishment of just eight companies rather than the usual ten mustered by regular units. Requiring to find only 480 rank and file, the duke was therefore in the happy position of being able to report his battalion complete by 14 April 1793, just six weeks into the three month period customarily allowed for the purpose.

Moreover pretty much all of the men drummed up in that first levy were apparently willing recruits, genuinely attracted to the very agreeable prospect of just a few short years of soldiering in their own country. While it is all too easy to overplay the downside of military life in the eighteenth century and dwell upon the supposed coercion sometimes employed in obtaining recruits, it is also important to remember that it held some very considerable attractions for fit young men chafing under the drudgery of farm work or weaving. To such men, standing in line on a gravelled parade ground held no terrors: long hours of drill was better than even longer hours of tedium at the plough tail or the loom. Service in the army provided an opportunity to travel far from home and perhaps away too from the claustrophobia of unchanging parish life and poverty. Indeed, if the pay itself was relatively poor it was at least constant, unaffected by bad weather, bad harvests or slumps in trade. Life in the army offered a certain security and rigorously scrubbed barrack rooms represented a considerable improvement to men accustomed to even more cramped and far less sanitary cottages; while the drabness of a countryman's shabby hodden grey was replaced by a fine uniform and by a sense of worth and self-esteem that could not always be found by staying at home. But in Scotland there was another, less tangible, factor: for while the army was all too often seen in England as the last refuge of the desperate, in Scotland enlisting was seen as something positive, representing an opportunity for a man to better himself – if the king's red coat was good enough for the laird, it was good enough for the loun.⁶⁰ In short, going for a soldier had few of the negative connotations associated with the army in England.

At any rate it was a splendid start and with the battalion reported as complete the duke was soon happily immersed in the much more agreeable minutiae of approving the fine uniforms for his brisk young men. They were to be dressed in short scarlet jackets, of course, and the same lemon-yellow facings worn by his earlier Northern Fencibles, and probably by Morris's 89th Highlanders before them. Only the tartan was going to be different this time around – on 15 April William Forsyth, noting that the duke was 'desirous to have patterns of the 42nd Regiment plaid with a small yellow stripe properly placed', sent him three samples, the second of which was duly adopted, first as the regimental tartan for both the fencibles and then for the regulars who followed, and then, after a lightening of some of the tones, as the Gordon clan tartan as well.⁶¹

Soon, however, that initial euphoria gave way to the inevitable problems and the happy amity that marked the early communing with the Laird of Grant quickly gave way to an injured sense of rivalry. It began in Holyrood House. The letters of service for all seven fencible regiments bore the same date, 1 March 1793, and in order to establish a proper order of precedence amongst them the commanding officers were summoned to a conference presided over by the Commander-in-Chief of Scotland, Lord Adam Gordon. There lots were drawn to decide the matter and the result of this aristocratic sweepstake was that Sir James's Strathspey regiment became the 1st Fencibles, while the duke's regiment had to settle for only sixth place. Aggrieved, the duke promptly and rather tediously complained to Lord Amherst that:

> having been an old colonel of Fencibles, I hope to have rank given me over those colonels who have not been in that situation before. From my never having resigned my commission as Captain in the 89th Regiment, and having been accordingly put on the half pay list, I cannot but consider myself in the same situation, and must hope that I shall not have my claim to priority of rank on that ground lessened, because I did not chuse to receive the annual stipend of the half pay, more especially as from an order in this late war for the posting of the officers in my regiment those even who had served at all in the army were to take rank of those who had never been in the Fencibles.

In point of fact Hugh Montgomerie of Coilsfield, commanding the Western Fencibles had also held the king's commission and unlike the duke he actually saw some proper active service in North America with the 77th (Montgomerie's) Highlanders away back during the Old French War. It was in any case all pretty immaterial, for as Amherst wearily explained, although 'Officers who served in the army certainly take the place of those who have not served,' that would have no bearing on the allotted seniority of their new regiments; and with that crushing response the duke had to be content.

Nevertheless, the ease with which they had raised their fencible regiments encouraged some of those colonels to go on and seek approval not only to augment them with second battalions, but also to raise regular battalions of the line with all the additional emoluments that would accrue immediately and the later certainty of half-pay for life if they should be disbanded on the outbreak of peace. Given their past experience with raising both fencibles and regulars, and with that gentlemanly agreement with the Laird of Grant then still in place, the Gordon family should have been in an unassailable position when it came to raising a regiment of the line. Yet there seemed an unconscionable delay in receiving the necessary paperwork – those all important letters of service – and in the meantime came Cameron of Erracht's interloping intervention in Lochaber.

The timing could hardly have been worse, for even without that official sanction, the duke's own plans were not only well advanced by November 1793 but were of sufficiently common knowledge for upwards of thirty applications to have already been addressed to him, all soliciting commissions in his proposed regiment. Many of these early applicants for commissions, including supposedly influential men such as Macdonald of Keppoch, and even a brother of Glengarry, were to be disappointed for one reason or another. Significantly, however, the successful ones included Simon Macdonald of Morar, a half-pay lieutenant of the old 76th who in February was endorsed as being '... in point of friends and connections extremely well calculated to raise a company'.

Fraser of Gortuleg continued:

> It would be particularly agreeable to him to be promoted in any corps to be raised by the Marquis of Huntly, as his brother is a captain the first

Royals, and owes much to Lord Adam Gordon, both from his original introduction and promotion in that regiment. Independent of his own tribe, which are numerous, and his remaining property by no means inconsiderable, he is by inter-marriage particularly connected with the Glengarry branches.[62]

In other words Morar was more than adequately supported by that extensive web of patronage both inside and outside the army that was an essential prerequisite to any successful military career. In this case that patronage, and not least the assistance of Lord Adam Gordon, saw him promoted from half-pay lieutenant to be the senior of the two majors appointed to the regiment.[63]

Equally importantly, there was also Ewen Cameron of Fassfern's son John, who would be the senior captain in the regiment when it was raised, and would eventually die leading it at the battle of Quatre Bras in 1815. With men like Morar and Fassfern, and of course Locheil himself, all working in the Gordon interest to milk Lochaber of its bounteous store of recruits, Erracht was as welcome at Fort William as the proverbial ghost at the feast. There was little wonder that his advent should arouse so much hostility or that he should make himself some dangerous enemies from the Duchess of Gordon on downwards.

Nevertheless, after inducing that momentary fright – which he was certainly not oblivious to, regardless of his later air of injured innocence – Erracht was seemingly well out of the way when the long-anticipated 'invitation' to form a regiment of the line finally arrived at Gordon Castle on 1 February. Confident that all was now going well, the duke had no hesitation in seconding his enthusiastic acceptance with the immediate nomination of his eldest son and heir, the Marquis of Huntly, to be the putative regiment's lieutenant colonel commandant.

It was understandable enough that the Duke should choose to bestow the regiment on his twenty-four-year-old son, for he himself was no longer a young man, and while it was gratifying enough to be the proprietor of a home-based fencible regiment, the commander of a marching regiment might occasionally be expected to lead it in person on active service. In any case the letters of service clearly specified that the commanding officer would hold the rank of lieutenant colonel commandant and while it would be a regular commission it would also have meant that the duke would have to lose a step in rank. Altogether better then to pass it on to Huntly, who as a serving officer in the Scots Guards (and before that a captain in the 42nd Highlanders) was therefore ideally suited to lead what was fondly hoped would be the family regiment.

Inconveniently for all concerned, however, it just so happened that young Huntly was not actually available to raise the Gordon standard – he was rather too agreeably laid up at Walker's Hotel in Edinburgh, where he had supposedly gone to seek medical advice for an unspecified injury to his leg. The genuineness of the complaint is far from clear – there is more than a suspicion in the correspondence of the day that it was no more than a highly convenient excuse to escape the drudgery of recruiting for the more congenial delights of Edinburgh society. A rather offhand (and somewhat belated) notice in the *Aberdeen Journal* for 23 March had to suffice:

> Lord Huntly presents his respectful compliments to the gentlemen who have obligingly interested themselves in his regiment. He sincerely thanks them for their exertions, and flatters himself that he will soon be permitted by his physicians to go to the north, and to have the honour to co-operate with them in person. In the meantime he requests that the recruits already enlisted may be sent to the headquarters at Aberdeen, where Major Erskine is appointed to receive them.

Unsurprisingly his own apparent equanimity over his absence appalled his supporters. At the very least it might be accounted as complacency, but once again the timing could hardly have been worse, for in the meantime a new and very real threat to the proposed regiment had emerged. This came not from an ancient clan feud in Lochaber, but from a much more recent rivalry – one rather closer to home, which had quite unexpectedly reared its head again.

In the six months since Allan Cameron of Erracht got his letters of service for the 79th Highlanders, no fewer than twenty other new infantry regiments had been authorised, besides a number of second battalions for existing units. Now, had he read Amherst's letter properly, the duke would surely have realised that the invitation to raise yet another regiment was not directed to him alone, but was more in the manner of a standard pro forma addressed to a number of the Highland proprietors. Another happy recipient, inevitably, was Sir James Grant, who seems to have enjoyed a rather better postal service, for the letters of service for his regular 97th (Inverness-shire) Regiment were signed off on 8 February. Two days later, just before signing the duke's letters for what would initially become the 100th (Gordon) Highlanders, the Secretary at War also granted Lieutenant Colonel Duncan Campbell of Lochnell the authority to raise what would eventually become the Argylls. Of itself, this news was bad enough, but now the duke's agent in Aberdeen, a former officer in the old 89th Highlanders named William Finlason, began worriedly forwarding news of proposals for yet another rival Highland regiment, this time being promoted in that very same burgh by Colonel Alexander Hay – an officer whom the duke had cause to remember far too well.

As Gordon rather petulantly pointed out to Amherst after that unfortunate meeting in Holyrood, he himself had been a colonel of fencibles once before, raising an earlier regiment back in 1778 at the height of the American War. At that time, barely twenty years on since the New York Yankee, Staats Long Morris, raised the 89th Highlanders on the young duke's behalf, Aberdeenshire and the rest of north-east Scotland was still very much regarded as an exclusive fiefdom of the Gordon family. Finding the men for a new regiment should therefore have been easy. His wife, the duchess, had of course already raised a company on behalf of her brother for Fraser's 71st Highlanders at the very outset of the war, and in 1777 he himself intended to go one better by raising a whole regiment for one of his own scapegrace younger brothers, Lord William Gordon. Instead, to the surprise of everyone and to the secret (and sometimes not so secret) delight of many, he saw the prize unexpectedly snatched away by a distant kinsman, Colonel William Gordon of Fyvie!

Fyvie was a swashbuckling and, to say the least, thoroughly eccentric character who actively enjoyed scandalising a remarkable variety of people during a long and often disreputable life. He is probably best known to history for once threatening to run his sword through the duke's even-more-unhinged youngest brother, Lord George Gordon – on the floor of the House of Commons, no less.[64] Originally a dashing cavalryman by preference, he became lieutenant colonel of the very short-lived 105th (Queen's) Highlanders in 1762; later on in Italy he was flamboyantly painted in a flowing toga-like kilt and plaid by Pompeo Batoni before becoming one of the Grooms of the Bedchamber to George III in 1775. As a favoured courtier he was obviously well placed to solicit the command of a regiment, and when the king very sensibly turned down the duke's nomination of the patently unsuitable Lord William, but then granted letters of service to Fyvie instead, the duke immediately smelled a rat: 'The King having absolutely refused to give Lord William Gordon the rank,' spluttered a furious and perhaps hungover duke on New Years Day 1778,

> Fyvie was appointed after having assured Lord George Germaine that he was to have my interest and support – and indeed he was sure of it, had he behaved properly – but he had named most of his officers and had wrote to them before he was sure whether he or Lord William was to command the battalion, and by that means made it impossible, if Lord William had got the command, to have changed one of Fyvie's nomination without making them enemies to him and friends to Fyvie; and you will see that he had an eye to Aberdeenshire in the list he has named. To this hour he has never had the civility to offer me the appointment of one officer, tho Lord Adam [Gordon] has named three and George Ross has named your namesake and his for a Major, [Major Alexander Ross] who was tried lately at Inverness . . .'[65]

What was more, he went on: 'When Sandy Gordon delivered me Fyvie's letter at Edinburgh with the list of officers I was very angry, and said I was surprised at his brother's having got a regiment through my interest and not giving me the nomination of one officer. He answered in a huff, "Well by God we can raise it without you."'

And so they did. In the meantime the duke even appealed unsuccessfully to the king (who very tactfully but not entirely truthfully expressed surprise at Fyvie getting the regiment) but it was all to no avail. In the end he had to settle for the decidedly thin consolation of a fencible regiment: a home service battalion that conferred no permanent rank upon its officers and, unless the French should actually land, no prospect of military glory.

At least, however, Lord William became his lieutenant colonel and at first the duke seems to have assumed that the traditional power of his family's name would be quite enough by itself to fill the ranks. Instead, like so many of the other Highland proprietors, he soon found his confidence was sadly misplaced and that extravagant promises, hard bargaining and occasional threats were the order of the day rather than unquestioning obedience. In any case the timing was bad – first the recruiting parties from Fraser's regiment had already carried off the likeliest of the young men, and then other recruiters, ever more predatory, had followed. Even the Duke of Hamilton's regiment, although notionally a Lanarkshire unit, was widely reputed at the time to have picked up anything between a hundred and three hundred stout young men in Badenoch alone, and now of course there was the new 81st to contend with. As Fyvie and his officers were able to begin beating up for their recruits as early as January 1778, they obviously had a clear head start over the duke, who had to wait for his letters of service until April. When he did finally get them, open warfare broke out, for despite the supposed power of his family, the duke had to fight for every man – sometimes quite literally.

As one historian later put it: 'The County took sides in the quarrel, the non-Gordon lairds rallying to the laird of Fyvie, not because they cared so much for him, but because they had the chance of wiping off some old scores with the head of the house.'[66]

In a typical incident one of the fencible officers complained how:

At a market in Clatt, John Couper was enlisted as a soldier by Ensign John Gordon of the Duke of Gordon's Fencibles. About an hour after Couper's enlisting, one Innes, a Serjeant of a recruiting party belonging to Captain Leith of the 81st interfered with him, said he was a fool for engaging with the Fencibles; it would be much better for him to enlist with his Captain, who would pay the smart money to Mr Gordon, give him 15 guineas and his obligation for a halberd [ie; he was promised he would be a sergeant].

Initially Couper resisted temptation but afterwards Innes cornered him again in a pub at Knockespock and, presumably with the aid of a quantity of whisky, persuaded him to join the regulars after all. That particular little dispute eventually ended up in a full-blown court of inquiry and it is far from clear who got Couper in the end. But one thing was certain: the duke was not going to pull his clansmen out onto the heather at the snap of his fingers.[67]

Thus it was that to make up the numbers he looked westwards to that ancient feudal superiority granted to his family in Lochaber, but even there it proved hard going. One of his recruiters, Alexander Cameron of Letterfinlay (the father of Erracht's ensign) disgustedly wrote of one reluctant recruit that:

> I hope he had not the assurance to tell he did it [enlisted] willingly. To the contrary it was the utmost compulsion. I offered him twice in your presence to engage and I would continue him upon the same footing with the rest of the subtenants ... His return always was a fflat denyall upon which I have sett his lands to other people and threatened to eject him instantly; which was the only cause that induced him to go to serve.[68]

Effective though the threat may have been in this particular case, it reminded far too many people of the way the duke's uncle, Lord Lewis Gordon, and all the other Jacobite leaders had raised their regiments for the Pretender in 1745 by threatening to burn the thatch and take the cattle of any man who refused to follow them. Times, as the proprietors were slowly realising, were certainly a-changing.

In the end, therefore, although Lochaber duly played its part, the duke was even glad to pick up conscripts. As in previous wars a dearth of recruits had eventually forced the government to pass an 'Act for the more Easy and Better Recruiting of His Majesty's Land Forces and Marines', known for short as the Comprehending Act since all those 'comprehended' within certain categories – the unemployed and petty criminals for the most part, were liable to be taken up by the local authorities and handed over to any recruiting officer who asked for them. Not surprisingly, very few officers actually wanted to touch such unsavoury recruits and one of them punningly declared that he thought it 'beneath the idea of Fencibles to incorporate Comprehensibles with them,' but all too often they had to take what they could get in the end.

There is certainly no doubting that the duke came off the worst in the contest between the two regiments and the absolute nadir of the struggle came when some of Fyvie's supporters and recruiting officers finally became so bold as to invade the town of Huntly itself, which spiritually at least was still regarded as the duke's private domain. Led by a certain Captain Alexander Leith of Leithhall and his cousin Captain Alexander Leith of Boharn, Fyvie's people actually had the audacity to parade through the streets of the burgh with flaming torches, music and whisky. Inevitably everyone in the place was soon rolling drunk. With Fyvie's supporters invading the town almost every other day most of them seemingly remained that way for nearly two weeks and the festivities were scarcely dampened even when one young man, making his unsteady way home one night fell into the River Isla and was drowned. Afterwards the duke's supporters unconvincingly tried to claim that in the end Fyvie's officers only got four recruits there, and one of his informants also sniggered that: ' . . . they recruited a female in men's clothes at Drumblade. She was kept a day or two and dismist.' That story at least might have afforded the duke some wry amusement but there was no disguising the scale of Fyvie's victory – or the prominent part played by the Leiths in the duke's humiliation.[69]

Now, that same Alexander Leith of Leithhall was back again. As a lieutenant colonel on the half-pay of Douglas's 104th Foot, where he exchanged at the end of the American War, he had altered his name to Hay as the result of a fortunate legacy in 1789 that brought him the estate of Rannes, but his bold character was unchanged and he was no more intimidated by the duke now than he had been in his youth –neither for that matter were his many friends and supporters.

Although Hay wrote to the War Office on 8 March 1794, reminding Sir George Yonge that he had offered at the beginning of the war to raise a regiment and was still willing to do so. Like the duke, he had already anticipated the granting of those letters of service by preparing the ground widely. Moreover he was sufficiently confident of success not only to promise commissions to his would-be officers but to actually begin recruiting the men to go with them while the letter was still in the post.

Having been disappointed in an earlier application for a commission in the Gordon regiment, Lieutenant Forsyth of the 72nd Highlanders was reported in March to be raising a company:

> . . . either for the Marquis or Colonel Hay – for the latter I suppose, as he made the first offer; but nothing may be feared from him, as his

brothers in London raise the men, and he does not propose braving odium here and only to pick up straggling doggs, and even this only privately, for, if he be in opposition to the Marquis, his father will not admit of a publick appearance.[70]

In the event Forsyth found it more prudent to avoid taking sides by bargaining his recruits into a captaincy in the rather more anonymous 60th Foot, but, just as in 1778, others were to be much less circumspect in their defiance.

On 11 March the duke's agent in Aberdeen, William Finlason, was dismayed to learn that the title of the Aberdeenshire Regiment, which he himself had suggested to Huntly, was instead to be assumed by Hay's as-yet-unauthorised corps. Worse still the town council had even been persuaded to endorse Hay's corps in preference to the Gordon regiment –although Finlason bravely tried to put a gloss on this by variously claiming that the decision had been a fix, and that the endorsement amounted to no more than a 'milk and water' letter, there was no getting around the fact that Hay had stolen a considerable march on his noble rival.

Furthermore, according to rumours already rife on all sides, the bounty being offered by the Gordons was going to be outbid by the opposition and Finlason was urging that 'we should get strong before they start.' Even before the news of the new regiment began to circulate, he had been complaining to the duke about the meagreness of the all-important bounty and the competition from rival recruiters from a whole variety of other corps – including the Laird of Grant's 97th: 'I struggle hard to make a good bargain,' he protested on 22 February, 'but I may as well attempt to change the system of the whole army as to ask recruiting officers here to alter their terms.' Nevertheless, he tried hard, rather hopefully writing on 1 March that: 'I have had nibblers from morning to night this day, and I think three have taken the bait. Monday is the first attesting day, so we do not count our chickens.'

A little over a week later he mingled hope and dismay, recounting how, typically:

This day I engaged George Gordon from the Cabrach, late a tenant of the Duke ... But I had to engage him thro' many windings – (1) a recommendation to the Marquis to solicit the Duke for his former tack to him on or after his discharge from the army: (2) and application ... for some tenement or bigging for his wife till his return: (3) promotion if he deserves it: besides (4) ten guineas bounty and three guineas to his pilot, Sergeant Reid ... Tomorrow he goes in high dress with his sword by his side to announce his new profession.[71]

Clearly, this new breed of clansmen were far from being the hapless victims of popular legend, forced into the army against their will. Not only were they just as ready as their supposed 'betters' to put on some swank and play up their Highlandness with kilt and sword in a manner quite impossible for their English counterparts to conceive, let alone emulate. They were also quite prepared to lay old loyalties aside and put their own interests first. Once they started putting a price on their services it was inevitable that, like that anonymous young man in the Grassmarket, they would soon look around for the best available offer. That of course set Finlason fretting again:

I am really much concerned that the Marquis does not come north instantly, as I cannot see how the material business of raising the regiment can be set going and put fairly on leg ... It is obvious that Sir J[ames] G[rant], or any undertaker who has been at the fountain head and a disciple under agents so long and versant in the publick market and traffick of the day, must start with every advantage.

By the middle of March it seemed certain that Hay would indeed get his letters of service and now Gordon of Coynachie added his voice to the chorus of dismay, gloomily predicting that: 'If Colonel Hay's beating orders come to this country before the Marquis makes his appearance, it will knock our recruiting on the head. Every man that has any inclinations expects such high bounty money from him.' On 1 April, Hay suddenly showed his hand by openly commencing his recruiting in Aberdeen itself, just the day before his letters of service were signed. Finlason was in utter despair:

The town is in a roar. We shall catch nothing till it settles. Nothing less than 30 guineas is spoken of; so we must have patience ... A bounty from the County will soon be noticed for the Aberdeenshire Regiment. Lord

Huntly's friends must equal it and not be outdone. For one emissary we have on foot, they have a hundred. The whole town is for them. We have no one to assist us . . . For God's sake, lay every oar in the water. Secure all the Strathbogie men. The Aberdeenshire Regiment will be about your ears, if every friend of the Marquis does not act with heart and hand and stop at no bounty.[72]

The old captain, who was clearly one of those eternal pessimists who positively revelled in predicting ever darker doom, gloom and disaster, again foresaw a bidding war. A month earlier he warned that: 'If friends to one Corps [Hay's] advertise gratuitys, the other, the Marquis's, will find some to do so too. It becomes necessary in such a case, and there is no help. It is inflaming the reckoning on both sides, but the Marquis will chuse to keep his ground, I daresay.'

There were certainly signs this might turn out to be the case. In early April a meeting of freeholders, commissioners of supply and other Aberdeenshire worthies met to appoint a working committee to assist Hay and to contribute a substantial bounty. In response the *Aberdeen Journal* noted on 28 April that:

At a meeting of some of the Duke of Gordon's tenants in the Parish of Kirkmichael and Strathdown, it was resolved in testimony of their gratitude and attachment to the noble family under which they and their predecessors had lived for generations, to exert themselves to assist in enlisting volunteers for the Marquis of Huntly's regiment, and for that purpose they resolved to give three guineas of additional bounty over and above every other bounty, to any good recruit from their own country, who shall voluntarily enlist with the Marquis of Huntly . . .

And much good it may have done him, for Hay shrewdly outmanoeuvred him once again by gladly accepting all the practical assistance offered by the committee, but publicly declining the top-up to the bounty – thus tacitly obliging the Gordons to do the same and so levelling the field in his favour.

What was more, in his eagerness to secure Lochaber against the threat from Erracht, the duke had mistakenly taken the support of the Aberdeenshire lairds for granted. A striking example can be seen in the case of Major James Urquhart, a younger brother of the Laird of

Craigston and a disappointed candidate for the major's job in the new regiment. The fact that he was an experienced half-pay officer from the 14th Foot who had seen active service in the West Indies and at Bunker Hill during the American War should have counted for a lot in itself, and possessing an extensive network of family connections both inside and outside the army ought to have clinched it. Instead he was turned down flat. Simon MacDonald of Morar, although junior to him in rank, may have been reckoned more important for securing Lochaber, but more likely it was because Urquhart's sister Jean had thoroughly upset the Gordons by marrying Staats Long Morris scandalously soon after the death of the old duchess back in 1779. Either way, turning Urquhart down was to be a bad move, for although 'Jamie' was reckoned by his siblings to have no great head for business, he and his family commanded considerable influence in north-eastern Aberdeenshire and alienating them was hardly calculated to advance the duke's cause.[73]

The fact of the matter was that for a variety of reasons, as Bulloch argues, a significant number of the local gentry were putting aside petty rivalries to rally against the Gordons. 'All people here are acting for [Hay],' warned Finlason in another letter, 'and the connection made with [Francis Garden of] Delgaty by his brother [Peter Garden] being second Major is powerful in Aberdeenshire . . . I hear Pitfour and Allardyce assisted strongly.' A week later he was again complaining that: 'The whole town high and low are at work for the Aberdeen Regiment. Tomorrow Hay gives a great dinner . . .'

Unlike the duke and his absent son, Hay was working hard:

> . . . so popular that one market day as many as eighteen men joined him. Mr Skene of Skene brought a large contingent drawn from his own estates and obtained at Rood Fair, Montrose, where he had liberally regaled all and sundry at the Market Cross. The Earl of Aberdeen was at Tarland to help on the work, and, punch being distributed in great abundance in the street, a number of 'very fine young men' were enlisted.[74]

And still Huntly remained in Edinburgh: 'Good God, why will he not come and be a Lion in his own cause?' wrote Finlason on 17 May. 'I wish to God I was stopped and officers appeared. It does not answer for me [not an officer in the regiment] to carry on such an oppositional business. Unsupported, too, is dreadful. I have not even a serjeant to keep my irregulars in order.' The Marquis's continued absence at this juncture was inexplicable to his supporters and could have been fatal to his regiment. Not until June did he finally put in an appearance and in the meantime his formidable mother, who had of course tried her hand in this line of business many years before, pitched in to help in person.

According to legend a quite improbable number of recruits surrendered to the bestowal of a guinea and a kiss from the Duchess's own lips, while another version of the story had her daughters speeding the work by dancing at Tomintoul market with any young man who would enlist. If either story was true then remarkably little was said or written about it at the time, although the velvet bonnet worn by the Duchess is still preserved and Stewart of Garth did refer in passing to her having assisted with the recruiting 'in person'. However, when Clerk came to write his memorial of Colonel John Cameron of Fassifern in 1858, he probably approached the truth of the matter by noting that:

> It is said that the celebrated Duchess herself was more active and more successful than any of her vassals or friends: that, equipped in semi-military costume, she rode from farm to farm, from hamlet to hamlet of her extensive estates, by an eloquent tongue rousing the martial ardour of her tenantry: and in rare cases where this failed offering the bribe of a kiss from her own lips. Such a bribe always proved irresistible.[75]

Whether she kissed many or just a few in those 'rare cases', or even none at all, there seems little doubt that it was largely through her personal exertions that the Strathbogie men were secured and the honour of the house preserved. However, eastwards into Aberdeenshire proper, it was pretty much a lost cause – in the face of this determined competition, in what was once his own back yard, there was no alternative but to once again look westwards to the fertile recruiting grounds of Lochaber.

The surviving description roll for 1794 records the parishes of origin for 894 of the original 940 recruits to the regiment. Of those, only 206 men

– rather less than a quarter of the whole – came from Aberdeenshire and Banffshire, and the majority of those from the Strathbogie area, where the Gordon influence (or at least the Duchess's) was strongest, rather than from further eastwards where Hay and his supporters held sway. Almost incredibly that number was matched, if not exceeded, by the southern recruits picked up in Paisley, Glasgow, Stirling, Edinburgh and thereabouts. There were even fifty-one Irishmen amongst them. It was indeed Lochaber, therefore, that proved to be the salvation of both the regiment and its Highland character, with no fewer than 271 men coming from Inverness-shire and Argyllshire, and another sixty-one from Ross, Caithness and Sutherland, where Sir Robert Sinclair of Stevenston had married the Marquis's sister, Madelina, and exerted himself manfully in his brother-in-law's service. No such record has survived for Hay's regiment but from the correspondence of the time there is no doubt that he was the clear winner when it came to recruiting in Aberdeenshire and in the burgh itself.

At any rate with the aid of the Lochaber men the Gordon regiment was completed first and duly inspected and approved at Aberdeen on 25 June 1794 by General Sir Hector Monro – who curiously enough had once been an officer in Morris's 89th Highlanders all those years before. By all accounts it was a lively affair: the previous day the Marquis, fully recovered at last from that mysterious injury, attended the laying of the foundation stone for a new barracks on the Castle Hill, together with the bretheren of seven lodges of freemasons, the magistrates and anybody else who could contrive an excuse for a place in the front row. One hopes they included Finlason, who deserved a place there if anyone did. The occasion was suitably celebrated thereafter in the New Inn on Broad Street and the principals may not quite have sobered up by the following morning, for one of the Gordon recruits, Daniel Nicol, declared that he and his comrades were each required to run fifty paces in front of the old general to prove their fitness!

Two months later Hay's regiment was also passed as fit for service at Aberdeen by the general on 5 September 1794, and shipped to Jersey in April 1795 for a spell of garrison duty before going on active service. Long and sometimes bitter experience had taught the army the importance of this procedure for introducing newly raised battalions to the somewhat arcane ways of soldiering, and in June they returned again to Southampton, or more precisely to the great tented camp on Nursling Common, where a great 'descent' was being prepared for the West Indies.

Whatever his feelings might have been about the prospect of a posting to the dread fever islands, Hay, like Allan Cameron of Erracht, reacted with anger and dismay when instead the Duke of York ruthlessly took the decision to draft the 109th out of existence. This was part of a massive exercise, sometimes referred to as the 'Great Drafting', and all the regiments and battalions junior in rank to the 90th Foot were to have been disbanded and their personnel turned over to other units. The fact that Erracht's 79th was also to have been included points either to an unfavourable view having been formed of it by senior officers, or more likely perhaps to that malign influence that he was so fond of complaining about. Unlike Erracht, however, Hay was unsuccessful in his appeal, despite the active support of the Aberdeen-born editor of the *Morning Chronicle*, who ominously warned that:

> However necessary for the public service it might be to draft the men from the new Regiments into old, it is much to be lamented that measures were not taken to obviate the discontents which it was easy to see it must occasion among the men who understood the terms of their enlisting to be that they should not be drafted. Nothing can be more dangerous than for the Government of a country to be suspected of breaking faith with those who are to fight in its defence. The late Mutiny of the Manchester and Birmingham Regiments in Dublin is imputable to this cause alone; and although the mutiny has been quelled, every military man knows that many of the men will carry their discontents to the regiments into which they may be drafted, and, instead of proving good soldiers themselves, corrupt others who but for such communication would have become good soldiers.[76]

In early correspondence the regimental agent, Hugh Donaldson, had referred to the 109th as a Highland regiment and the officers certainly wore feathered bonnets, and although it is uncertain whether the men had kilts, white trousers were served out in the summer of 1795 in preparation for going to the West Indies. So there was no practical impediment to their being drafted into the otherwise depleted ranks of the 53rd Foot on 24 September 1795 – thus making something of a mockery of that corps' notional 'Shropshire' title.[77] A number of the regiment's officers also went over to the 53rd along with their men, and it is nice to record that Hay also secured a commission (dated that same 24 September 1795) for the regimental sergeant major, Hugh Douglas. On the whole the matter was probably rather better handled than most exercises of this kind and at all events the fate of the 109th was certainly better than that of Sir James Grant's 97th, which was broken up completely, with the flank company men going to the 42nd and the rest being scattered to no apparent purpose between the 21st, the 74th and even the marines.

Surprisingly, however, the Gordons escaped, and their very different experience reveals that once again some powerful strings were being pulled on their behalf. Soon to become famous as the 'Ninety-Twa', the regiment was at this time numbered as the 100th Regiment in the Army List and so lay well outside any safety margin when the time came to consider their fate. By any reasonable expectation the regiment should have been included amongst those units scheduled to be drafted, but as it happened, they were safely abroad when the axe fell.

Having been formally embodied, the Gordons were first posted to Southampton before going on to the Gibraltar garrison and the excitement of a minor and happily bloodless expedition to Corsica in June of 1795. These circumstances were in themselves enough to win for the regiment a temporary stay of execution, for it was hardly practical to bring them home simply to disband them, particularly as that would in itself require the diversion of another battalion to replace them at Gibraltar. Nevertheless, as Harry Dundas was explaining to Huntly, as late as December 1796, the regiment still remained in very real danger and only some determined string-pulling could save it:

> You know that your regiment is considerably beyond the line of those which are to be kept up on the limited establishment. The latest number not drafted is the 90th and the only exemptions is your regiment and one at the Cape, [the 98th, later 91st Highlanders] which we could not spare from that quarter at present. Your Regiment will still be continued undrafted, and at Gibraltar till the Peace; but you will recollect that the only ostensible ground of doing so is that it is a Regiment raised

by your family, which would therefore be hard to draft, as the same exertions which raised it were able to keep it at its full compliment. In consequence of a conversation I had with the Duke of York, I think it right to mention these particulars to you with a view that you will omit no exertions on your own bottom to keep your Regiment complete to its full establishment. I need not tell you that in a Regiment circumstanced as yours, it is impossible to give to it any of the men levied under the Act of Parliament. It being, however, a material part of the garrison of Gibraltar, it is very essential that you should exert yourself both for your credit and to prevent your Regiment from being drafted, and, allow me to add, to prevent any reflections being cast on those who, it may be said, ought to have drafted yours at the same time they did the others below the number 90.[78]

That urgent advice was no doubt prompted not only by the very pointed questions currently being asked in Parliament about the Gordons' continued survival, but also by the rumour that the regiment was after all going to be drafted into the ranks of the 42nd; a rumour which was still going the rounds for some time afterwards and greatly retarding Huntly's efforts to act on Dundas' advice to fill up the ranks.

In January an 'advertisement' which he had posted around all the parish kirks in Kingussie proclaimed that:

His Lordship, being anxious to have a few young handsome fellows to complete his Regiment, entreats and expects the assistance of his friends in Badenoch. He can assure such young men as are willing to go along with him that the Regiment is *not* to be drafted during the war, and that they may depend on every attention from him while they continue in service; and that on their return to the country they and their relations will have preference upon equal terms, from the Duke of Gordon for such farms on his estate as they are inclined to settle upon. His Lordship will be found at Aviemore during the whole of the day on Monday.

Nevertheless those rumours still would not go away and as late as 11 February 1797, Todd the factor at Fochabers had to write that:

The story of Lord Huntly's regiment being drafted into 42nd, is an infamous falsehood, and you'll see it contradicted in all the papers by authority. Some of his Lordship's rivals in the recruiting line have thought such a tale might be of service to them, but I can assure you that Lord Huntly has the most positive assurance from the highest authority that his regiment shall not be drafted during the war.[79]

And so of course he had, and from Dundas himself no less, but nevertheless it was not until October 1798, after some useful service in Ireland, that the threat of drafting was finally lifted and the regiment famously re-designated as the 92nd Foot.

~ 5 ~

Mutiny: The Strathspey Fencibles

That pointed allusion in the *Morning Chronicle* to the mutinies of the Birmingham and Manchester regiments serves as a useful reminder that such disturbances were not by any means confined to the British Army's Highland battalions. By studying the Highland mutinies in isolation, as has been done in the past, it can be very easy to gain the impression that they were the product of a fatal clash of cultures, in which the Highlanders were hapless victims of cynical exploitation by an indifferent government and ambitious chieftains turned landlords. It would also be a highly misleading impression, for English and Irish regiments also mutinied with some frequency throughout the eighteenth century, usually for exactly the same reasons that provoked their kilted colleagues.

So far as the Dublin affair was concerned, the disturbances were directly linked to the enforced drafting of those units into the ranks of other regiments. It had, of course, happened many times before. In an earlier incident in 1779, for example, a party of recruits originally destined for the 42nd and 71st Highlanders had mutinied at Leith when they were ordered to be drafted into the 83rd Royal Glasgow Volunteers instead. At first the mutiny amounted to nothing more than a noisy refusal to embark on the boats intended to carry them out to the transports, but when the South Fencibles were called on to restore order, shooting broke out, and a total of fourteen men were killed and twenty-eight wounded on both sides. Both the violence and the resulting casualty list were far from typical – the Dublin affair by contrast, although noisy, produced no fatalities and was perhaps untypical only in the scale of the drafting that provoked it.

Although contemporary critics such as General Tarleton and historians like Fortescue liked to portray both the officers and men that were swept up in the recruiting boom of the early 1790s as a worthless rabble, the reality was that many of the new battalions were actually made up of some very fine materials indeed. As we have already seen, there was a genuine popular impulse to raise some of these units, often sponsored as they were by local corporations, landowners and businessmen. Thus, to take just a few examples: L'Hoste's 104th Manchester; Bulwer's 106th Norwich; Montgomerie's Royal Glasgow Regiment; and a score of other similar units – including of course Hay's 109th (Aberdeenshire) – could in many ways be regarded as the precursors of the locally-recruited 'Pals' battalions raised by those same local communities in the heady opening months of the Great War a century later.

Consequently it was actually the new regiments that were harvesting the cream of the recruits, whilst the older more established units, unable to deploy either the money or the resources being lavished on their rivals, had to make do with the left-over dregs. In the circumstances it was hardly surprising that the old regiments should now cast covetous eyes on the infinitely better materials forming the new battalions, or that the Duke of York should be persuaded to oblige by drafting these fine recruits into the struggling veteran units.

For the most part he got away with it. So far as the new Highland regiments were concerned, the 78th and 79th were senior enough to escape, although the latter was temporarily drafted for entirely practical reasons, while the Argylls and the Gordons contrived to be safely overseas and protected by friends in high places when the blow fell. The rest, on the other hand, mostly passed out of existence with a certain quiet dignity, and indeed only Breadalbane's 116th Highlanders, or at least some of them, joined with their English colleagues in the Dublin riots –the fact that they did so in concert only underlines the commonality of their experience.

Drafting of course was not the only cause for protest. Overseas postings of any kind could also be fraught with difficulty. Quite apart from the original Black Watch mutiny of 1743, one particular cause célèbre some years before had been the refusal of the 77th Highlanders to embark for India in 1783, just after word came through that peace was signed, ending the America War and thereby entitling every man in the battalion to receive his discharge. However, notwithstanding the drama of that particular incident – involving both mobbing and rioting in the traditional eighteenth-century style and the seizure for a time of the port's fortifications – the regiment's defiance was far from isolated. Other regular units quartered in the Portsmouth area at the time were equally reluctant to embark for further service abroad and the 77th's violent protest ashore was mirrored by an equally mutinous attempt by the already embarked 68th (Durham) Regiment to run *their* transports onto the beach! The Government was forced to acknowledge itself to have been in the wrong; in the end the fact that the 77th just happened to be a Highland regiment had not had any bearing at all on the causes, course and successful outcome of the protest.

This, generally speaking, was also true of all the other 'Highland' mutinies, but this aspect of their story is nevertheless an interesting one, especially as there was another round of trouble connected with embarkation orders early in 1794, which is well worth re-telling in a little detail. First, through the brief and rather anti-climactic experience of the Duke of Gordon's 6th (Northern Fencibles) in March 1794, and then, by way of contrast, through the undoubted mutiny of a part of Sir James Grant's 1st (Strathspey Fencibles) just a few days later. Both regiments were amongst those raised at the outbreak of war a year earlier and solely intended, as their letters of service proclaimed, 'for the internal protection of North Britain'. That stipulation was rather sensibly qualified by the statement that they might also be called upon to serve in England in the event that the French should actually land there, but there was no provision for their going south in anticipation of such an invasion. This, as the gentlemen at the War Office quickly realised, was a touch inconvenient. Realistically there was no great expectation of the French sailing across the North Sea to land in Scotland, but the English Channel was a different matter entirely – should the Royal Navy fail in its duty, it was the beaches of Kent and Sussex where the invader would be greeted.

The challenge was finding enough men to meet them there, for as we have also seen it was not until August of 1793 that any additional regiments of the line were authorised. Even then the first of them, Erracht's 79th Highlanders, was not accepted as complete until January

1794, let alone passed as fit for service. Yet just at that very moment the government was worriedly convincing itself that a French invasion might be a distinct possibility and that if no regulars were going to be available to stop them there was no realistic alternative but to stiffen the English militia with Scottish fencibles.

To its credit the government made no attempt to ignore or circumvent that unequivocal stipulation as to restricted service, and in the circumstances the answer must have seemed obvious enough. The fencible regiments could not be obliged to go to England but there was nothing whatever to prevent the men themselves from being asked to volunteer for service in the south, just as a later generation of home service territorials could volunteer for 'Imperial Service' abroad.

Accordingly, to start off with, it was proposed by Dundas to ask for just 250 men from each of the eight battalions (the Earl of Breadalbane having contrived in the meantime to obtain letters of service for a second battalion to his regiment), and if this plan had been persevered with, all might have been well. Instead Lord Adam Gordon decided in the interests of efficiency – by which he meant retaining strong garrisons in Edinburgh and Glasgow – to ask just four of the regiments for five hundred men apiece, reckoning that 'it will more readily be gone into than if a separation took place, for Highlanders do not like to part company.'

This might very well have been true in theory, but when only two hundred and fifty men were required from each battalion, those who did not want to go south could comfortably stand aside and cheer the volunteers on their way. Instead, with none of the fencible battalions mustering more than six hundred rank and file and usually a little less, Lord Adam Gordon was to all intents and purposes asking for entire regiments to volunteer for service. It might still, nevertheless, have been possible for individual dissenters to remain in Scotland with the depot and any other non-effectives, but it is all too clear from what followed that the men themselves did not see the question in that light. Their consent might be required but it was being taken for granted and they were effectively being drafted for service in England, in what seemed on the face of it to be a clear breach of their terms of service.

In turn this apparent demonstration of bad faith had the unfortunate effect of implying that a degree of coercion would be involved, or at the very least undue pressure exerted to ensure compliance. Soldiers who might otherwise have willingly gone south not only joined with the genuinely reluctant in holding back, but worse still began to treat other official pronouncements with some quite-unwarranted suspicion. As Stewart of Garth rather ponderously commented:

> Measures were accordingly taken, but unfortunately not with that care, precaution, and ample explanation, so necessary when men's feelings and prejudices are to be consulted, and any previous agreement or understanding to be altered or renewed on another and different basis. In this case, [he was speaking specifically of the Strathspeys] when the commanding officer issued the orders on the subject, some officers thought it unnecessary to offer any explanation to their men; others entirely mistook the meaning and import of the proposals. The consequence was a degree of jealousy and mistrust; and as busy and meddling advisers are not wanting on such occasions, the soldiers became alarmed; they knew not what to believe, or what was intended; and even the explanations of those officers who understood the nature of the proposed measure lost much of their effect.[80]

Nor were matters improved when it was also proposed by his lordship, again simply in the interests of efficiency, to embark them and carry them south by sea, rather than to march them there by land. In Lord Adam's sensible view, a few days' voyage by sea was going to be far quicker and far easier to organise than a lengthy road march requiring detailed route planning, and all manner of tedious but necessary arrangements for feeding and accommodating the troops en route. Inevitably, on a march of such a length there was also sure to be a certain degree of wastage: worn-out shoes and worn out men, and perhaps the odd deserter or two. Much better entirely to send them quickly and comfortably by sea – but to the soldiers themselves, accustomed all their lives to walking everywhere, the supposed advantages were perhaps less apparent. There was a tendency to ask why they were to be carried aboard ships when they could easily go dry-shod to their destination, and inevitably to then go on to question whether once embarked they might not perhaps be carried off to somewhere else entirely.

Consequently, on 8 March 1794, when Lieutenant Colonel John Woodford paraded the 6th (Northern) Fencibles at Edinburgh Castle and had the appeal for volunteers read out to them, not a man stepped forward. And that was all that happened – or rather didn't happen. The Highlanders simply declined to volunteer, and although the officers, being quite unable at first to account for this lack of response, immediately leapt to the conclusion that there was some kind of premeditation, perhaps stirred up by shadowy external agitators, there is no real justification for labelling the affair as a mutiny. There was no refusal to obey orders, no murmuring, no shouted defiance, no angry tumult, far less any mobbing, violent behaviour or shots fired. It is rather hard in fact to avoid the impression that in the days that followed the officers were as baffled by their soldiers' continuing good behaviour as by their initial flat refusal to volunteer.

Not so Colonel Hugh Montgomerie of Coilsfield's West Lowland Fencibles stationed up at Inverness – there was no ambiguity at all about *their* behaviour. Coilsfield's early service in his kinsman Archibald Montgomerie's old 77th Regiment in the 1750s seems to have led him to identify with Highlanders far more closely than might have been thought proper for a representative of one of Scotland's most ancient Lowland families. During the American War he again served with a kilted battalion, this time of Argyll Fencibles, and when he was granted letters of service to raise his very own regiment in his native Ayrshire in 1793, he not only dressed the rank and file of the West Lowland Fencibles in tartan trews and feathered bonnets, but personally went for the full fig of belted plaid, broadsword and all the other outward trappings of a Highland officer.[81] Never was there a clearer example of the growing impulse to assert *Scottish* identity through the wearing of tartans and other Highland dress, so that in Macauley's words Scotsmen and Highlanders were to be 'regarded as synonymous words'.

Nevertheless, no matter how much they might outwardly resemble a Highland regiment (or at least be mistaken for one by untutored Englishmen), Montgomerie's men were all Lowland Scots, through and through, and this simple fact needs to be firmly kept in mind when considering what happened next. At first, wrote Lieutenant Colonel Donaldson on 12 March, he had been confident the men would respond positively to the appeal for volunteers, but:

> ... about 8 o'clock I was surprised by a number of men getting together, with their arms and their bayonets fixed, huzzaing, and in liquor, saying

they never would embark, that they would march to any part of England, but embark they would not, as that was no part of their engagement, that they were sold... They forced the Guard, obliged a fifer and drummer to beat to arms, broke open the stores, and took the made-up cartridges and served them out amongst themselves. I find they have now mounted a Guard, have placed Sentries on the stores, and thus the matter now rests at 12 o'clock at night.[82]

That was indeed as far as it went for the moment, although fear of a similar outbreak led the officers of Lord Hopetoun's South Fencibles – another Lowland Scots unit – to lose their heads and hastily dump that battalion's ammunition into Banff harbour.

By contrast, back down at Edinburgh meanwhile, the Gordons were still behaving impeccably, except that as news of the Lowlanders' disturbances filtered southwards, some of them were 'seen in knots talking Gaelic with an air of mystery' and others were going so far as to exchange letters with friends and relatives in the Strathspey Fencibles at Glasgow. It would hardly be surprising if they were discussing the extraordinary news from the north, but neither their English commanding officer, Lieutenant Colonel John Woodford, nor many of his officers could actually speak enough Gaelic to know what they were actually talking about and so they perhaps quite naturally assumed the worst, as our friend Pryse Lockhart Gordon recalled:

> Ours being locked up in the Castle, had less communication with the malcontents and was the last to exhibit discontent... The Lieutenant Colonel fancied himself actually a Highlander, and, piquing himself on his popularity, he imagined his eloquence would bring the men to reason. He marched them by detachments into the garrison chapel, and, mounting the pulpit, lectured away with great vehemence for a couple of hours, but, as might have been expected, without effect.[83]

Consequently the duke himself was sent for from Gordon Castle and, interrupting his efforts to raise the family's new regiment of the line, took just forty-eight hours to get from Speyside to Edinburgh, where he immediately wrote to his uncle, Lord Adam, to say that: 'If my Regiment, or 500 of them, had been asked to march into England they would readily go, but whether they will boat is more than I will answer for.'[84] He may or may not have been aware when he wrote this that a personal appeal by Sir James Grant of Grant to the Strathspey Fencibles had just failed, but nevertheless, having paraded the battalion on 19 March:

> He explained in a few words the nature of the service they were called for, 'the defence of their country'; and he trusted that any soldier who was such a disloyal dastard as to refuse such a service he would step out of the ranks and he should have his discharge, for, although they were raised for the defence of Scotland, England was now in danger, and none but cowards would refuse the call. He could assure them that, wherever they went, they would find him at their head; and, if they preferred marching to England by land, rather than being transported by sea, that they had their choice. This short harangue was received with the greatest applause, and every bonnet was elevated, and every voice cheered, that they were ready to follow his Grace to the world's end.

'Thus', remarked a sardonic Pryse Lockhart Gordon, 'terminated the dreaded mutiny ...'[85]

It was also pretty much the same story up at Inverness, although sadly the West Lowlanders lacked an equally talented diarist to record what happened there in any detail. Having responded to Donaldson's plea for assistance, Montgomerie of Coilsfield, perhaps passing the duke en route, hastened northwards and made what must have been a very similar personal appeal to his regiment, with the same effect. They too cheered him and agreed to go to England if they were ordered, and eventually the full 500 men duly embarked with him for Chatham at the end of March, accompanied by 181 men of Hopetoun's regiment.

The readiness and indeed the speed with which both battalions had been turned around by rousing speeches from their commanding officers, indicates that there had always been an underlying willingness to extend the terms of their service if they were appealed to honestly, but any satisfaction obtained by Lord Adam Gordon from this happy outcome was tempered by some shocking news from Linlithgow.

Sir James Grant of Grant entered into the business of raising regiments for the Crown comparatively late in life, but with some success. The Grants were one of those ancient Scottish families who eschewed grand titles of nobility but nevertheless enjoyed far more power and influence than their humble addresses might suggest. What was more, Sir James himself was something of a paradox. He was unquestionably a Highland proprietor in the modern style and a shrewd businessman, but yet one who still exercised a genuine paternal responsibility for his tenants –in that respect at least he behaved far more like a genuine Highland chieftain than many of his contemporaries who aspired to the romantic trappings of such a title while caring nothing for their *soi disant* clansmen. Even John Prebble could find nothing about him worthy of criticism beyond the entirely innocuous fact that on succeeding his father in 1773 he was forced to sell off some of his family estates (which naturally enough went with the benefit of sitting tenants) in order to pay off some of the debt he had also inherited! Stewart of Garth, who tended to be equally condemnatory of the degenerate chieftains of his day, was in positive raptures when it came to describing the good Sir James, who in his eyes embodied everything a clan chief should be. 'He was the worthiest master, the best husband, the best father, and the best Christian of the district to which he was an honour and a blessing,' he gushed, paraphrasing Clarendon's celebrated encomium on King Charles I, and wound up by declaring, 'Few men could with more confidence step forward with an offer to his King.'

He referred of course to Grant's offer to raise a battalion of fencibles, and like his neighbour, the Duke of Gordon, Sir James completed his battalion swiftly enough: on 9 May 1793 he reported from Forres that he had enlisted 24 sergeants, 24 corporals, 10 drummers, 2 pipers and 480 privates in the eight companies, and another 150 supernumeraries besides. Interestingly enough, however, many of them seem at first have been part-timers, for he went on to admit that:

> As yet, neither the drums, arms, or cloathing are come down, which is of the less consequence as I am convinced His Majesty would think it improper to withdraw many of the men who are engaged from the necessary labours of the spring, to whom we gave such assurance. The seed time has been very backward this season, and makes it indispensably necessary to give all possible indulgence to the Farmers.[86]

In other words a significant proportion of his recruits had promised to enlist with him, but only after the spring planting was complete – an arrangement that would on the one hand have been incomprehensible to English recruiters, and on the other hand clearly demonstrates the degree to which that enlistment was far from a one-sided bargain. Grant's regiment might be raised, at least in part, from amongst his tenants and the tenants of his friends and relations further afield – but they all came willingly. It was certainly not an old-fashioned clan levy with old and young alike harried out at the chief's command, like the 'perfect herd boys' reported standing in the ragged Jacobite ranks at Culloden.

In spite of this, Sir James seconded this happy news with a successful application to put those supernumeraries into two more companies and when the regiment was formally inspected and embodied by Lieutenant General Leslie on 5 June it paraded fully six hundred private soldiers, complete to establishment.

Although he was successful in raising a respectable number of his tenants, or their sons, and those of the other Grant gentlemen who rallied to his banner, there was still a limit to just how many young men on his own estates could be found to enlist; or rather who met the ordinary physical criteria for soldiers of the Crown. Thus, like the Duke of Gordon, Sir James too had found it necessary to range far and wide in search of recruits to complete the regiment. According to Stewart of Garth, forty-one of the men came from Lowland Scotland (a rather inexact term, which he seems to have defined as being anywhere south of the Forth), three men from England and an obligatory two from Ireland.[87] But once again, in emulation of the duke, he had gone westwards into the Great Glen and Lochaber to find the rest.

The similarities did not end there, for just as the duke was joined by Cameron of Locheil, Sir James had the far-from-unalloyed pleasure of welcoming his nineteen-year-old ward, Alasdair Ranaldson McDonnell of Glengarry, into his regiment as a captain. Like Locheil, Glengarry was the representative of an old Jacobite family and he too was 'puffed up ... with ideas of chieftainship and power which no longer existed', although it might perhaps be admitted in his favour that he at least carried those ideas off with far more swagger and panache than the rather colourless Locheil. He was also, however, a dangerously disruptive element, who shared Locheil's bitter resentment of his subordinate position within the regiment – a resentment that must have been sharpened by the fact that his immediate superior was Major John Grant of Glenmoriston. The irony of that particular juxtaposition being that historically the Glenmoriston Grants had been rather more accustomed to marching behind Glengarry's banner, than before it.

Even as the regiment was being formed he was disputing his precedence amongst the other captains. With that particular cause for petty resentment aside, young Glengarry then also insisted, to an even greater degree than Locheil, on treating the seventy men of his company as his personal following, as though they had, as it were, accompanied him into the army but were not of it. 'He has a cursed trick of laughing & speaking to the men, which does much harm,' complained the lieutenant colonel on one occasion, 'but I hope we will cure him of it by degrees.' Another time he spoke of his 'going on in his accustomed folly, such as coming to the parade in brown breeches, plain Hat, Sash & Gorget, & when reprehended for it, saying he didn't like the duty & would resign, if he could only be allowed to name his successor.'[88] Such behaviour could not fail to be prejudicial to good order and discipline: while it might not perhaps in itself have led directly to what followed, Glengarry's behaviour unquestionably went a long way to creating the conditions that made it possible. Not surprisingly the lieutenant colonel wound up one particular tirade by remarking to Grant that: 'I rely if he offers to resign to you, that you will not refuse him, for the Regt. will never be quite the thing while he is in it.'

In the meantime the lieutenant colonel, who rejoiced in the name of Alexander Penrose Cumming of Altyre, and Major John Grant of Glenmoriston were, as was customary in those days, taking turn to go on extended leave. When the crisis broke it was initially Glenmoriston alone who was in charge of the battalion, for Sir James had been detained in London by Parliamentary business and a heartbroken Altyre was detained by a fatal outbreak of whooping cough amongst his children.

Surviving regimental correspondence between Glenmoriston, Sir James, the paymaster and the adjutant shows that he and the other officers at least had been aware of the proposed posting to England as early as the beginning of March. The battalion was then at Glasgow and the usual preparatory steps of calling in outposts and recalling officers from leave had already been set in train when, on 6 March, Sir James instructed the paymaster to clear the men's accounts. There had already, according to Glenmoriston, been 'reports in town from Edin. that we are to march for England' and now these instructions were the clearest possible indication to both officers and men that a major move was indeed in prospect, for long experience had taught the army that the surest possible recipe for trouble was to draft men or order them overseas without first settling any outstanding issues relating to pay and allowances. On 9 March the battalion received its orders to march for Linlithgow, 'from whence,' wrote the surgeon's mate, 'it is supposed 500 will go for England'. The first division accordingly moved off on 13 March, much to the relief of at least one young subaltern, who declared:

> Heavens be thanked free of Glasgow and I had much rather go to the Plains of Flanders than return to it ... I did not nor wd not believe that there were such places as Glasgow and Paisley in Scotland before I saw them ... There are 1 Lt. Colonel 4 Captains & 15 Subalterns of us ordered wt the 500 men for England.[89]

Dangerously, the battalion's departure for the south was therefore already being spoken of as an accomplished fact, although nothing had actually been said to the men, either officially or by way of informal explanation. Glenmoriston, newly returned to the battalion and by all accounts pre-occupied with a new girlfriend, was still getting to grips with administrative matters. Only Sir James, it appeared, had the necessary authority to actually ask for volunteers, but despite Lord Adam's urging he was not able to join the battalion until it was strung out along the road to Linlithgow. Still split into two divisions it was therefore not until 16 March that the Strathspeys were fully concentrated in the burgh, and not until the following morning that they paraded together as a battalion for the first time since leaving Glasgow.

It was at this point that Sir James finally appeared in front of his regiment and made the long-anticipated official announcement. 'My Friends and fellow soldiers,' he began, reading from a carefully drafted script, 'You know we are come here in consequence of a call from His Majesty to go to the South of England, where in the present exigency of Public affairs he thinks our aid of most consequence ...' He acknowledged thereby that the plan to send two thousand fencibles was common knowledge, and went on to explain that transports had been ordered for their convenience. He asked for the required five hundred rank and file, who 'must undoubtedly be the chosen men of the Regiment, for abilities, good looks, vigour, youth, and strength of constitution'. He extolled too the benefits of serving in England, where 'the soldier lives much better there than he can do here,' and he once again assured them that he ever had their welfare and happiness at heart. His speech was warmer, far more paternal in tone than the tub-thumping appeal to patriotism that the Duke of Gordon would deliver two days later, but he was evidently no orator, and perhaps for both those reasons it failed. Just as at Edinburgh, not a single volunteer stepped forward.[90]

At first it seemed it was going to be a repeat of the Gordon business, for the battalion was otherwise quiet and obedient, although there was certainly more than a suspicion that men from both regiments were in correspondence and seemingly colluding in presenting a united front in their defiance. The extent to which those suspicions may have been justified is perhaps debatable, but it could well be significant that on the evening of 20 March, just the day after the Gordons agreed after all to go to England, the Strathspeys' light company announced their willingness to do likewise.

'We were flattered yt the Light Company to a man were coming forwd,' wrote Lieutenant Grant. 'And after drawing up in proper order before the Colonel's window unanimously expressed their readiness and willingness to follow him & their officers anywhere – the Cols own Company joined & were almost unanimous in doing the same as were a great many of the majors – you may believe we now thought matters wd come round as we wished.'[91]

In fact things just were about to become infinitely worse. Encouraged both by the news from Edinburgh and by this evidence of an apparent change of heart amongst his own men, Sir James decided to make a renewed appeal of his own next morning. However, as he explained to Lord Adam Gordon just before setting out for the parade ground, he was still not entirely confident of the outcome. The Strathspey men, he said, all intended when they got there 'to express their sorrow and their resolution to go to England in any way I saw proper.' However, if Lord Adam was being encouraged thereby to think that Sir James had persuaded the whole Strathspey Regiment to embark he was quickly disabused of that happy notion, for Grant immediately qualified his news by revealing that the 'Strathspey men' in question were only those of his tenants belonging to his own company. Other companies he felt sure would follow their example, including of course the 'Light Infantry, led by Captain Fraser, their Captain', but there was still a certain anxiety over the grenadiers, and, 'I cannot however be so sanguine as to the Macdonnell Company, whose animosity to the measure, & proceedings, supported by some of the Grenadiers, and heightened by the reports and Letters they received as to the other regiments had made the whole so seemingly backward.'[92]

The emphasis that Sir James placed on the role of Captain Fraser in bringing about the change of heart by the light company was significant, for he clearly believed that their conversion was not the spontaneous impulse suggested by Lieutenant Grant. His own appeal to the battalion had failed, perhaps because he was a poor orator, but if Fraser could bring his own men around, he reasoned, then similar personal appeals by the other company officers might be equally effective.

It was a disastrous miscalculation, for while he himself might have used a combination of his own authority and the splendid example of the light infantry to rally the battalion, by placing the decision back in the hands of the individual company commanders he robbed the appeal of any cohesion.

As ever it can be difficult to separate out behaviour that was actually recognised as ominous at the time and those missed warning signs helpfully dredged up afterwards. The first inkling of trouble came, as Sir James had half expected, from the grenadiers. In older battalions of the line this company was an elite, formed of the steadier old sweats who could be relied on in a crisis. In newly formed battalions such as this one, however, there was no such pool of old soldiers to draw upon and instead the grenadiers were picked from the other companies for their height and for how well they matched up to a fashionable obsession with 'fine looking' or 'good looking' men. Consequently, far from being solid and dependable, the grenadier company may have lacked the social cohesion of the ordinary battalion companies still serving under the officers who had recruited them, while at the same time allowing themselves airs and graces as a fashionable, if not a military, elite. It was a recipe for disaster and '... next morning at 10,' continued Lieutenant Grant, 'we marched to the field of exercise near Linlithgow and after drawing up the companies separately as usual began wt putting the question to the Grenadiers when we found we could prevail on only a very few to join the colours and those who declined in a dastardly manner broke from their Ranks run off huzzaing.'

Exactly what provoked the outburst is unclear, but interestingly enough Lieutenant Grant relates that

> ... once their brain was afloat thousands of ideas each wilder than the other gender'd in it – one among the rest was that Capt. Frank [Sir James's son, Captain Francis William Grant] had brot. a stand of the Duke of York's Colours along wt. him & that they were all to be sold and sent to Flanders, What gave rise to this was that our Regimental embroidered Colours were unpacked that day and displayed for the first time – we had only the temporary Painted Colours before that.

John Prebble, in his classic account of the mutiny, suggests that it was when the colours were uncased and the order given to form the battalion by companies, that the grenadiers broke ranks, shouting that they were sold. In point of fact the colours should have been visible to the men long before, for the procedure laid down in the regulations was that once the companies were reported as present and correct they were to be formed in line and the colours posted before, not after, they had marched to the field of exercise.[93] Nevertheless that march would have given plenty of opportunity for the rumour to spread through the ranks and by the time Captain Robert Cumming spoke to his grenadiers, they had already convinced themselves they were sold abroad and were in no mood to listen when he spoke only of England.

On the other hand, afterwards no-one was in any doubt that although the trouble may well have begun with the grenadiers, it was really Glengarry's people who were at the centre of it all. The chaplain, for one, went so far as to complain that 'they have been the source of every evil,' and rather imaginatively wished 'Glengarry & his men had been in Botany Bay when they joined our Fencibles.'[94] Consigning them to an Australian penal colony probably sounded like a good idea to some of the other officers as well, for there is certainly no doubt that that company was slackly led by an arrogant and immature young officer who ostentatiously paraded his indifference to his duties, and that it was consequently ill-disciplined and indeed encouraged to be so. There was also another factor.

Glengarry also considered that as a Highland chieftain he ought to have a whole regiment of his very own – surprisingly enough, at this juncture there was an outside chance that he might get one. Roman Catholics were still excluded by statute from public life and although individuals such as Glengarry might enlist or even obtain commissions, providing they did so quietly and did not draw attention to their religion, this was done tacitly, rather than openly. However, faced with a growing manpower crisis the Government was now contemplating the possibilities of raising overtly Catholic regiments, tapping a huge pool of potential recruits in Ireland, and also a supposedly large Catholic population in the West Highlands. A six-battalion-strong Irish Brigade, officered by Catholic gentry once accustomed to serving in the Wild Geese of France, was actually in the process of being raised – as a serving officer, albeit a thoroughly bad one, Glengarry considered himself to be an obvious choice to recruit a similar regiment from amongst his clansmen in Lochaber. However, whilst the prospect of losing the chieftain may have filled Altyre and his brother officers with unalloyed joy, the men of his own company may have been encouraged to view the prospect of his going with rather less enthusiasm.

Oddly enough, when Sir James sounded out his company commanders the night before, Glengarry declared he could offer no assurances about the behaviour of his company, for: 'he says their having heard of his intention of offering to raise a Regiment and so leaving them had deprived him of his former influence amongst them.' That, as we shall see, and indeed as Sir James himself undoubtedly recognised, was pure humbug. They had all of them come into the army, and into Sir James's regiment, as followers of their clan chief and there is no doubt that they now figured in Glengarry's own plans as a nucleus for his proposed clan regiment. However, he would only be able to have them transferred across with him if they were still in Scotland rather than guarding a beach in Sussex – and in that light, what followed assumes an interesting complexion.

I Highland officer *c.*1760; print by MacIan based on a portrait of the
Duke of Sutherland as colonel of the Sutherland Fencibles

II *The Advantage of Shifting the LEG*; print by Rowlandson depicting a Highland officer about to decapitate a French grenadier

GRENADIERS of the XLII.º or ROYAL, and XCII.º OR GORDON HIGHLANDERS.

III Grenadiers of the 42nd and 92nd Highlanders –
print after Charles Hamilton Smith, 1815

IV 42nd officer, 1750s; Victorian print by MacIan, although clearly based on Van Gucht, this careful reconstruction includes some interesting details such as the broader bonnet and the red overstripe in the plaid

V   Colonel Francis Grant, depicted here by John Kay as the colonel of the Inverness Militia. He originally served in his father's regiment, the Strathspey Fencibles, before moving on to the 97th Inverness-shire Highlanders and finally the Fraser Fencibles

VI Highlanders; print by Atkinson. The regiment is unidentified, but the tartan has a red and possibly a white overstripe. They may therefore represent the 73rd prior to losing the kilt, but on balance they are most likely men of the 71st sketched before that regiment went into tartan trousers. (Private collection)

SEVENTY SECOND
OR
DUKE OF ALBANY'S OWN
HIGHLANDERS.

VII The first of the de-kilted regiments to regain Highland dress was the 72nd, as illustrated in Cannon's Historical Records. A number of units raised in the 1790s had also worn tartan trousers

VIII Wellesley at Assaye; a contemporary and reasonably accurate illustration. Although the Highlanders are wrongly shown wearing caps, the officers, including Wellesley, have the round hats favoured in the tropics

Unfortunately we know nothing of what Glengarry actually said to his men. It is unthinkable of course that he would have openly incited them to defy the appeal for volunteers, but he certainly had no incentive to encourage a favourable outcome. It is hard to avoid the feeling that Stewart of Garth was hinting at something when he wrote how 'when the commanding officer issued the orders on the subject, some officers thought it unnecessary to offer any explanation to their men; others entirely mistook the meaning and import of the proposals.'

At any rate, whether it was with Glengarry's tacit encouragement or not, whether he tried to hold them in their ranks or quietly stood aside, there was no doubting what happened next. Had the protests been confined to the grenadiers, Sir James and his officers might still have carried the business off. The night before, he had been encouraged by assurances that his own company and Glenmoriston's were ready to follow the example of the light infantry. Therefore he believed that with a little more time the whole battalion would have followed them, and that a happy result was only frustrated by the evening growing too dark. Unfortunately, that morning seniority placed Glengarry's company next to the grenadiers and when the shouting began they were 'immediately joined by the Black Sett the Macdonells & many others put the whole Regt in confusion,' said Lieutenant Grant. And then to the astonishment of all, they ran around the side of the loch to the roofless but still substantial Linlithgow Palace, where, continued Grant, 'after seizing upon the ammunition & made up Ball Cartridges several of the Rascalls came to the opposite side of the Loch betwixt us and began to fire upon the men & officers who had remained in the Park.'[95]

Since the McDonnells clearly accounted for most of the mutineers, a reluctant Glengarry, according to Grant, was sent off after them, together with his second-in-command, Lieutenant James Watson, who also happened to be the regiment's adjutant. Significantly, however, Watson, a former ranker appointed to that position on the strength of his experience and commonsense, said absolutely nothing about his captain or anyone else accompanying him in his account of the affair.

When the shooting began, he wrote:

I had absolutely Resigned myself to anything and I was ordered of from the main body single handed to go in among the insurgents which was at once a novel undertaking and not at all likely to succeed – at least not without Loosing the Life ... I made my appearance at the gate accompanied by no other person at that moment when I was accosted by the Sentinels which were by this time numerous what my business was – I told them I came as a <u>friend</u> and if they would admit me amongst <u>them</u> I would Endeavour to do them a service after a council of war being held in the inside I was admitted after making such concessions as you may be assured hurt me much particlary one, that no officer was even to make his appearance amongst them but myself not even the Colonel ... I must acknowledge I feeld myself very awkwardly situated not withstanding their pretensions and in fact it shews you clearly to what a pitch they had wrought there Tempers to before I arrived amongst them that they were Determined to sally out and Repell force by force to those who would not join them.

One wonders how any other officer would have fared in these circumstances, but as an experienced former NCO, Watson was equal to the occasion:

After a great deal of altercation amongst them I had the good fortune to Establish a little order – and I proposed that falling in and Exercising would shew the world at once that they meant no <u>harm</u> to any individuals who was not of their way of thinking – this they at last agreed to although god knows neither my heart nor Inclination was Equal to the Task – at that time however I did the best I could and had the good fortune to Divert their minds from commiting any more outrages and although every man's piece was properly flinted and for the most part loaded there was not the smallest accident happened and I Exercised them until they said they were tired and wish'd to Rest themselves this motion I of course agreed to as I was tired enough myself.

His tactics had worked: by simultaneously working off their surplus energy and imposing a degree of normality upon them he defused the situation sufficiently that 'towards the evening after many couriers had pass'd betwixt them and the Commanding Officer they agreed that I should go for him for they wished to speake to him ... the Colonel came – honest man with a heavy heart and Granted them all they wanted they then insisted on marching out with flying <u>culars</u> which was also Granted and they have in some measure Remain perfectly Quite since.'[96]

The colours were presumably the same that had aroused that absurd fear that they were all sold to Flanders – if so marching out behind them neatly saved a certain amount of face on both sides, but unsurprisingly the battalion remained in an edgy mood for some time afterwards. A couple of weeks after the mutiny Glenmoriston was assuring Sir James he was confident nearly all of the men would be willing to go to England by land, but he and the other officers were still wary of the McDonnells. Altyre, now back with the battalion, resolved to deal with them in a surprisingly modern way, which was quite at odds with the popular image of an unbending martinet unsuited to command Highlanders. He wrote to Sir James on 10 April:

> After evening parade, I went up to the palace with the Major, Adjutant, Doctor and Capt. MacDonell's company and after putting sentries on the Gate told them that I had called them together to speak with them as their Commanding Officer and friend – that I shd treat them as I had ever done with civility and kindness – that I had a few propositions to make to them and that I expected and relied what I said to them would be listened to respectfully and meet with a cool and civil answer – That I had it in command to inform them that a very considerable part of the Regiment sensible of their late misconduct, had come forward and offered to march to England with their officers – That if they would handsomely and voluntarily do the same, that the whole of us would esteem it as a mark of affection and attachment that you would be much flattered with it, and that it would go far to re-establish us in the publick esteem in which I was sorry to add we were at present very low – as I went on with the different sentences the other officers translated it literally to the circle.[97]

The upshot, however, was that while they responded very positively to this civil way of speaking to them they still unanimously, but very politely, declined to go to England. On the other hand, said Altyre:

> The leading speakers among them said they were happy to have this opportunity of assuring me that they were willing to seal it with any oath, that Capt. McDonell was unjustly traduced by the suspicion of it

having been said that he had any hand in their declining the expedition (to England) for he had used his utmost influence and exertion to bring them to do it.

Interestingly enough, Glengarry himself was absent and Altyre 'mentioned his being gone to England on the idea of promotion in another Corps, which they bore with unexpected sang froid, and seemed to think they could be as well with any other officer'.

There had already been a shrewd suspicion amongst the other officers as to Glengarry's culpability in the mutiny, but although he had now ostensibly been exonerated by what his men said, as Altyre grudgingly admitted to Sir James, the truth was soon out. Having resigned his commission on 4 May, to the unspeakable relief of all concerned, the young chieftain soon bounced back again when his coveted letters of service were granted on 14 August for the raising of the Glengarry Highlanders and amongst those petitioning to transfer into the ranks of his new regiment were no fewer than seventy-two men of his old company in the Strathspeys.

In an almost pathetic echo of those hard bargains driven by the Gordon and Grant tenants, they also assured Glengarry that '. . . we expect to enjoy those possessions which our ancestors so long enjoyed under your ancestors though now in the hands of Strangers, as we do not wish that you should loose by us we shall give you as high rent as any of your Lowland Sheepherds ever give' and thereby admitted that they were not quite so indifferent as to whether he led them as they once artlessly claimed.[98]

Notwithstanding those assurances given to Altyre, they at least were still uncomfortably aware that if their landlord was intent on behaving as a Highland chieftain of old, then, in the words of Robert Louis Stevenson: when the piper plays, the clan must dance. Whether they were dancing to Glengarry's tune that March day in Linlithgow we will probably never know, but the suspicion that they were was certainly there – and it was strong enough to cast real doubts as to whether the mutiny really was a spontaneous reaction to imagined betrayals of trust, or a cynically manipulated affair that got badly out of hand.

Glengarry's brother officers certainly thought so.

~ 6 ~

Castlebar Races: The Fencibles at War

Altyre's efforts to bring the Strathspeys around were ultimately to be in vain, for although he soon convinced himself that everyone except the McDonnells was now willing to serve in England after all, the battalion itself was regarded by the authorities as quite unreliable and no longer wanted there. Consequently it spent the rest of its unhappy existence in Scotland, confirming officialdom's poor opinion by briefly mutinying for a second time at Dumfries in the following year.[99] Despite offering to go to Ireland, it was disbanded together with all the other first generation battalions in 1799.

In the meantime, having learned its lesson, the Government proceeded instead to raise an entirely new generation of fencible regiments, this time extending the scheme to both England and Ireland and abandoning the original restrictions on their deployment – by first widening their terms of service to include anywhere within the British Isles and the Channel Islands, and eventually to Gibraltar and the Mediterranean garrisons as well. Thus, between 1794 and 1799 some fifty new fencible battalions were raised, of which around twenty were Highland units in name at least.

This continuing heavy preponderance of Highland units was still in part a reflection of the fact that Scotland had as yet no statutory militia force to serve as a second line behind the regulars, but there was also another explanation. Encouraged by the apparent success of the original 'chieftains', the Government resolved to see if the others could also raise their clansmen as of old and so letters of service were freely offered to those Highland proprietors understood to retain some of their traditional influence, no matter whether they were actually fit to be entrusted with a regiment. Thus it was intimated, for example, that the Government anticipated a regiment might perhaps be raised by the Mackay gentry in 'Lord Reay's country' – despite the fact that Lord Reay himself was generally considered quite mad. Similarly, of course, young Glengarry, who although comparatively sane was equally unfit to command anything at all, was another who got himself a regiment, as eventually did his rival, Locheil, with the Lochaber Fencibles in 1799. Breadalbane, not content with two battalions (and his regular 116th Regiment) raised a third fencible battalion; Hay's brother, James Leith, raised the Aberdeen (Princess of Wales) Fencibles, while two entirely new regiments were raised in Argyle and a third in Dumbarton. A Caithness Legion was recruited to rival Sir John Sinclair's Rothesay and Caithness Fencibles, which itself gained a second battalion, and there were Loyal Inverness Fencibles, Banffshire Fencibles, Fraser Fencibles, McLeod Fencibles and Elgin Fencibles; a Regiment of the Isles, the dashingly titled Ross and Cromarty Rangers, and several others besides, all of them bravely dressed in either kilt or tartan trews, and feathered bonnets.

It is very easy to be cynical about these new clan regiments and the readiness with which so many Highland proprietors and other gentlemen 'nearly related' to them took up commissions as fencible officers, but it would also be wrong to portray the battalions as nothing more than a vehicle for the enrichment of the local gentry at the expense of their hapless tenantry. Very few of those involved in the business found the monetary and social rewards equal to their considerable trouble and expense, or indeed the disruption to their everyday lives. Some landowners, such as Glengarry and Locheil, were undoubtedly exercising their own vanity in raising regiments, but for the most part the others were honestly undertaking what was genuinely regarded as their patriotic duty to serve and defend their country and constitution in time of danger; since Scotland had no citizen militia at this time the natural place to discharge that obligation was in the fencibles.

Duty or not, in the circumstances, there was no prospect of Lord Reay himself being offered a commission, even to act as a figurehead, and so on 24 October 1794 command of the fencible regiment bearing his name was confided instead to the confusingly named Mackay Hugh Baillie of Rosehall, while George Mackay of Bighouse became its lieutenant colonel. Stewart of Garth would later go into raptures about this particular battalion, floridly claiming that of the 800 men originally recruited no fewer than 700 'had the word *Mac* prefixed to their names', although in fact the true figure turns out to have been just 381! Nevertheless there is no doubting that it was indeed a proper Highland regiment by any standard and very largely comprised of men from its notional recruiting area in the far north, despite fierce competition from both the older established regiments in the area and from other newcomers such as the Fraser Fencibles and the Caithness Legion.

As we have seen there was nothing new in this competition for recruits and perhaps because all of them were at it this time around, rather than just the rival partisans of two great feuding factions, the business seems to have been conducted a good deal more civilly than it had been in Aberdeenshire and in Lochaber. To all appearances, of course, the new battalions were also competing strongly for recruits with the regular army and on that count alone the fencibles were roundly denounced by the usual critics, both at the time and afterwards. However, this particular charge may not be entirely fair, for there is no certainty that those men who were joining the fencibles were being diverted away from the regular army at all. Experience both with the original regiments formed back during the American War and with those being raised during the present one strongly suggests that the fencibles were actually attracting a quite different class of recruit: young men who were willing to spend a limited period on home service, but who would not necessarily enlist for unlimited service in the regulars, particularly given the prospects of a posting to India.

What is so striking about all those bargains being made between tenants and landlords, for preferential treatment at the time or at a later date in return for enlisting, is not just the fact that men were confident enough to place such conditions on their enlistment, but also the unspoken assumption that they would indeed return home to enjoy that favour within a foreseeable time-frame. No such certainty was attached to service abroad – while those 'respectable farmers' sons' might be prepared to take their chances on a short but glorious campaign in Flanders or even North America, India – where so many of the regular

Highland battalions ended up – was a different matter entirely. It was certainly not perceived as a potential death-trap in the way that the Caribbean was sometimes viewed; quite the reverse – it was somewhere a man might make his fortune. The real problem with a posting to India was the uncertainty and length of service inevitably associated with it. Lord Macleod's regiment, for example, after being raised in the far north went to the East Indies as the 73rd Highlanders in 1779 and did not return home (as the 71st Highlanders) until early in 1798, close on twenty years later, while the 2/42nd not only metamorphosed into the new 73rd but after twenty-odd years in India then went further out to serve as a garrison for Botany Bay! Similarly the two Highland regiments that were specifically raised for service in India in 1787, the 74th and 75th, would not return to Scotland until 1805; the 78th likewise went out to the Cape in 1796, proceeded from there to India, and then out to Java before finally coming home long after the wars were finally over. Obviously enough, many individual officers and soldiers did come back in the meantime, occasionally perhaps having indeed made their fortune out there, but otherwise it was widely recognised that to all intents and purposes any soldier going to India was effectively lost to his friends and family – and to the girl he may have left behind him.

Consequently the authorities hoped, with good reason, that those men who shunned the regulars – either through simple prejudice, as in England, or because they feared the very real prospect of lengthy service overseas – might still be persuaded to serve their country for a short time by becoming fencibles. Like it or not there was still a pressing need to find thousands of men to defend the British Isles themselves from the twin threats of foreign invasion and domestic insurrection – nowhere more so at this time perhaps than in Ireland.

That country, it will be remembered, was still administered quite separately during the eighteenth century, with a royal viceroy in Dublin Castle and its own notoriously corrupt Parliament. What was more, for the last hundred years it had also paid for and looked after no less than fifteen thousand soldiers, in order that they might maintain law and order in the countryside and help the Protestant gentry sleep soundly in their beds at night. Unfortunately, the emphasis thus placed on policing an unruly population meant that the Irish garrison had long since degenerated into little more than a rural gendarmerie of questionable military effectiveness. It was well known, in short, that once posted to Ireland and resigned to the lax control of Dublin Castle, otherwise fine regiments rapidly went to the dogs. Far away from the pomp and ceremony of the capital and colourful field days in Phoenix Park, or even proper garrison towns such as Limerick, regiments were all too often broken up and scattered far and wide as tiny detachments in little villages and country police stations. There they quietly went to seed – and moved at least one inspecting officer in the 1750s to issue a stern order that no officer was 'to appear in the Barrack Yard, on the Parade or any where out of doors, in his Night Cap or Slippers!'[100]

This bucolic state of affairs, which made the Irish establishment a laughing stock on the other side of the water, was reluctantly tolerated by the army only because in peacetime it also served as a very convenient place to 'hide' all those regimental cadres that might otherwise be disbanded by an ever-parsimonious Westminster Parliament. Naturally enough, however, with war now raging at an unprecedented level in almost every corner of the globe, the army was anxious to dust off all those cadres, bring them back up to strength and send them on their way to glory. But how then to comply with the very laws that had preserved them, by still maintaining that 15,000 man permanent establishment? The obvious answer of course was to replace the regulars with home service fencibles.

And so the Reays and others like them were posted to this peculiar backwater, to find themselves keeping the peace in a country where all the old political certainties had been turned on their heads. Back in the 1750s, when the Earl of Rothes only had those carpet slippers and some scandalously bad drill to exercise him, it was straightforward enough. Ireland was run by a tiny Protestant oligarchy and any threat to its peace and stability came from a dispossessed Catholic underclass – specifically from agrarian terrorist groups sporadically calling themselves 'Whiteboys' or 'Defenders', if indeed they bothered with a name at all. Then had come the American War and with it dangerous notions of democratic reform, which saw the radicalisation of a hitherto quiescent Protestant middle class, and the spectacular growth of a volunteer movement ostensibly created to protect the country from the imminent threat of a French invasion. Instead, once organised, armed and uniformed, those loyal volunteers proceeded to turn themselves into a pointed demonstration that where the American colonies had gone, Ireland might well follow if the existing political deficit was unaddressed.

That particular crisis was headed off by allowing a far greater measure of autonomy to the old Irish Parliament, and by extending the franchise to a very limited extent. In the longer term, this hasty settlement not only removed any real checks and balances on the ruling elite in Dublin but also sharpened the differences between the newly enfranchised Protestant middle class and the larger Catholic population, especially in the cities. In a final effort to head off trouble, when war with France came, Pitt persuaded a reluctant Irish Parliament to relax most of the penal laws still excluding Catholics from public life, but they remained barred from sitting in Parliament itself and instead many became involved in a secret revolutionary group calling itself the United Irishmen.

Like the similarly named United Englishmen and United Scotsmen, this left-wing organisation was pledged to a total overthrow of the existing regime and the establishment of a French-style republic dedicated to the Rights of Man. However, although the Scottish Jacobins had provided very convenient scapegoats for the unrest amongst the original fencible regiments culminating in the original Strathspey mutiny, neither they nor the United Englishmen really represented a serious threat to anyone. In Ireland, however, it was a very different matter because over there the revolutionary intellectuals were able to tap into and largely take over the existing agrarian terrorist groups in the name of 'Liberty'. Under the Government's collective noses a secret army was soon taking shape, pledged to rise up in bloody insurrection when the moment came – a moment that was to be signalled by the arrival of a French army!

Oblivious to these developments, the Reay Fencibles, properly resplendent in red jackets with bluish-grey facings, and Mackay tartan kilts, were inspected and embodied at Inverness on 18 June 1795 and shortly afterwards marched for Port Patrick and thence across the water. For the next eighteen months their experience was to be typical of any regiment serving in Ireland: sometimes living in tents, sometimes in barracks. Perhaps the most exciting moment came one fine day when the commanding officer decided it would be a splendid idea if the officers as well as the men turned out in full Highland dress – only to be told they had been parading in breeches, boots and round hats for so long that none of them actually possessed the requisite bonnet, plaid and hose![101]

That happy Irish complacency vanished in a brief moment of panic in December of 1796 when a French invasion fleet turned up like the Devil at prayers in Bantry Bay, but then providentially sailed off again without landing any of the troops it carried. Suddenly the threat of insurrection became disturbingly real. Despite their obvious disappointment at the French failure, the United Irishmen continued to grow in strength, and by February 1798 their secret army amounted to the curiously precise figure of 279,896 armed men – on paper at least –all of them supposedly organised into proper regiments in each county. Spurred on by heightened terrorist activity and by other increasing indications that something was badly amiss, the army found itself becoming involved in a haphazard, unco-ordinated and increasingly brutal counter-insurgency operation. Lacking any proper intelligence of exactly who the rebels were and what they might be up to, all across Ireland little detachments of English, Welsh and Scots fencibles, Irish Protestant yeomanry and Protestant-officered Catholic militia were set to rooting them out.

Sometimes they did so intelligently. Jamie Urquhart of Craigston, after having been turned down by the Gordons, had somehow contrived to get the command of a regiment of Essex fencibles and later boasted of how he had succeeded 'from my great exertion and fatigues in the Countys of Fermannah and Donegal where I commanded with my Regiment in keeping down Rebellion and preventing the United Irishmen from rising and disturbing the peace of those parts'. Not only that, he claimed, but when the French eventually arrived,

> a deputation from the Catholicks of the Parishes of Kilbannon and Ballyshannon waited on me with an offer of 1000 men fit to Bear Arms to act under my orders in any manner I should be pleased to order against the common Enemy the French so well had my Conduct in my Command been approved of by all partys, the like offer was not made to any officer in Ireland but myself, I furnished these Catholicks at the desire of Government with Arms and ammunition out of the stores at

Ballyshannon, and to their credit and Honor, not one of them left their homes or attempted to join the French, but remained ready & steady to join me and defend Ballyshannon.[102]

By all accounts, however, his experience was indeed exceptional. All too often units were simply embarking upon what can only be described as a reckless campaign of terror. Ominously, while there is no doubt that the conduct of many detachments was absolutely deplorable, some of them were getting the results to justify their behaviour. A growing haul of pikes and other arms only served to hint at the true scale of the danger, yet paradoxically the very success of this brutal repression was increasing that danger, for the rebel leaders were becoming steadily more desperate, and ultimately reckless.

Just at that moment, Sir Ralph Abercromby, freshly returned from the West Indies, was appointed commander-in-chief of the Irish army and promptly set about trying to do something about the developing crisis, or rather the dire effect it appeared to be having on his forces. Dismissive of the shadowy threat from the United Irishmen, his first priority as he saw it was to ensure that his army was capable of facing up to a real French invasion, like the one it had so narrowly escaped in 1796. Unfortunately, in his jaundiced view it was instead degenerating into a 'state of licentiousness which must render it formidable to everyone but the enemy'. Tact, as we have already seen, was never his strongest suit and he seconded this intemperate denunciation by going on to explicitly instruct all commanding officers to enforce the strictest discipline and very pointedly reminding them that standing orders expressly forbade troops to act against suspected rebels unless called upon to do so by the civil magistrates, or if they were actually under attack. This critical general order, justified though it certainly was in strictly military terms, provoked an immediate political crisis. There was no obvious threat from the French at that moment, but the increasingly beleaguered Protestant ruling classes were by now living in daily terror of an uprising. They wanted to see the smack of firm government in the shape of continuing oppression of the rebellious lower orders and, faced with growing evidence that their fears of insurrection were on the point of being realised, they loudly clamoured that any slackening of the pressure now would only result in disaster.

In retrospect the result was quite inevitable. Abercromby was reluctantly forced to resign and was replaced by Lieutenant General Gerard Lake, an Anglo-Irish Protestant who had no compunction at all about turning the army loose on the countryside in an effort to disarm the so-called 'disturbed' districts. Indiscriminate floggings, beatings and other forms of casual (and occasionally ingenious) torture became ever more commonplace. Arms seizures duly increased, seemingly vindicating the increased brutality, but so did the disturbances, finally culminating in the long-feared eruption of a full-scale rebellion on the night of 24 May 1798. Yet astonishingly enough, when it did happen the outbreak seemingly took the authorities totally by surprise, for they thought they had nipped it in the bud with a wave of arrests in Dublin itself, which had seemingly wiped out the rebels' national leadership.[103] In fact they were just too late, for the orders had already been given, but crucially the arrest of the leaders momentarily paralysed the insurgents and although the capital awoke next morning to find itself surrounded by armed camps, the rebels in those camps at first did little beyond hoisting green flags and plundering the adjacent countryside.

This was just as well for the army, and the yeomanry were initially too scattered and too disorganised to deal with any but the smallest groups. A number of minor but well-publicised massacres took place and although a number of isolated posts successfully fought off attacks by local insurgents, they could at first do nothing about the bigger 'armies'. In County Meath, just a little to the north-west of Dublin, one such host established itself above the main road on the Hill of Tara: an ancient fortress famous as the seat of the old High Kings of Ireland. Alone and unsupported, the local yeomanry could only look on impotently, until quite by chance Captain Hector Maclean and Captain John Scobie turned up at Navan on the evening of 25 May with three companies of the Reay Fencibles, en route to Dublin. The yeomanry officers immediately urged the Highlanders to join in an attempt to recapture the nearby village of Dunshaughlin – at first Maclean agreed but then the following day, when the little expedition found the place deserted, he insisted on resuming his march to the capital. According to some accounts, he claimed that his orders took precedence and did not allow him to go wandering off around the countryside in the faint hope of stumbling over an elusive enemy – an excuse that, although strictly true, seems a touch disingenuous given that the enemy in question was all too visibly posted on the Hill of Tara at the time.

Be that as it may, off he went despite the yeomanry officers' angry protests, only to run straight into Captain Aaron Blanche. Like James Watson of the Strathspeys, Blanche was no Highland gentleman but a tough and resourceful ex-ranker who had been brought into the Reays to serve as their adjutant[104] and he was taking no nonsense from any Irish rebels. The day before, some of those rebels had attacked a twenty-strong baggage party belonging to the regiment at Dunboyne, killing eight and taking the rest prisoners. Now he was determined to get them back – along with the nine thousand rounds of ball cartridge they had been transporting.

Exactly what passed between Blanche, Maclean and Scobie is unclear and glossed over in the adjutant's report, but it may not have been an altogether happy meeting and it probably didn't help matters that when he first arrived and loudly demanded to know why they were marching away from the enemy, the men all gave him three hearty cheers. Strictly speaking, of course, Blanche was not a line officer and freely admitted he was currently acting without orders. Maclean on the other hand did have his orders – very explicit ones directing him to march to Dublin, but nevertheless the upshot was that in the end he and Scobie, however reluctantly, agreed to join with Blanche and the yeomanry in attacking the rebels.

All of the Loyalist forces, fencibles and yeomanry combined, amounted to just 190 men of the Reays and Captain Molloy's Lower Kells Infantry[105], and a single 6-pounder cannon, besides six assorted troops of Yeoman cavalry, accounting for a hundred troopers between them. The rebels on the other hand were said to number about four thousand, or perhaps as many as eight thousand by some estimates – but, led by Captain Blanche, the little band of redcoats bravely set off towards the Hill of Tara, about five miles away.

'On arriving at the large fort at Mr Lynch's,' said a contemporary account, 'the army got in full view of the rebel camp on the Hill of Tara; the fields around appeared black with rebels. On perceiving the army, they instantly got into motion – their chiefs mounted, and in about ten minutes formed their line, which was extended very far, and very deep, with three pair of green colours.'[106]

* * *

The rebel position was in fact centred around a walled churchyard on the summit of the hill, dominating the Dublin road and extending outwards, taking advantage of the ancient earthworks surrounding the hill-top. The surge forward from the camp to take up this strong position was at first thought to be the start of a general attack, but instead of flooding straight down the hill and overwhelming the Highlanders and their yeoman friends, the rebels seemed curiously content to merely stand at bay. Numerous as they were, the fact was that they lacked both the training and proper organisation needed to turn them from an unruly armed mob into a proper fighting force. Rather like the Scottish patriot William Wallace at Falkirk, their leaders had brought their men to the dance, but then had no idea what to do with them beyond exhorting them to 'hop gif ye can.' This was unfortunate because very few of them had firearms. About twenty muskets had been seized from the ambushed baggage party, but otherwise all they had were shotguns and sporting pieces and most of them not even that, trusting instead to home-made pikes – effective only at close quarters.

Captain Blanche on the other hand was seemingly in an even more daunting position. By any reckoning he was seriously outnumbered, with something less than three hundred men all told, facing upwards of four thousand insurgents. Yet any wavering now, far less a retreat, would be instantly fatal. Nor was there going to be much future in trying to hold the village or any other kind of hasty defensive position against such a host. In the circumstances, therefore, he took the only possible course open to him and decided upon an immediate frontal attack, trusting to discipline and the bayonet to carry the day as it had so often done in North America. Thus he simply drew up his four companies of infantry in a single line, placed three troops of cavalry on either flank, and then calling the yeomanry officers together, 'informed them he had no orders to give, except to lead on their divisions with courage to the action'.

'It was half past six of the clock when the action commenced – immediately some of the army lay dead from the fire of the rebels,' said our unknown correspondent, and as Blanche and his little band bravely advanced up the long grassy slope, the rebels 'put their hats on their pikes, the entire length of the line, and gave three cheers'.[107] However, only a few scattered groups launched unco-ordinated and unsuccessful little rushes against the Highlanders while the rest remained behind the walls and banks – so the Captain took advantage of their seeming immobility by sending a party of yeomanry to work around their flank, directing his lone 6-pounder to fire on their centre, and then led the Reays straight towards the old churchyard marking the summit.

'On approaching the churchyard gate,' he reported, 'we met with the most obstinate resistance ... At one period the King's troops did not gain the least advantage ...' As often happens in close-quarter fighting his advance had stalled as soon as he and the enemy began trading fire and this, as he readily admitted, was the defining moment of the battle: '... finding the men's ammunition almost expended,' continued Blanche, 'and our situation getting still more critical, I found it absolutely necessary to make one decisive effort by charging the rebels which was gallantly executed by the Grenadiers.'[108]

Not for the first or the last time, resorting to the bayonet instead of trying to shoot it out with a foe far superior in numbers proved effective. That one gallant rush headed by the Reays' grenadier company got the Highlanders into the walled churchyard and then something quite extraordinary happened. When Blanche and his men disappeared into the churchyard the 6-pounder was left outside and Captain Molloy hastily ordered it to follow, but there was a delay because the gunner in charge was killed and Molloy himself had to put his hand to the wheel to get it up onto the road. Seeing him struggling, a party of rebels immediately rushed forward and one supposedly laid his hand on the barrel before, as Blanche dryly remarked, Molloy 'returned their cordial invitation, which crowned our operations with a complete victory'.

There was a little more to it than that, of course. The first discharge at murderously close range killed or wounded ten or twelve of the insurgents, and then while Blanche and his Highlanders plied their bayonets inside the churchyard, Molloy sent round after round of canister into the packed ranks of rebels milling about outside. After a few minutes of this murderous work the insurgents started giving way, and with no proper leaders to rally them, the whole rebel line swiftly crumbled outwards from the centre. It was a near-impossible victory won by sheer courage and discipline. It might have been more complete still if some of the yeomanry he had sent around the flank had done their duty by falling on the fugitives instead of somehow getting themselves 'lost', but in the circumstances no-one could really complain about the result.

Against a total loss of just thirteen killed and twenty-eight wounded, mainly amongst his Highlanders, Blanche reported that three hundred and fifty rebel dead were found on the field next day (which if true means that between them his men killed rather more than their own number), together with vast quantities of pikes and other weapons. Just as happily, he also rescued the surviving members of the baggage party and even recovered that portion of the stolen ammunition not actually expended during the fighting.[109] Strategically too the battle was a great success, for not only were the Meath rebels totally dispersed by this unexpected defeat but the ring of rebel camps around the capital was thereby broken and the road to the north re-opened.

There was still much more fighting ahead of the Reays and the other 'Scotch Fencibles' such as Colin Campbell of Stonefield's Dumbarton Fencibles, who first helped save the day at Arklow and afterwards served in Wexford under Colonel John Moore, the future father of the British light infantry. It was a scattered, disorganised war, which lasted through the summer. It was also a dirty war, marked by blundering and atrocities on both sides – which occasionally amounted to ethnic cleansing – and although Stewart of Garth never served there, he was still, more than twenty years afterwards, moved to write how 'the unpleasant feelings which many of the events of the late unhappy insurrection creates, with so few circumstances to relieve them, I wish to abstain from all the details of the particular duties of the different corps employed on that occasion.'[110] Only the Reays' fight at the Hill of Tara was worth a brief mention in his narrative and even then he ascribed the victory not to the intrepid Blanche, but to the more obviously Caledonian Captain Maclean. Otherwise he preferred simply to stress – perhaps protesting rather too much – how well-behaved his beloved Highlanders were and how happy were their relations with the inhabitants.

At last, by the middle of August it was all but over and the rebel armies destroyed: their leaders for the most part dead, captured or fled. Throughout the three months that followed Blanche's victory on the Hill of Tara, the Highland fencibles had played a crucial role in the victory, fighting as well and as hard as any regular units. Thus far, that fighting, although often fierce when it was not one-sided, had only been against the

Irish insurgents themselves. Now, quite unexpectedly, with the original rebel armies defeated and scattered, and an air of complacency returning, the French came after all, and the question of how the fencibles would fare against a 'real' enemy was dramatically answered.

They landed quite unexpectedly at Killala in County Mayo on 23 August, in the one remote part of Ireland that had so far remained calm and unaffected by the troubles – just one regiment of infantry: the 70th Demi-Brigade, some horseless troopers of the 3rd Hussars and a few gunners, totalling just 1,099 men. Those who came ashore were seemingly only the vanguard of a much larger force, several thousand strong, and exactly when the rest would actually arrive was uncertain. But their commander, General Joseph Humbert, had of course brought a tolerable quantity of rusty muskets and other obsolete equipment to arm the hundreds of men who were confidently expected to come flocking in to march behind Liberty's banner. Sadly, all too many of them did so, and while Jamie Urquhart was confident enough to arm the Catholics at nearby Ballyshannon, hundreds of others joined the French at Killala.

In the meantime the local commander, Major General John Hely-Hutchinson, lost no time in warning Dublin that the long-awaited French invasion was finally begun and, having done so, he then very properly called in his outposts and marched for the strategically important town of Castlebar with every man he could muster. Humbert, for his part reckoning that passively waiting for the rest of the fleet to turn up was not an option, took the equally soldierly decision to leave a small garrison in the little town and marched out to meet him with nine hundred of his own men and an estimated two thousand local volunteers enlisted into an optimistically titled Irish Legion. On 25 August the local yeomanry abandoned the nearby town of Ballina without a fight and fell back on the crossroads town of Foxford. However, Humbert declined to launch a head-on attack and when he set off for Castlebar under cover of darkness on the night of 26 August, instead of taking the easier and therefore more obvious route, he swung around the west side of Lough Conn by way of a rough hill track. Warned by a chance sighting of a long column of men in blue coming over the hills, Hutchinson sent Major James Fraser of Kincorth out to a defile at Barnageeha with fifty men of the Fraser Fencibles.

The Frasers were another of the new generation of 'clan' regiments. Major General Simon Fraser – the sometime Master of Lovat who cannily managed to avoid fighting at Culloden but took his 78th Highlanders to Quebec and afterwards raised the original 71st Highlanders – was long dead by now. Since he left no acknowledged children, legitimate or otherwise, the Lovat estates went to one of his half brothers, Archibald Campbell Fraser. As was considered right and proper, brother Archie also succeeded Simon as one of the Members of Parliament for Inverness, but when war broke out and the invitation to raise a Fraser regiment was offered, he very sensibly admitted himself far too old for military adventures. Instead it was another kinsman, Major James Fraser of Belladrum who was persuaded to come out of retirement and accept letters of service for 'His Majesty's Fraser Fencible Regiment of Foot' on 29 November 1794.

Although he could hardly be regarded as a sprightly young buck himself, having been born way back in 1732, Belladrum was a good choice to command the regiment. Briefly a Black Watch officer, he had served with Keith's and Campbell's Highlanders in Germany during the Seven Years' War and with Simon Fraser's 71st in North America, before retiring on to the half-pay in June 1782. In-between times he had also been a captain in the Duke of Gordon's original Northern Fencibles and so he had a pretty shrewd idea of what he was now letting himself in for – and an equally shrewd notion of the necessity of relying on his friends and family to raise the regiment.

In all there were nineteen officers named Fraser, including Archie's son John, often referred to as 'Young Lovat', who was that very same Captain John Fraser who persuaded the light company of the Strathspeys to volunteer for service in England.[III] Although there were only 122 rank and file bearing that name rather than the 300 predictably claimed by Stewart of Garth, the regiment was indeed chiefly recruited in the old Fraser country of Kiltarlity, Stratherrick and the Aird, just to the west of Inverness. As such it might justifiably appear to have some claim to being a clan regiment of sorts, but nevertheless it also picked up a fair number of men from further afield as well: especially along Glen Urquhart, where Kincorth had married a daughter of Mackay of Auchmonie; from Forres and Nairn; and from the Black Isle and further north towards the Reay country.

Like the Reays, their service in Ireland had been quiet enough at first and they too were well scattered when it all began. However, four of the companies under Kincorth were at Tuam when the French arrived and so were snatched up as part of the rag-tag little army that Hutchinson took to Castlebar. Some months later, a Colonel Scott tried to find out what happened next – he began, rather crushingly:

> I could not find an officer of the Frasers sufficiently intelligent to give me an exact disposition of the Troops. I got a countryman to walk with me the track the French took, by which it is plain the enemy were suffered to march along the front to turn the left. Major Fraser told me he commanded 50 men at the Barny Gee pass about seven miles advanced . . . He said the Brigade Major gave him orders on approach of the French to retire without firing, which he observed, tho' the whole ground back to Castlebar is wild country with some enclosures where he might have disputed the ground to the best advantage. The French came on at night, but it was light soon after they got possession of the pass.

In the meantime Lieutenant General Gerard Lake had arrived at Castlebar to take over command, which may have hindered any delaying action – indeed the overall impression is of a certain paralysis at headquarters. To be fair, Lake and Hutchinson may have had little confidence in their troops. They amounted in total to some seventeen hundred men and so they probably outnumbered the French and their Irish auxiliaries, but the problem was that most of them belonged to two Irish militia regiments, from Kilkenny and Longford. There were also some equally dubious Galway yeomanry infantry and a few cavalry, including a handful of the 6th Dragoon Guards, but seemingly the only troops to be relied upon were a single company of sixty men ('a remnant') from the regular 6th Foot, the four companies of the Fraser Fencibles, amounting to no more than one hundred and fifty men, and a small detachment of Royal Irish Artillerymen.[112]

Scott continued:

> Our troops were drawn up in close order about 50 yards from the Fenc[ibl]es. Those on the right were in the way of the guns. Instead of moving them up to the hedges and firing over them, they made them all fall back, which was the first retrograde movement. [Major] Fraser

coming in without firing, the Generals would not believe his report. The first disposition was for the Foxford Road … The loss of the day seems principally from not having the command of the Mountain Road.

Notwithstanding Scott's low opinion of the Fraser officers, as narratives go it was hardly a model of clarity, but seemingly the army was originally drawn up covering the Foxford road. Once the Major managed to convince the two brave, but not overly imaginative, general officers in charge that the French were actually coming over the mountains, it had to hastily change its front and in the process initially ended up with the front line blocking their own guns. Nevertheless the 'retrograde movement' over which Scott shook his head must have done the trick, for when the French advanced at about 8 a.m. the redeployment was complete. The largest unit, the Kilkenny Militia, was in the front line together with the detachment of the 6th Foot and another of the Prince of Wales Fencibles. The Frasers and some Galway yeomanry infantry formed the second line and the four companies of Longford Militia were posted in the right rear of the Kilkennys, while Captain Shortall and his two curricle guns were out in front with a clear view of the French.[113]

By all accounts he did well, for the advancing French were twice halted by unnervingly accurate artillery fire, which not only disabled Humbert's own gun, but also sent most of his unenthusiastic Irish allies running for home.

In desperation, at the third attempt one of the French officers, a Colonel Sarazin, put himself at the head of his regiment's grenadiers, formed into one of those solid blocks or columns that had become a trademark of the French armies and charged the guns with the bayonet. Just as on so many other battlefields across Europe this determined rush proved too much for the militia. Like many raw troops they began firing too early, too quickly, and quite ineffectively. The Kilkennys must have broken and run without fighting, for Humbert afterwards made a point of praising the stand of the Longfords, but no-one else was very complimentary about either regiment and the general consensus was that they, together with most of the cavalry, simply bolted, leaving just the four companies of Fraser Fencibles and the 6th Foot detachment to face the enemy alone.

At that point the result became inevitable and amidst the wreckage of the shattered militia the Highlanders fell back slowly and in good order. Somewhere along the road they had to abandon their two guns, but Kincorth managed to halt and make a stand for a time on a bridge just short of the town. It was a brave attempt to give the rest of the army some breathing space, and it probably cost them their colours as well as the majority of their thirty-two casualties, but it was also futile because the rest of the army was broken beyond all rallying. Lake was reportedly 'overwhelmed with grief at the unsteady behaviour of the regiments under him', and some of the yeomanry rode so hard and so fast for Athlone that the battle was ever afterwards dubbed the Castlebar Races!

Unsurprisingly, there were, as the saying goes, some wild scenes within the town itself, and afterwards Musgrave related how the Frasers had their own counterpart to the boy who stood on the burning deck:

4   Gerard Lake, as he fled the field during the Races of Castlebar. He was said to have lamented that the outcome would have been different if the Reays were there.

The French approached the new goal in Castlebar to break it open. It was guarded by a highland Fraser sentinel whom his friends desired to retreat with them; but he heroically refused to quit his post, which was elevated, with some steps leading to it. He charged [loaded] and fired five times successfully and killed a Frenchman at every shot; but before he could charge the sixth time, they rushed him, beat out his brains, and threw him down the steps, and the sentry box on his body.[114]

In the retreat that followed, the Frasers, like the rest of Lake's defeated army, were reported to have behaved badly, robbing countrymen and burning cottages, but they soon redeemed themselves again. At Tuam, the new viceroy, Lord Cornwallis, was already assembling another army around the regular 100th Foot, as the Gordon Highlanders were still officially designated. At first he expected to have to prise Humbert out of Castlebar, but the French general was only too keenly aware that he needed to find more men – he first headed north, hoping to raise Ulster once again and then after a skirmish at Collooney, just as abruptly turned south again on hearing the news of an actual uprising in the Midlands. Those rebels, however, were intercepted at Wilson's Hospital near Cavan on 6 September, by yet another Highland fencible regiment. Major John Porter of the 1st Argyle Fencibles[115] was supposed to be holding Cavan itself, but hearing that the rebels were approaching he stoutly marched out that morning with one hundred of his Highlanders, some two hundred and fifty yeomanry and one of the ubiquitous curricle guns.[116]

The battle that followed, as a correspondent identified only as 'T. S.' reported, was as brief as it was decisive:

> As soon as the rebels were convinced the army had arrived at this place, they sent five hundred of their stoutest men from the hospital armed with musquets and fowling pieces, and a large body of pikemen, to attack them. The Highlanders were at the time posted on the high road near Bunbrusna, drawn up in very close order, with the field piece in their centre.
>
> A desperate party of rebels issued from the main body, and ran with violence towards the cannon, advancing almost to its muzzle, with a determination to sieze it; but by a discharge of grape-shot, they were made to pay dearly for their temerity ... The infantry now made so good

a use of their musquets, that the rebels broke, and were pursued by the cavalry in all directions.[117]

And that was more or less that. Lake, with a new army, was now pressing hard on Humbert's heels, encouraged by a lengthening trail of guns, wagons and stores abandoned on the road. Ahead of him lay Cornwallis, but it was Lake who did the business when the French eventually turned at bay at a place called Ballinamuck two days later, on 8 September. He had with him a provisional battalion of light infantry, the Armagh and Kerry Militia and a detachment of the Prince of Wales' Fencibles, but the core of his army were our old friends the Reay Fencibles. At Castlebar he was said to have lamented that: 'If I had my brave and honest Reays here, this would not have happened.' Now he did. Recognising it was hopeless, Humbert and his men fought only long enough to satisfy honour before surrendering – while Lord Roden's yeomanry were turned loose on the Irish Legion.

Thereafter there was still a little more fighting to be done, but by now it was just a matter of mopping up. Castlebar had been re-occupied by fifty-six men of the Frasers led by Kincorth's son-in-law, Captain David Urquhart, and on 12 September he was attacked there by an estimated two thousand rebels. This time the town was held, but sadly Musgrave provides no details and only relates that: 'The garrison, consisting of fifty-six Fraser fencibles, thirty-four volunteers (including boys), and one troop of yeoman cavalry, was so judiciously posted by Captain Urquhart of the Frasers, as to completely rout the assailants.'[118] The end, inevitably, came at Killala itself. Once again the French fired a few volleys and then, with honour satisfied, laid down their arms and left their Irish friends to their fate. The Reays and the Frasers, fittingly enough, were there to see it happen.

Throughout the Irish rebellion, the Highland fencibles had more than proved themselves to be good soldiers, not least during Blanche's desperate storming of the Hill of Tara, and had shown that they were at the very least the equal of the regulars – indeed, given the tendency for regular units in Ireland to be made up of broken cadres, they were probably better.

Moreover, in answering the old charges that their men would have been better employed in those regular units, Stewart of Garth not only re-iterated the argument about the fencible regiments largely being formed of men who would not otherwise have enlisted, but went on to make the point that a considerable number of them did in fact later transfer over to the regular army. '... the Highland Fencibles furnished a most excellent and seasonable nursery of men for regiments of the line,' he claimed. 'The 72nd regiment was in a few months filled up from 200 to 800 men by Fencible volunteers. Upwards of 350 men volunteered from the Clan Alpines into different regiments; 200 men of the Caithness Highlanders joined the 79th and 92nd; and so of the others ...'[119] More remarkable still, of course, was the case of the regular 93rd Highlanders, who actually began their existence in 1793 as the Sutherland Fencibles. That particular battalion, like all of the first-generation fencibles was disbanded in 1798. However, in May 1800,

> Major General William Wemyss of Wemyss, who had been Colonel of that Corps, received authority to raise a regiment of 600 men, with instructions to endeavour, if possible, to prevail on the men of the Fencible corps to return to their ranks in this new regiment, which was to be of the line. This was an arduous undertaking, for the men had been already eighteen months settled in different situations, which they were unwilling to relinquish. However, the complement required was raised (of which ... 460 were men of Sutherland,) and the corps was soon afterwards augmented, first to 800, and then to 1,000 men, with officers in proportion.[120]

The brutal coercion by Lady Stafford of the Sutherland Estates, so necessary to ensure that the men turned out again after being settled into their civilian occupations, was thus hinted at but otherwise glossed over by Garth. Unlike the tenants on the Duke of Gordon's lands and those of the Good Sir James's, there were no bargains to be made, no promises of secure leases held out to those invited to enlist – just straightforward threats of eviction from what would shortly be the most notoriously 'cleared' of all the Highland estates. Yet for all that, the 93rd would paradoxically develop a reputation as one of the better Highland regiments.

Meanwhile, half a world away in India, Arthur Wesley was renewing his tenuous acquaintanceship with the 73rd Highlanders.

~ 7 ~

The Tiger and the Elephant

Amidst all the noisy clamour of the French wars and that eventual crowning glory on the ridge at Waterloo, it is all too easy to forget the parallel, but quite unconnected, series of wars being fought half a world away in India. Nevertheless, the sub-continent has a very special place in the early history of the Highland regiments: a place summed up by a single word – Assaye.

There were no fewer than five Highland regiments serving in India when the French War began in 1793 and it is sometimes fashionable to draw a close parallel between those regiments and the Indian soldiers they served alongside. In an age when empires are frowned upon, it is convenient to pretend that having been defeated at Culloden the erstwhile clansmen were themselves turned into sepoys: that they were unwilling slave soldiers compelled by force or by economic circumstances to serve their conquerors in the drive to create a global empire. Yet any attempt to disassociate Scotland from its imperial past in this way wilfully ignores the incontrovertible fact that far from being the involuntary victims of England's ambition, it was Scots – and more frequently than not, Highland Scots at that – who probably did more than anyone else to first build and then run that empire.

That was largely because the process of creating what became the British Empire was started off not by any deliberate government policy, but by the maverick actions of the men actually on the ground: the employees of the grandly titled United Company of Merchants of England trading to the East Indies, better known simply as the East India Company. At first the London-based company was primarily concerned with the lucrative spice trade of South-East Asia, but then the vast markets of India beckoned, and so too did all the tea in China. By the beginning of the eighteenth century the Company was firmly established on the fringes of the Indian subcontinent, where it underwent some deep and significant changes. Outwardly, and indeed to the very end of its existence, trade, not conquest, was the East India Company's principal *raison d'être*; tea from China became its outward symbol and the price of it was the barometer by which the Company's share price was gauged. Nevertheless, as it rapidly expanded to become the first and arguably the greatest multinational trading corporation the world has ever seen, with commercial interests stretching right around the globe, it also evolved (more by accident than by design) into an increasingly important territorial power in its own right.

The initial catalyst for this remarkable transformation was a desperate rivalry with the French Compagnie des Indes, which for a time threatened the British company's very existence. The only way to survive the competition was by cultivating and manipulating local allies, and the Company's servants did so to such good effect that in a few short years not only were the French decisively taken out of the game, but in the process the Company found itself ruling vast tracts of land and enjoying a growing political importance across the entirety of the subcontinent. What was more, despite that bold proclamation of Englishness in its official title, the Company also came at the same time to be increasingly dominated by *Scots* soldiers and entrepreneurs. Scotland had once had its own company for trading with the Indies and its spectacular wreck on the shores of Darien was in large part orchestrated by the rival English company. However, that wreck and the national bankruptcy that followed led directly to the Union, and that in turn opened the English company to all those Scots seeking an outlet for their skills and energy outside the 'newly United' Kingdom. What was more, within an astonishingly short length of time they had also turned it into something of a Scottish mafia.

By way of illustration, an early and surprisingly important Scottish recruit for the Company – yet in his way an entirely typical one – was Captain Alexander Grant, of the Shewglie family. In 1745 he led the Glen Urquhart men during the last Jacobite Rising and afterwards, finding it expedient to put some considerable distance between himself and Scotland, he obtained employment with the Company – which, as a commercial undertaking, very conveniently did not require its soldiers to take an oath of loyalty to the Crown. Ten years later he then had the dubious distinction of literally being the last man into the last boat to get away from the doomed garrison of Calcutta. Thus, Flashman-like, he avoided death at Culloden and incarceration in the Black Hole, and so survived both to persuade another imperial adventurer named Robert Clive to fight at Plassey and thereby bring all of Bengal under the Company's sway. Despite falling out with Clive soon afterwards, Grant also made his fortune in the process and encouraged many other members of that large but tight-knit Glen Urquhart family to follow his example – although he could hardly have expected that one of his protégés, Charles Grant, would not only rise to become a director of the Company but ultimately would be the most able and influential chairman in its long history.

However, if eighteenth-century India offered seemingly limitless opportunity for Scotsmen on the make, albeit at some personal risk, the Company's nascent 'empire' increasingly needed to be bolstered by regular forces of the Crown. In the early days the Company had been accustomed to recruiting the few soldiers it required to guard its 'factories' or trading establishments by itself. At first the rank and file largely came from amongst the shifting collection of European and Eurasian mercenaries and adventurers already drifting about the East, supplemented by odd drafts from home – sometimes trawled from Newgate jail, and nearly all of them leaving their country for their country's good. Not surprisingly, despite the occasional brilliance of Robert Clive, and the bravery and determination of other individual officers like Alexander Grant, this rather dubious private army had tended to perform badly when left to its own devices – the debacle at Calcutta being an obvious case in point.

A hastily raised expeditionary force sent from Britain had to bail the Company out after the French seized Madras in 1746; continuing hostilities, despite the signing of peace in Europe afterwards, necessitated the long-term deployment of a regular battalion: Colonel John Adlercron's 39th Foot. Four companies of that regiment served under Clive at Plassey and, as the war against the French and their allies escalated, yet more regular units were committed, including Staats Long Morris's 89th Highlanders.[121] While all of them had been withdrawn or absorbed into the local East India Company forces by the time the immediate hostilities ended in the mid-1760s, fresh conflicts with the Marathas and with the sultanate of Mysore in the following decades demanded the deployment of yet more regular troops, just as the army was at full stretch coping with the crisis in North America.

This time they included no fewer than three new Highland battalions – not because they were thought particularly suited to the role but simply because they were the first troops available. The senior one, albeit by only a few months, was raised by John Mackenzie, Lord MacLeod, as the 73rd Highlanders in 1777. Like Simon Fraser he once marched behind the Pretender's banner, but after his mother secured him a conditional pardon he took himself abroad to enter the Swedish service, where he eventually rose to the rank of lieutenant general before coming home and tactfully offering to recruit a Highland regiment for the Crown. In the circumstances the offer was accepted as graciously as it was made and no sooner was the battalion completed and taken into the line as the 73rd Foot than letters of service were granted for a second battalion. The latter was to form part of the Gibraltar garrison during the Great Siege and came home, like so many other battalions, to be disbanded in 1783, but in the meantime the original battalion, after an uneventful period of garrison duty on Jersey had embarked for Madras in January 1779.

There they found the East India Company engaged in a new war for survival, not with the French this time but with the sultanate of Mysore and its warrior ruler, Haidar Ali Khan. The background to the struggle need not detain us, except to note that Haidar Ali's forces were strong and well organised by Indian standards, and he himself was a soldier of extraordinary ability. Having for the moment dished the rival Maratha Confederacy in the north, he turned his attention to the temptingly weak British possessions to the east: opening his campaign with a shattering raid that swept into the very suburbs of Madras itself. For a time it was touch and go – had a rumoured French expeditionary force arrived at that juncture, the British defeat would have been complete.

Instead, to the unspeakable relief of all concerned, the arrival of the 73rd Highlanders just ahead of the French saved the day and enabled the local commander, Sir Hector Monro, to go on to the offensive himself. In late August he marched with the Highlanders to Conjeeveram where he intended to rendezvous with another force led by a Colonel Baillie. The latter, however, was late and by 6 September 1780 was still some fifteen miles away when he was attacked by Haidar Ali's equally capable son, Tippu Sultan. After several hours of fighting young Tippu broke off the engagement but remained hovering dangerously in the vicinity and a thoroughly intimidated Baillie decided to stay put and call for help. Monro for his part, hampered by a desperate shortage of food, felt equally unable to move to his assistance with his whole force and instead sent off a small detachment, under a Colonel Fletcher, which included the flank companies of the 73rd Highlanders, the light company commanded by the Honourable John Lindsay, and the grenadiers under a certain Captain David Baird. It was to be a fateful encounter.

At first all went well. Fletcher was competent enough to avoid an ambush on the way in and rendezvoused successfully with Baillie, but despite this reinforcement the latter still hesitated and was lost. On the night of 9 September the combined force, now some four thousand strong, was surrounded by Tippu at Polilur and next day was totally wiped out. Some two thousand men were killed and a thousand more taken prisoner, and the true magnitude of this disaster, 'which cannot be paralleled since the English had possessions in India,' may be judged by the fact that sixty out of eighty-six European officers were killed, while the rest, including Davie Baird, were captured.

Baird was also wounded and according to the traditional version of the story, the bullet would not be extracted from his thigh until his eventual release more than three years later in March 1784. If true, this fact alone might be enough to account for his later irascibility, but it is also significant that, on learning that all the prisoners were fettered together, his mother is said to have remarked, 'God help the chiel chained to ma Davie.' Just who, if anyone, *was* chained to him is, alas, unknown to history, but neither his long imprisonment nor his undoubted suffering hindered Baird's career and by the time he finally got his revenge at Seringapatam in 1799 he was a major general.[122]

In the meantime the 73rd were joined out there by a new 78th Highlanders, raised in 1778 by Kenneth Mackenzie, Lord Seaforth. Unlike Simon Fraser and Lord MacLeod, Seaforth was no Jacobite, for although support for the Stuarts once ran strongly in the family, his cautious father had been more or less successful in keeping his clansmen out of the rebellion – as a result Kenneth regained the once forfeited Earldom of Seaforth, albeit in the Irish peerage. The regiment might therefore be seen as grateful payment for the favour thus shown; or more likely it was a simple reflection of the fact that he was regarded as being exceptionally well placed to raise a badly needed regiment of infantry for the American War.

In all, he did not do too badly. He raised the regiment in the far north for the most part, of course, and in the Outer Hebrides, where the Mackenzie chieftainship still meant something in a trackless wilderness, remote from the modern Scotland of the Enlightenment, where his tenants for the most part still considered themselves to be his clansmen. His letters of service were granted on 8 January 1778 and by May, just a few days over the four months allowed, he was able to assemble 1,130 men at Elgin. According to Stewart of Garth some five hundred of them came from his own estates and another four hundred were raised by other Mackenzie lairds; including those of Scatwell, Kilcoy, Applecross and Redcastle. The remaining two hundred, he allowed, were found in the Lowlands and included forty-three English and Irish recruits. Garth's figures always need to be taken with a certain pinch of salt and it is likely that the real proportion of non-Gaelic speakers in the regiment may have been rather higher; but nevertheless there it was, the regiment was complete.

Notwithstanding the usual bargaining with his tenants, Seaforth's recruiting efforts had been greatly assisted by the confident expectation that the regiment was intended to go to North America. Today the depopulation of the Highlands is routinely ascribed solely to the enforced Clearances of the early nineteenth century, but those emotive evictions by Highland chieftains-turned-'improving'-landlords were preceded in the latter half of the eighteenth century by what has been called a 'people's clearance': a wave of emigration from the Highlands forced by the twin pressures of overpopulation and economic failure. The poor gravitated as they always had done to the Lowlands, swelling the population of cities such as Glasgow (and often enlisting under Highland recruiters there), while those who could afford the fare emigrated to take up the near limitless lands being offered in North America. The events of Lexington, Concord and Bunker Hill obviously put something of a brake on this voluntary transatlantic migration, but the raising of the new regiments now offered another route to the Americas. It was remembered how, when Montgomerie's and Fraser's regiments were disbanded after the previous war, the remaining men were offered substantial land grants if they chose to stay on in Canada rather than come home, and the prospect of exchanging service for land, not in Scotland but in North America, was now a powerful incentive to enlistment.

The trouble was that as the months passed there was no sign of the 78th Highlanders going anywhere near America and when their embarkation orders finally came, they promptly mutinied.

The catalyst, supposedly, was the news that they were to go not to America but to the Channel Islands. There they were to relieve Lord MacLeod's men, who were in turn ordered to India. Whether this particular detail was taken as being a precedent or was confused with their own orders, the rumour spread through the regiment that they too were going to India, and on the morning of 21 September 1778, a number of men suddenly broke ranks, loudly demanding their arrears of pay and the bounty money due to them.[123] Others quickly joined them and within minutes some three hundred men were shouting, jostling, mobbing their officers and exuberantly loosing the odd shot off into the air, all in traditional style.

It could hardly have been a more public demonstration of disaffection, for the tumult broke out on the parade ground in front of Edinburgh Castle, where the esplanade now stands. What was more any lingering doubts as to whether the mutineers might be deliberately playing to the gallery was removed by their decision to establish a camp on Arthur's Seat, the mighty volcanic crag overlooking the capital. Someone, clearly, was using his imagination – while their grievances were understandable, there was nothing peculiarly 'Highland' about them. The fact that their accounts had not been settled was straightforward enough – and all too common – and the complaints that soon circulated of unduly harsh discipline were added simply to gain public sympathy.

Regarding the latter, it is frequently argued that Highland soldiers required gentler treatment than that meted out to the general run of soldiers and that they expected and responded to honeyed words and easy familiarity better than harsh discipline and savage punishment

– or at the very least, the constant threat of it – popularly associated with King George's army. While there was no doubting that this was so and very largely still is so, there is always a happy medium and a considerable difference between relaxing the bounds of discipline and failing to impose it in the first place – as the unhappy example of young Glengarry and the Strathspey Fencibles illustrates only too clearly. In reality, as new recruits, they were very properly being treated relatively gently, but the simple fact of the matter is that, however it is handled, the transition from civilian to military life is invariably a shock to the system, and often an unhappy one at first.

In all the circumstances the Commander-in-Chief of Scotland, Sir Adolphus Oughton, had no alternative but to surrender to their demands. The claims of unduly harsh treatment he very sensibly ignored, but the complaints about their unsettled accounts were a different matter entirely. They at least were entirely legitimate and despite the summoning of reinforcements by way of a proper show of force, there was never going to be any question of laying on a real battle for the entertainment of the good citizens of Edinburgh just because the battalion's paymaster had been negligent! All that Oughton could realistically do was extend the customary promise of amnesty for any specific offences committed during the disturbances, and most important of all ensure that the outstanding money was swiftly paid over.

A combination of good sense and hard cash therefore sufficed in the end to get them to the Channel Islands; after an uneventful few years in garrison learning the habits of soldiering, they were finally ordered from there to Madras. When those particular orders came through it no doubt helped that Seaforth himself was something of an exception, and an honourable one at that. Unlike most of the landed proprietors who raised the later Highland regiments, he took his soldiering seriously and while most of his counterparts were content to wave their men off to glory from the quayside, he too embarked with his regiment for India on 26 May 1781. It was a pity, therefore, that three months into the voyage he died suddenly in the night. The cause of death, beyond a comment as to its suddenness, was not noted in the log of the East Indiaman *Deptford*, but the log did record the first symptoms of scurvy amongst the soldiers on 25 July. By 2 September it was reported to be spreading fast and by the end of the month there was a cryptic note of 'much fever' and the first of what became a lengthening daily death toll. With the situation rapidly worsening, there was no alternative but for the convoy to put the troops ashore on the lonely island of St Helena and lay over until 3 December. Thus it was not until 1 April 1782 that they were carried through the surf to land on the open beach at Madras – not surprisingly, for some time afterwards the regiment was in no condition to fight anybody. The few fit men were temporarily drafted into the ranks of the 73rd Highlanders and it was not until October that the regiment was finally declared fit for service, just in time for a gruelling day-long battle against the French at Cuddalore.[124]

The third of the original 'Indian' regiments, arriving just a month after them, was 2/42nd, the second battalion of the Black Watch, embodied at Perth on 21 March 1780. The fact the battalion existed at all was, as Stewart of Garth points out, quite remarkable in itself, for in the preceding eighteen months some 12,500 men had been raised in the Highlands north of the Tay, including the short-lived 77th (Athole) Highlanders, but if the Black Watch men expected to join the regiment's other battalion in North America they were sadly disappointed, for they were first earmarked for an abortive expedition to take the Cape of Good Hope and then diverted to India and a gruelling nine-month siege in Mangalore.[125]

Two other Highland regiments, Murray's 77th and Gordon of Fyvie's 81st, were also slated to go to India at this time, but just as they were on the point of embarkation the American War officially ended ,and the men of both battalions unilaterally opted to take their discharges instead. Indeed, despite having originally expressed some enthusiasm at the prospect of going out to the East, the 77th actually mutinied rather than embark and so triggered off a whole string of similar protests amongst the other regiments – both Scots and English – gathered at Portsmouth. Both the 77th and the 81st were therefore disbanded, having been enlisted, as was customary, for only three years or the duration of the war. Despite that same stipulation in their letters of service, there was no question, however, of dispensing with the services of the three units already out in India. Instead, on 18 April 1786 all three were re-numbered as they shuffled up the Army List to fill the vacant spaces left by two others.

One of those vacancies, sadly, was created by Simon Fraser's 71st Highlanders. Its fighting record in North America was second to none and from first to last it had arguably seen more and harder fighting there than any other regiment, the Black Watch included. Unfortunately it was also shattered by defeats such as Tarleton's disaster at the Cowpens and at the war's end there was no stomach for rebuilding it. Instead it was disbanded and so Lord MacLeod's 73rd assumed its number instead.

According to a curious regimental legend the change in their designation was at first so unpopular with the men that Davie Baird had to go through the ranks with a bonnet full of the new cap-badges in one hand and a cocked pistol in the other! As always there is actually a factual basis to what might at first seem an unlikely story, even if the pistol is an apocryphal embellishment – strictly speaking, the battalion, having been raised for the duration of the (American) war *was* now being reduced. The men were therefore offered a choice: they could re-enlist with a bounty of £10 or they could take their discharge. In times past it was customary for regiments in such a situation to ceremonially ground arms, thus signifying the passing of the old order, and then after a suitably reverential pause, briskly take them up again in their new guise. Instead, here the men were being asked to individually signify their re-enlistment as soldiers of the new 71st by accepting a token – presumably a suitably numbered regimental button since cap-badges had not yet been invented.

As the next battalion in order of seniority, the 78th followed hard on their heels to take up the vacancy left by the short-lived Manchester Volunteers and so become the 72nd Highlanders, while 2/42nd, instead of being consolidated with its parent in far-off Canada, was split away from it entirely to step into the number only just vacated by MacLeod's and so become a new and entirely different 73rd Highlanders, with dark-green facings on their scarlet jackets instead of blue. Once again, every man in both of these battalions was theoretically entitled to his discharge, yet all but a handful took the bounty and re-enlisted for unlimited service under the new designations.[126]

This reshuffle was actually only the start of a much bigger scheme. In the following year two additional Highland regiments, and two English ones besides, were ordered to be raised specifically for service in India –at the entire expense of the East India Company. In the short term the new regiments were justified as a form of outdoor relief for at least some of the many officers and soldiers made redundant by the ending of the American War, but there was also a far deeper purpose behind them as well. They were intended to form the nucleus of an entirely new King's Indian Army which would see the eventual integration of the Company's forces into the British Army. As the multi-talented Harry Dundas at the Board of Control not unreasonably wrote, he 'could not conceive anything more preposterous than that the East India Company should be holding in their hands a large European Army exclusive of the Crown'. In point of fact, strictly speaking, there was now very little that was European about the Company's armies except the officers, for in the years that followed Clive's victory at Plassey it had been transformed by a massive increase in the number of sepoy units – native Indian soldiers organised and trained on European lines. Nevertheless, Dundas could hardly fail to be moved by the fact that, in 1784, the Company theoretically commanded some 116,110 white and Indian soldiers: more than many a European power. His concern that they be brought under some proper control was therefore understandable, but in the end the complete integration of the two services was thwarted by the determined resistance of the Company's officers. Far from being permanently stationed in India the four regiments therefore remained a part of the regular line and in due course all four would eventually be rotated home again like any other.

In the meantime the two new Scottish regiments were Sir Archibald Campbell's 74th (Argyle) Highlanders and Colonel Robert Abercromby's 75th Highlanders. The first directly replaced an earlier, but quite unconnected, 74th (Argyle) Highlanders, raised by John Campbell of Barbreck back in 1778, which had fought in America and was disbanded as recently as 1783. While the second would eventually bear the territorial designation of Stirlingshire. Even Stewart of Garth was reluctantly forced to concede that only about half of the four hundred men originally enlisted into the 74th were proper Highlanders, and that 'a considerable proportion of the men had been raised in Glasgow and Paisley, not the best nurseries for robust soldiers.' The 75th, for their part, evidently fell even further from his ideal. Colonel Abercromby, a younger brother of Sir Ralph, came from Tullibody, 'close to the base of the Grampians, on the southern side, where,' explained Garth, 'short as the distance was, the inhabitants differ so materially in their manners and dispositions from those within the range, Colonel Abercromby could not raise his men as has often been done in the Highlands:– that is, without money ... To the south of those hills, no recruits could be obtained without money.'[127]

Given Garth's remarkable ability to find Highland virtue in the most unlikely places, both descriptions are quietly damning and only serve to underline the fact that while they were unquestionably Scottish regiments, they were not Highland regiments as the term was originally understood and they therefore illustrate perfectly how those regiments were becoming assimilated into the British Army rather than standing apart from it. They were no longer tribal auxiliaries, as the original Black Watch had once been, but regular infantry of the line. It was indeed now sufficient that they were raised north of Edinburgh and west of Glasgow for 'Scotchmen and Highlanders [to be] regarded as synonymous words.'

However if there was any doubt as to the 'Highlandness' of the new regiments, there was none at all about their prowess as fighting men. Ever since that disaster at Polilur, Mysore was unfinished business so far as the East India Company, the British Army and Davie Baird were concerned. To be sure, Haidar Ali was soon dead – carried off by 'a great carbuncle' rather than in battle, as everyone expected – but to the frustration of all concerned, his son Tippu emerged alive and victorious from the war in 1784. No-one can have been surprised therefore at the resumption of hostilities just six years later and the 71st and 72nd (as they now were) went to war once more, winning all-too-transient renown at Dundegul, Palacatcherry, Bangalore and Nundydroog, before being joined by the new 74th and 75th, for what turned out to be an unsuccessful siege of Tippu's fortress capital of Seringapatam. An uneasy peace was then negotiated, which saw Tippu lose much of his territory, but it took another seven years – when Napoleon Bonaparte's invasion of Egypt raised the awful spectre of French troops coming to his assistance – before the final reckoning. This time there could be no half measures and fittingly it fell to Davie Baird to lead the storming party that finally broke through the walls of Seringapatam and gave Tippu his quietus on 4 May 1799. What was left of the 71st had finally gone home the year before, but the 74th and the new 73rd Highlanders followed Baird into the breach – watching his triumph was a former officer of the latter regiment, Arthur Wellesley.[128]

As all too often happens, victory brought some awkward problems in its wake. Few seemed to mourn Tippu's passing, but Baird and Wellesley were bitter rivals and the upshot of their rivalry was that Baird went off to Egypt, while Wellesley (whose elder brother Richard just happened to be the governor general) stayed on, first to govern Mysore and then to confront a new threat –in taking over that state the Company had also inherited its traditional enemies: the Marathas.

Thus far the Marathas had presented little real threat to the Company; indeed, apart from a brief war between 1778 and 1782, relations were generally friendly rather than otherwise, but the Maratha state was actually an unstable confederation of semi-independent fiefdoms uncertainly presided over by a Peshwa or hereditary chief minister. British diplomacy and British bayonets were therefore committed to supporting him against the various rival chieftains who represented the real power in the confederacy; in 1803, when one of those chieftains, Scindia, marched on the capital at Poona, Major General Arthur Wellesley was tasked with stopping him.

From the outset he knew it would not be easy – like all the Maratha chieftains, Scindia had built up a proper army comprised of well-drilled and disciplined sepoy regiments, led by European mercenaries and supported by an impressive train of properly handled artillery. Nevertheless, he considered his own forces entirely adequate for the purpose. A formal integration of the two services might have been thwarted, but experience of Indian warfare had long since taught the value of combining King's and Company units into mixed brigades rather than deploying regulars and sepoys as discrete formations. Thus, although the majority of Wellesley's men were sepoys drawn from the Madras army (and in theory at least no different in character or quality from those serving Scindia), he also had two battalions of British regulars under his immediate command and a third close at hand. By an odd coincidence all three were Scottish units and when the two armies met at Assaye both of Wellesley's regular battalions on the field were Highland ones: the 74th and the 78th.

The 78th were not of course the old Seaforths, which had been re-numbered as the 72nd nearly twenty years before – but by another of those curious coincidences associated with the 'Indian' regiments, they *were* raised by a later representative of the house: Francis Humberston Mackenzie of Seaforth. Although not a military man by profession, Seaforth's family, social and political connections were impeccable. When the last Earl of Seaforth died while en route to India with his regiment in 1781, the title fell to his cousin: Colonel Thomas Mackenzie-Humberston, of the then 100th Foot. When Thomas in turn died of wounds in Bombay two years later, both the chieftainship and the parliamentary seat for Ross-shire fell to his brother Francis Humberston Mackenzie (without the hyphen).[129] Whether the fact that what may have been regarded as the family regiment passed into other hands was a source of grief to him is not entirely clear, but it may perhaps be inferred from his eagerness to obtain a new regiment of his very own. At any rate it was as the head of the clan Mackenzie and a pillar of the establishment, rather than as a soldier of renown that Seaforth obtained his letters of service on 7 March 1793 – from a government anxious to make an appropriate gesture to demonstrate that it was taking the war very seriously. He promptly translated them into a splendid regiment of Highlanders. He equally promptly had himself painted in their uniform, but the ridiculously overblown pose entirely belies the fact that, being deaf and practically dumb as a consequence of Scarlet Fever when aged 11 (he was consequently known as 'McCoinnich Bodhar' – Deaf Mackenzie), he would never lead them in the field and his name would only be remembered again when the 72nd and 78th were happily combined in 1881 as the Seaforth Highlanders. In the meantime the regiment actually became more familiarly known as the Ross-shire Buffs – a secondary title they derived from the milky-white facings on their jackets.[130]

At any rate although they were relatively recent arrivals in India, they arrived out there with a good reputation. In 1794 they had gone to Holland, under Lieutenant Colonel Alexander Mackenzie, undergone a mercifully light baptism of fire at Nijmeguen in November and then fought at Geldermalsen, where they lost slightly more men than the Black Watch when the picket line was overrun by those French hussars. Meanwhile Seaforth's recruiting efforts had been rewarded by the granting of letters of service for a second battalion, which went straight to the Cape of Good Hope. After Geldermalsen, the already-lukewarm

Dutch had changed sides and so the British government snatched the opportunity to send a small expeditionary force to seize the Cape: a strategically important prize long coveted both by the Crown and by the East India Company. However, this happy success also coincided with the commencement of the Great Drafting and inevitably 2/78th was one of the casualties, but rather than bring the junior battalion home to be disbanded or scatter its men amongst strangers, as had happened to the 97th and 109th, it was decided to send 1/78th out to the Cape as well and then consolidate both battalions on the spot.

Consequently in June 1796 the pick of the officers and men were combined into a single very strong battalion under Colonel Alexander Mackenzie,[131] comprising, according to Stewart of Garth, 970 Highlanders, 129 Lowlanders and just 14 Englishmen and Irishmen, which then sailed for Bengal in November. There, as it turned out, the 78th were to have a relatively quiet time in contrast to some of their predecessors, so that when they were eventually summoned south to march against the Marathas in 1803 they were well rested and accustomed to India. This was just as well because the fight ahead of them was to be harder and bloodier than anyone imagined.

For all that it began promisingly enough. Major General Wellesley required a base of operations; the fortress of Ahmednuggar fitted his requirements and when the *killadar*, or governor, refused to surrender, he – or rather his Highlanders – stormed the town on 8 August so briskly that a visiting local dignitary wrote in some amazement that: 'These English are a strange people, and their General a wonderful man. They came here in the morning, looked at the pettah wall, walked over it, killed all the garrison, and returned to breakfast!'

It was not quite as easy as that: Captain Duncan Grant was killed at the head of the light company of the 78th, while Captain Mackenzie-Humberstone of the grenadiers was also shot dead as he mounted his ladder, and his second-in-command, Lieutenant Colin Campbell, only got them in at the third attempt. All in all, reported their commanding officer, the 78th lost fourteen killed and forty-one wounded in a thoroughly vicious fight with the Arab mercenaries that were defending the place. Wellesley and his officers may have enjoyed their late breakfast afterwards, but by comparison with what was yet to come, those casualties were going to seem comparatively light.

The battle of Assaye that followed was essentially brought about by one intelligence failure and shaped by a succession of others. Anticipating that the Marathas would try to avoid fighting for as long as possible in order to wear down their attackers, Wellesley was anxious to catch Scindia and beat him at the earliest opportunity. Reportedly he was now at a place called Borkardan and Wellesley accordingly planned to rendezvous near there on 23 September with another force, under Colonel James Stevenson, and fall upon the Marathas next day before they could move off again. Unfortunately, what Wellesley's scouts failed to realise was that the Maratha camp was not actually centred around Borkardan, but stretched for some four miles eastward from it along the north bank of the river Kaitna towards another village called Assaye. As a result Wellesley blundered into them twenty-four hours earlier than he expected – while Stevenson and the 94th Foot[132] were still well out of supporting distance. Nevertheless, convinced that any delay would allow Scindia to escape, he decided to attack anyway.

With just six battalions available to him, (and another left behind in camp to guard his massive supply train) it went without saying that he was going to be badly outnumbered and there could be no question of mounting a frontal assault straight across the river. Happily, a hasty reconnaissance revealed the likely presence of a ford linking two small villages just beyond the Marathas' left flank. Displaying a boldness that totally belied his later – and quite undeserved – reputation for caution, Wellesley immediately resolved to emulate Frederick the Great by throwing his army across the river at that point and then rolling up the Marathas' left flank.

Unfortunately, despite all the intelligence about the Marathas that had been gathered over the years, he seems to have completely underestimated his enemy. Far from being a tumultuous rabble, the Maratha infantry were well organised, properly trained and, as he now discovered, perfectly capable of rapidly changing their front to form a new and equally formidable battle-line to oppose his flanking move. What was more, they were also able to do so before Wellesley himself was properly in position, and there the trouble really began, for the formation adopted by the Marathas was an odd one. Their first line was now entirely comprised of artillery – variously estimated at between sixty and ninety guns,[133] all of them nine or twelve pounders, and as soon as Wellesley began crossing the river he came under a heavy and sustained fire that quickly silenced his own far lighter artillery and gave him little time to reconsider his next move.

The initial deployment on crossing the Kaitna was necessarily untidy. The advance was led by the pickets of the day, a small ad hoc duty battalion comprised of a half company drawn from each regiment, commanded by Lieutenant Colonel William Orrock of 1/8th Madras Native Infantry. Once across the river, they were pushed forwards just far enough to leave room for a complete infantry brigade, drawn up on a north–south alignment, between their position and the river. Wallace's brigade, comprising the 74th Highlanders and two sepoy battalions then followed and took up a covering position somewhat to their east and directly above the ford, while the remainder of the army got across and deployed into line to the south of Orrock. Wellesley's original plan was then to go forward in two lines with his left flank guiding off the river, but finding the Marathas extending their line as they wheeled around to face him, he next ordered his men to conform by drawing out into a single line with his two regular battalions anchoring either flank – the 78th on the left and the 74th on the right, and the six sepoy battalions sandwiched in-between. He was, we are assured, cool and calmly collected, but there is more than a hint of nervous excitement in the way he brusquely ordered Colonel Orrock and the other battalion commanders to abandon their own bullock-drawn light artillery when it lagged behind, and then ordered an immediate advance without waiting for the deployment to be completed. He may have reasoned that there was no need to wait, playing a ponderous game of grandmother's footsteps, for such a manoeuvre was one that was well practised by both King's and Company troops, but if so, it was a decision he was soon to regret.

At any rate this meant that the 78th began the attack while the 74th, at the other end of the line, were still moving out obliquely towards their right. Wellesley for his part placed himself by the right flank of the 78th and accompanied the Highlanders straight towards the Maratha guns. It was a brave gesture, which would twice lose him his horse, nearly cost him his life and, as we shall see, nearly cost him the battle as well. On the face of it the strong and well-disciplined 78th had no need of his personal encouragement and supervision, even if they were likely to come into action first, but Wellesley may have decided he had no alternative but to lead them in, for their brigade commander, Lieutenant Colonel William Harness of the 80th Foot, was in the early stages of a nervous breakdown!

At first the advance was brisk but steady. The Highlanders halted some fifty metres away from the Maratha gun-line and fired a volley: not the old rolling fire of the now-obsolete system of platooning, but a single crashing discharge. Then, in a studied display of unconcern, they stood still, coolly reloading and waiting while the 1/10th Madras Native Infantry came up into line on their right, before stepping off again, this time with arms ported and bayonets flashing in the sun. It was no wild Highland charge, for they deliberately kept their ranks, only gradually quickening the pace before the front rank levelled their bayonets and took the final ten metres at a run, preserving their breath for the fight.

The Maratha artillerymen meanwhile stood to their guns manfully, fighting them to the last without any assistance from their infantry, before being quickly overwhelmed as each successive battalion rolled over them and then reformed into a new battle-line beyond.

Thus far, despite having his horse shot from under him, Wellesley had good reason to be satisfied: the Maratha guns were taken without undue loss and their infantry stood dismayed, having done nothing to save them. The British were still heavily outnumbered but already they had achieved an unshakeable moral ascendancy over the enemy – this time when the Highlanders fired, the Marathas visibly wilted under the volley. Two battalions on the extreme right of the Maratha line broke at once, setting off a progressive collapse towards the centre as each sepoy battalion came up and delivered its fire.

Scindia's military commander, a German mercenary named Anton Pohlmann, did his best to stem the rout, swinging backwards to establish a new battle-line running westwards from Assaye. In order to cover this movement a large body of Maratha cavalry came forward, but while the sepoy units had temporarily become scattered and disorganised in pursuing the defeated infantry, the 78th remained in their ranks, presenting a sufficiently bold front to keep the Maratha horsemen at bay until some of their own guns came up.

Mounted again, Wellesley then began issuing orders for a renewed advance when he became uncomfortably aware that something had gone horribly wrong on his right flank. As he later explained to Colonel Monro:

> When the enemy [first] changed their position they threw their left to Assaye, in which village they had some infantry, and it was surrounded by cannon. As soon as I saw that, I directed the officer commanding the pickets to keep out of shot from the village; instead of that, he led directly upon it. The 74th, which were on the right of the first line, followed the pickets . . .[134]

For some reason Orrock had misunderstood his instructions – probably thinking Wellesley intended him to form just out of range of *musket*-shot rather than cannon-shot – and the circumstances certainly point to the general being altogether far too impatient to explain himself properly. At any rate, instead of halting and forming just at sufficient distance for the two brigades to form between his position and the river, he steadily kept on going towards Assaye. Worse still, Major Samuel Swinton of the 74th, who was under orders to form on Orrock, blindly followed after him. The brigade commander, Colonel William Wallace, for some reason failed to stop him, while Wellesley of course had abdicated his overall responsibility in order to go gallivanting off with the 78th. So both the 74th and the pickets soon found themselves entirely isolated – and well within range of the guns of Assaye.

In his letter to Monro, Wellesley (who surely had a guilty conscience) professed himself unable to condemn Orrock, for he never saw a man 'lead a body into a hotter fire' and the consequence was that the little battalion was to all intents and purposes quite literally shot to pieces in a matter of minutes. The 1/2nd Madras Native Infantry had been left behind to guard the baggage, yet they afterwards reported the loss of forty-six men killed and wounded, all of whom must have belonged to the half company with Orrock. This in turn also suggests that most of the twenty-eight killed and eighty-one wounded reported by the 78th Highlanders (exactly double their casualties at Ahmednuggar), fell here rather than in the battle on the left, but they were moderate enough by comparison with the losses suffered by the 74th.

It is impossible, and indeed quite pointless, to separate the casualties suffered by the half company with the pickets and those suffered by the rest of the battalion. Caught in a heavy crossfire between the Maratha guns to their front and those surrounding Assaye, they marched steadily on, forced their way through a cactus or prickly pear hedge (where according to Garth, 'many of the men having lost their shoes, their feet were much torn and pierced'), and were finally brought to a halt about a hundred metres short of the village with half their number down. Wounded himself, Swinton ordered them to fall back and once beyond the hedge he rallied the survivors on their shot-torn colours, just as the Marathas came forward to finish them off – a large body of cavalry at first and at least two of Pohlmann's regular infantry battalions as well. Too battered and too exhausted to run, the Highlanders formed a ragged square and fought off the first attack. A second might indeed have finished them, but just at the right moment Colonel Patrick Maxwell charged at the head of the 19th Light Dragoons and two regiments of Madras Light Cavalry, completely sweeping away the Marathas, both horse and foot.

The battle was still far from over at that point, but the respite gave Colonel Wallace time to find his missing battalion and pull the survivors out of range of the enemy guns. To all intents and purposes the 74th had been destroyed. Altogether 11 officers, 9 sergeants 7 drummers and 127 rank and file were killed on the spot and a further 7 officers, 11 sergeants, 7 drummers and 270 rank and file returned as wounded, for a total of 449 casualties. Not one of the battalion's officers had escaped unscathed and, in commenting on the 105 casualties returned by their comrades in the 78th, Garth stated that only those officers unable to 'keep the field' were actually returned as wounded. If the same was true of the 74th then the remnants of the battalion must have been brought off by the surviving sergeants – and many of them too must have been uncounted walking wounded.

Having arrived on the scene just in time to witness Maxwell's charge, Wellesley immediately had to double back again to where the 78th were experiencing an unusual problem. Not all of the Maratha cavalry had been driven off by Maxwell, for after their initial repulse by the 74th a large body had swung around behind the British line to retake some of the guns captured in the opening assault. The result was that the 78th suddenly found themselves fired on from the rear and had no alternative but to face about, and while the sepoy battalions covered what was left of the Marathas' main position, the Highlanders, led by Wellesley, wearily tramped across to assault the gun-line for a second time. Again Wellesley lost his horse, this time run through with a pike, but otherwise the affair was just a matter of mopping up, as was the final advance which followed.

There was still more fighting to come: another battle at Argaum two months later and the storming of the fortress of Gawilghur on 15 December, but nothing matched the sheer horror of Assaye. Both Highland regiments gained it as a battle-honour almost as a matter of course, and both were awarded a third colour by the East India Company, bearing an elephant on it, which they subsequently adopted as a badge. But it was the 74th alone who, with a certain bitter pride afterwards, referred to themselves as the Assaye Regiment.

~ 8 ~

The Glasgow Highlanders and the Corsican Ogre

The French War, which called so many Highland regiments into being, officially ended in 1802 with the Peace of Amiens, and this happy event inevitably led to the immediate disbandment of the last of the fencible battalions. They had certainly fulfilled their original purpose of home defence and more than proved their worth in Ireland. Nevertheless, leaving aside odd little contretemps such as the bad behaviour of the Strathspeys, the limitations on just where they could serve were more than a little inconvenient. Therefore, when hostilities not unexpectedly resumed within just a few short months, an entirely new plan was adopted. A whole army of reserves would be created, but unlike the fencibles this was not to be a separate force. Instead it would be formed by raising second battalions for all the existing regiments. Such additional battalions had existed before of course: for as long as anyone could remember, the Royal Scots had two battalions and the 60th (Royal Americans) had four, but to all intents and purposes these battalions were entirely separate units. Indeed, as we have just seen, the second battalion of the 42nd was so separate that in 1786 it was re-designated as the 73rd Highlanders. Now, the new battalions were to be much more closely linked to their parent. They were to serve in the first instance as a depot and as a feeder for recruits, but in the event of invasion or insurrection they would also, obviously, be available for actual service. It didn't work out quite so neatly as that in practice, of course, but the point was that there were to be no more private armies raised by the great and the good on either side of the Highland line. All the available resources in men and money were to be devoted to the regular army, and home defence was to be once more entrusted to the militia.

Wars and rumours of war aside, it was a timely change in policy so far as most of the Highland regiments were concerned, for all of them needed rebuilding after the long years of war. None more so than the 'Indian' regiments such as the 71st (Glasgow) Highland Regiment, now home at last after twenty long years away. It was a cruel irony, therefore, that no sooner was it recruited back up to strength – and a second battalion duly formed – than it was sent off again under Davie Baird, or rather Major General Sir David Baird as he had now become, to reoccupy the Cape of Good Hope. This was accomplished without any difficulty in January 1806, but then the Highlanders found themselves a vital component in a cunning plan to liberate South America from Spanish rule.

It all looked promising enough. Spain's navy had effectively been destroyed at Trafalgar two months earlier, leaving its vast American empire invitingly open to attack, and if Britain lacked the resources to do so immediately, there was always the colonists themselves. Not entirely coincidentally, a would-be revolutionary named Francisco Miranda was then in England busily telling anyone who would listen that the South American colonies desired complete independence from Spain. Encouraging unrest, if not outright rebellion, in those colonies was clearly a desirable object in itself, and was all the more desirable in the light of a burgeoning trade between Britain and South America that could only improve if Spain and her punitive customs regime were cut out of the picture. However, what really clinched the matter for those actually involved in planning the whole thing was the perception that the province of De La Plata was awash with silver. And so, without any official authorisation, in June 1806 Admiral Home Popham persuaded Davie Baird to lend his old 71st Highlanders for an unauthorised filibustering expedition to conquer South America.

The story of what followed – and of the experience of serving in a Highland regiment during the campaigns in Portugal and Spain, which paved the 71st's long road to Waterloo – would be told in one of the most remarkable soldiers' narratives to come out of the Napoleonic Wars: the ponderously entitled *Journal of a Soldier of the 71st or Glasgow Regiment,*

Highland Light Infantry from 1806–1815. It was published anonymously in Edinburgh in 1819 and the search to identify its author is a fascinating story in itself. The editor was a jobbing writer and occasional inventor named John Howell, and according to an inscription that he left in a copy of the third edition (now in the possession of the Royal Highland Fusiliers): 'James Todd is the individual I got the greater part of the journal from.'

At first sight that seems straightforward enough, for, as it turns out, there was indeed a man named James Todd serving in the 71st during the Napoleonic Wars.[135] Moreover the author tells us that he was born in Edinburgh in 1790, and sure enough a search of the capital's parish registers reveals a James Todd was born there on 29 July 1790, the son of Alexander Todd and Janet Brown. However, there is a major problem with this easy identification, for Howell went on to say that: 'When he [Todd] left me I got one Archd Gavin to fill in any part we had missed and to establish any fact I doubted I had recourse to the testimony of a party of the 71st at the time in Edin.'[136] Clearly it was a composite effort and, as we shall see, the evidence of the 71st's muster rolls leaves no doubt whatsoever that the 'Thomas' of the journal who went to South America and Private James Todd are *not* one and the same man.

Be that as it may for now, our Thomas begins his story by relating how, despite having been brought up for better things by his poor but honest parents, he resolved to become an actor, only to make a disastrous debut on the stage at the age of just sixteen. Crushed, he explains: 'I wandered the whole night. In the morning early, meeting a party of recruits about to embark, I rashly offered to go with them. My offer was accepted and I embarked at Leith with seventeen others, for the Isle of Wight in July 1806.'[137]

At this time the Isle of Wight was being used as a massive transit camp where recruits could be securely assembled and given some basic training before being shipped out to their regiments abroad. Quite typically then, according to our hero he remained on the island for just three weeks before sailing for the Cape of Good Hope – and sure enough the muster rolls for the 71st do indeed record a draft of recruits embarking for the Cape on 11 August 1806.[138] However, when Thomas and his companions arrived after what seems to have been an unremarkable voyage, they found the 71st had already gone to South

America with Popham, and so they had no alternative but to go to sea once more.

Unbeknown to them, Popham, and a Colonel William Beresford, had duly seized Buenos Aires in June and at first everything looked very promising. However, rather than confine himself to just liberating the citizens, the gallant admiral also chose to liberate over a million dollars in silver, which was promptly forwarded to a grateful Treasury by way of justifying his initiative. A suitably mollified Government promptly responded by dispatching further troops to reinforce his success, but in the meantime the Spaniards and the less-than-revolutionary colonists launched a counter-attack, retaking the city and capturing most of the 71st Highlanders in the process.

Thus, relates Thomas, 'We arrived in the River Plate in October 1806, when we were informed the Spaniards had retaken Buenos Aires and that our troops only possessed Maldonado, a small space on the side of the river, about five or six miles farther up than Monte Video'. Worse was to come:

> Soon after our arrival at Maldonado, The Spaniards advanced out of Monte Video to attack us. They were about 600, and had, besides, a number of great guns with them. They came upon us in two columns, the right consisting of cavalry, the left of infantry, and bore so hard upon our out-picquet of 400 men that Colonel Brown, who commanded our left, ordered Major Campbell, with three companies of the 40th regiment to its support. These charged the head of the column. The Spaniards stood firm and fought bravely; numbers fell on both sides; but the gallant 40th drove them back with the point of the bayonet. Sir Samuel Auchmuty ordered the rifle corps and light battalion to attack the rear of their column, which was done with the utmost spirit. Three cheers were the signal of our onset. The Spaniards fled, and the right column, seeing the fate of their left, set spurs to their horses and fled, without having shared in the action ... This was the first blood I had ever seen shed in battle; the first time the cannon had roared in my hearing, charged with death. I was not yet seventeen years of age, and had not been six months from home. My limbs bending under me with fatigue, in a sultry clime, the musket and accoutrements that I was forced to carry were insupportably oppressive. Still I bore all with invincible patience. During the action the thought of death never once crossed my mind. After the

firing commenced, a still sensation stole over my whole frame, a firm determined torpor, bordering on insensibility. I heard an old soldier answer, to a youth like myself, who inquired what he should do during the battle, 'Do your duty.'

It was stirring stuff, even if some of his apparent equanimity at his first battle probably stemmed from the fact that, like the other raw recruits, he was serving in Auchmuty's headquarters guard at the time, and therefore never in any immediate danger. The minor victory at Maldonaldo enabled Auchmuty (who, despite his Scottish name, was actually an American) to capture Montevideo on 3 February 1807, but there, surrounded by a hostile countryside, he sat tight and waited for those promised reinforcements. In due course they arrived, led by a General Whitelocke, who was one of those bluff, stout-hearted soldiers perfectly capable of leading a battalion into the hottest of fights, but hopelessly out of his depth when it came to commanding a brigade, let alone an army, as he now proceeded to demonstrate.

On 28 June 1807 the army assembled near Ensenada de Barragon and commenced its ill-fated march on Buenos Aires. By this time Thomas had been posted to the light company of the 71st, which had avoided the earlier debacle there:

We remained under arms on the morning of the 5th of July, waiting the order to advance. Judge our astonishment when the word was given to march without ammunition, with fixed bayonets only. 'We are betrayed', was whispered through the ranks. 'Mind your duty, my lads; onwards, onwards, Britain for ever,' were the last words I heard our noble Captain Brookman utter. He fell as we entered the town. Onwards we rushed, carrying everything before us, scrambling over ditches, and other impediments which the inhabitants had placed in our way. At the corner of every street, and flanking all the ditches, they had placed cannon that thinned our ranks every step we took. Still onwards we drove, up one street, down another, until we came to the church of St Domingo, where the colours of the 71st regiment had been placed, as a trophy, over the shrine of the Virgin Mary. We made a sally into it, and took them from that disgraceful resting place, where they had remained ever since the surrender of General Beresford to General Liniers. Now we were going to sally out in triumph. The Spaniards had not been idle. The entrances of the church were barricaded, and cannon placed at each entrance. We were forced to surrender, and were marched to prison.

As a summary of what went wrong it was probably better than most. Just as in the earlier battle the British troops found themselves bogged down in fighting through streets that were not only barricaded but lined with flat-roofed houses stuffed with enthusiastic citizens who would have fled at the first volley in an open field but were more than happy to blaze away from their own rooftops.

Several months of captivity deep in the interior then followed, but eventually all were released, and Thomas and his comrades safely landed at the Cove of Cork on 25 December 1807. Vivid and convincing as the narrative goes thus far, and backed up as it is by the regiment's own records, the adventures just recounted were certainly not those of James Todd, or for that matter Archibald Gavin.[139]

As the greater part of the 71st had already been captured at Buenos Aires before they ever embarked from the Isle of Wight, the ten men belonging to the 11 August 1806 draft were identified quite separately on the regiment's quarterly rolls for some time afterwards. They were:

> William Farquhar
> David Faulds
> Edward Floyd
> William Mackee
> James Moody
> Joseph Mulholland
> Joseph Shuder
> Joseph Sinclair
> David Walker
> Peter Yellet

James Todd, it will be observed, was not one of their number, for he was in fact serving with the regiment's second battalion at the time. Yet one of the ten, clearly, must be the Thomas who fought at Buenos Aires – but which one?

Four of the men – David Faulds, James Moody, David Walker and Peter Yellet – can be eliminated at once, for over the next few years all four of them would subsequently be returned as killed in action or otherwise dead, while Joseph Shuder was discharged – or deserted – on 24 July 1809, just as the regiment was embarking for Walcheren. This obviously whittles the possibilities down to just five, and, as we shall see shortly, all but one of them can be dismissed equally confidently.

In the meantime the long months of captivity in Argentina obviously took their toll on the 71st with unexpected consequences in a particular direction. By all accounts they were a pretty sorry sight when they disembarked, for their uniforms were at best worn and shabby and in some cases entirely lacking. What was more, being British soldiers and therefore inclined to regard dress regulations as being no more than optional guidelines, they had also quite characteristically supplemented or replaced their tattered regimentals with locally acquired garments such as serapes and ponchos. Something, decided a horrified authority, would have to be done and done quickly.

It is not entirely certain whether, having been stationed in South Africa, they actually went across to Argentina in their kilts, but they certainly needed new ones when they came home. However, their commanding officer, 'Sweet' Dennis Pack advised the Adjutant General's Office that he intended to cloth the men in tartan trousers as these could be run up more quickly than kilts. His confidence that this measure would be approved was not misplaced, for back in October 1804, the Adjutant General's Office had already been discreetly canvassing the Highland colonels for their private opinion on 'the expediency of abolishing the kilt in Highland regiments and substituting in lieu thereof the tartan trews, which have been reported to the Commander in Chief, from respectable authority, as an article now become acceptable to your countrymen, easier to be provided, and both calculated to preserve the health, and promote the comfort of the men on service.'[140]

It was later to become an article of faith amongst romantically inclined historians, starting with Stewart of Garth, that Highland soldiers were passionately attached to their kilts – even to the point of mutiny. Yet in 1794 Sir John Sinclair of Ulbster had dressed his Rothesay and Caithness Fencibles in tartan trousers in the curious belief that they were more authentic and that 'bare knees [seem] to have been a Roman, rather than a Celtic fashion.'[141] It was to be even more common still for ordinary trousers to be substituted, especially on active service.

Not only were trousers worn in North America during the Revolution, but the 'East Indian' regiments had them too. The army's clothing regulations in the 1790s sensibly specified that troops serving in both the East and West Indies were to have short single-breasted jackets, linen trousers and wide brimmed hats – without any mention of an exemption for Highlanders. (As we have already seen the 109th Highlanders adopted white trousers in anticipation of embarking for the Caribbean.) To be sure there were exceptions: the three Highland regiments who went to Egypt in 1801 kept their kilts, and according to a so-far-unsubstantiated legend, the 78th may still have had their kilts at Assaye, but for the most part there was more than enough precedence for the wearing of trousers.

However, the present proposal was not inspired by an altruistic desire to improve the lot of the common soldier, or even driven by considerations of economy. Apart from the Black Watch, all of the Highland regiments were originally raised by the great, would-be great or once-great men of the Highlands, but neither they nor the patriotic corporations and county associations who had also done so much to raise Mr Pitt's army at the beginning of the last war were in the picture this time around. The old patriotic enthusiasm was exhausted and without their unstinting aid the Government was hard-pressed to establish a mechanism for creating that new 'Army of Reserve'. The solution, and an obvious one, was to lift the old restrictions on the army enlisting men who were already serving in the militia.

This was definitely one of the Government's better ideas, for the ranks of the militia regiments were recruited and maintained by conscription. The old objection to taking men from the militia for the regulars was two-fold: in the first place, the ballot was far from popular and might be strongly resisted at the outset if it were believed that, once taken for the militia, men then might be drafted or at the very least coerced into serving abroad. Secondly, every man who did volunteer into the regulars had then to be replaced by a further, and inevitably more difficult, round of conscription.

However, these quite understandable objections were outweighed by the obvious advantages: not only did such men come ready trained, but the fact of their having been balloted from a relatively wide cross-section of the population meant that by and large they presented a much higher standard than the ordinary run of recruits. Some militiamen (and officers) were happy to stay at home, but a consistent theme in the memoirs of men such as James Anton, a Huntly weaver who volunteered from the Aberdeenshire Militia into the Black Watch, is that having once become adjusted to military life they soon took the view that they might as well do it properly, and literally thousands volunteered from militia battalions into the regulars, compared to the small numbers of individuals found by ordinary enlistment.[142]

Outstandingly successful as the scheme was for building up the ordinary regiments of the line, the Highland ones, unfortunately, still presented a problem. Thanks to those earlier patriotic gentlemen, they accounted for some 10 per cent of all the infantry units – and the kilt, which had once been reckoned an inducement to recruits, was now thought by the Government to be a stumbling block to maintaining them.

In short, because there were now more Highland regiments than were warranted by the size of the general population, the only realistic way to keep them up to strength was by taking recruits from the English and Irish militia. However, while most Scotsmen were seemingly happy to wear the kilt, irrespective of which side of the Highland line they were born and bred, Englishmen and Hibernians were understandably less keen. Pack, the Anglo-Irish son of the Dean of Ossory, was therefore only going along with what he understood was the official thinking on the question by offering to put his men into tartan trousers. The suggestion was duly authorised but if he thought that his early initiative would ensure the proper preservation of the regiment's Highland character, he may have been reckoning without a characteristically intemperate intervention by Allan Cameron of Erracht!

The 79th, it will be recalled, had been all but destroyed in the West Indies, with those men who had not succumbed to the twin perils of the climate and the rum being drafted into the ranks of the Black Watch, thus leaving Erracht with just a bare cadre of officers and NCOs. Nevertheless, he had succeeded, through a combination of his own boundless energy, a burning sense of grievance and his father-in-law's money, to recruit the regiment afresh. Understandably enough, at that stage in the war it had not been easy, and a 1799 return revealed there were at that point only 268 Scots in the ranks (presumably by no means all of them Highlanders). The Scots were somewhat outnumbered by 273 Englishmen, 54 Irishmen and 7 foreigners[143] – proportions that illustrated the Government's present point only too clearly. Not surprisingly they were dressed in blue trousers at the time rather than his own tartan and it is far from certain that they wore kilts during the subsequent campaigns in Holland and Egypt. Consequently when the adjutant general had enquired politely on 13 October 1804 about the prospects of abandoning the kilt, Erracht was in no mood to co-operate and two weeks later penned a characteristically bombastic response:

> ... in the course of the late war several gentlemen proposed to raise Highland regiments – some for general service, but chiefly for home defence; but most of these corps were called upon from all quarters, and thereby adulterated by every description of men, that rendered them anything but real Highlanders, or even Scotchmen (which is not strictly synonymous) and the colonels themselves being generally unacquainted with the language and habits of Highlanders, while prejudiced in favour of, and accustomed to wear, breeches, consequently adverse to that free circulation of that pure wholesome air (as an exhilarating bracer) which has hitherto so peculiarly benefited the Highlander for activity and all the other necessary qualities of a soldier, whether for hardship upon scanty fare, readiness in accoutring, or making forced marches – besides the exclusive advantage, when halted, of drenching his kilt in the next brook as well as washing his limbs and drying both, as it were, by constant fanning, without injury to either, but, on the contrary, feeling clean and comfortable; whilst the buffoon tartan pantaloon, with its fringed frippery (as some mongrel Highlanders would have it), sticking wet and dirty to the skin, is not very easily pulled off, and less so to get on again in case of alarm or any other hurry, and all this time absorbing both wet and dirt, followed by rheumatism and fevers, which alternately make great havoc in hot and cold climates; while it consists with knowledge, that the Highlander in his native garb always appeared more cleanly and maintained better health in both climates, than those who wore even the thick cloth pantaloons.

Clearly the fact that his Highland regiment had been revealed to contain rather more Englishmen and Irishmen than Scots still rankled, but he still plunged on in his usual breathless manner:

> ...from my own experience I feel well-founded in saying that if anything was wanted to aid the rack-renting Highland landlord in destroying that

source which has hitherto proved so fruitful in keeping up Highland corps, it will be that of abolishing their native garb, which his Royal Highness the Commander in Chief and the Adjutant may rest assured will prove a complete death warrant to the recruiting service in that respect; but I sincerely hope His Royal Highness will never acquiesce in so painful and degrading an idea (come from whatever quarter it may) as to strip us of our native garb (admitted hitherto our regimental uniform), and stuff us in a harlequin tartan pantaloon, which, composed of the usual quality that continues at present worn, useful and becoming for twelve months, will not endure six weeks' fair wear as a pantaloon, and when patched makes a horrible appearance; besides that, the necessary quantity to serve decently throughout the year would become extremely expensive, but, above all take away completely the appearance and conceit of a Highland soldier, in which case I would rather see him stuffed in breeches and abolish the distinction altogether.[144]

It was vintage Erracht of course, breathless, bombastic to the point of incoherence and composed with a fine disregard for the facts. Unfortunately, if it was sufficiently frightening to persuade the Duke of York and the Adjutant General to leave the 79th (and its Englishmen) alone, the irony of it is that they may also have taken his advice literally when it came to stuffing the Highland regiments in breeches, for what emerged was a compromise. Like it or not, the fact remained that there simply were not enough Scotsmen enlisting in the army to support twenty-two battalions of Highlanders, so something had to give and on 7 April 1809 the axe fell:

As the population of the Highlands of Scotland is found insufficient to supply recruits for the whole of the Highland Corps on the establishment of His Majesty's Army, and as some of these Corps, laying aside their distinguishing dress, which is objectionable to the natives of South Britain, would in a great measure tend to facilitating the completing of the establishment; as it would be an inducement to the men of the English Militia to extend their service in greater number to these regiments it is in consequence most humbly submitted for the approbation of His Majesty, that His Majesty's 72nd, 73rd, 74th, 75th, 91st and 94th Regiments should discontinue to wear in future the dress by which his Majesty's Regiments of Highlanders are distinguished; and that the above Corps should no longer be considered as on that establishment.[145]

The 94th, the old Scotch Brigade, had never been a Highland regiment so their inclusion in the list must be a clerk's mistake for the 93rd, who thereby had a fortunate escape, but otherwise it was the 'Indian' regiments who accounted for most of those selected for 'de-kilting' and opened the way for men like Thomas Morris from Middlesex to join the 73rd. Given that these regiments had already been wearing trousers for most of their existence this was only logical, and while no mention was made of the 71st in the order, that was almost certainly down to Pack's pre-emptive adoption of trousers a year earlier.

Thus, some eight months after his return from South America, Thomas, wearing tartan trousers rather than a kilt below his feather bonnet, landed at Mondego Bay, near Lisbon. Enemies just months before, the 71st Highlanders and the Spaniards were now to be allies in what would become known as the Peninsular War.

Sir Arthur Wellesley was in command, pending the arrival of more senior officers. Never one to sit idly, he fought and defeated the invading French at Roleia on 17 May and four days later again at Vimeiro, where a piper named George Clarke, anticipated Finlayson of the Gordons at Dargai ninety years later by playing the men on even after he had been shot through both legs. Thomas, for his part, relates how just as the regiment was preparing for divine service, the French turned up:

> On the 21st, we were all under arms an hour before day-break. After remaining some time we were dismissed, with orders to parade again at 10 o'clock, to attend divine service for this was a Sabbath morning. How unlike the Sabbaths I was wont to enjoy! Had it not been for the situation in which I had placed myself, I could have enjoyed it much.
>
> Vimeira is situated in a lovely valley, through which the small river Maceira winds, adding beauty to one of the sweetest scenes, surrounded on all sides by mountains and the sea, from which the village is distant about three miles. There is a deep ravine that parts the heights, over which the Lourinha road passes. We were posted on these mountains, and had a complete view of the valley below. I here, for a time, indulged in one of the most pleasing reveries I had enjoyed since I left home. I was seated upon the side of a mountain, admiring the beauties beneath. I thought of home: Arthur's Seat, and the level between it and the sea, all stole over my imagination. I became lost in contemplation, and was happy for a time.

Soon my day-dream broke, and vanished from my sight. The bustle around was great. There was no trace of a day of rest. Many were washing their linen in the river, others cleaning their firelocks; every man was engaged in some employment. In the midst of our preparation for divine service, the French columns began to make their appearance on the opposite hills. 'To arms, to arms!' was beat, at half-past eight o'clock. Every thing was packed up as soon as possible, and left on the camp ground.

We marched out two miles, to meet the enemy, formed line, and lay under cover of a hill, for about an hour, until they came to us. We gave them one volley, and three cheers – three distinct cheers. Then all was as still as death. They came upon us, crying and shouting, to the very point of our bayonets. Our awful silence and determined advance they could not stand. They put about, and fled without much resistance. At this charge we took thirteen guns, and one General.

We advanced into a hollow, and formed again: then returned in file, from the right in companies, to the rear. The French came down upon us again. We gave them another specimen of a charge, as effectual as our first, and pursued them three miles.

Unfortunately, the two victories were then followed by the Convention of Cintra, which allowed the defeated French to evacuate Portugal unmolested and then quite inevitably saw Wellesley and the two more senior British generals responsible hauled before a court of inquiry. As an immediate result command of the army passed to Sir John Moore, and his own second-in-command, who happened to be none other than Davie Baird. Moore for his part then advanced with the army into Spain, hoping to co-operate with his new allies, only to be forced by Napoleon himself to turn around and retire not into Portugal, but into Galicia and over the bleak winter mountains to Corunna in northern Spain. Thomas's description is one of the most harrowing and evocative narratives of what followed:

There was nothing to sustain our famished bodies or shelter them from the rain or snow. We were drenched with rain or crackling with ice. Fuel we could find none. The sick and wounded that we had been still enabled to drag with us in the wagons were now left to perish in the snow. The road was one line of bloody foot-marks from the sore feet of the men; and on its sides lay the dead and dying. Human nature could do no more.

Donald McDonald, the hardy Highlander, began to fail. He, as well as myself, had long been barefooted and lame; he, that had encouraged me to proceed, now himself lay down to die ... We sat down together; not a word escaped our lips. We looked around, then at each other, and closed our eyes. We felt there was no hope. We would have given in charge a farewell to our friends; but who was to carry it? There were, not far from us, here and there, above thirty in the same situation with ourselves. There was nothing but groans, mingled with execrations, to be heard, between the pauses of the wind ... We had not sat half an hour, sleep was stealing upon me, when I perceived a bustle around me. It was an advanced party of the French. Unconscious of the action, I started upon my feet, levelled my musket, which I had still retained, fired, and formed with the other stragglers ...

Towards the close of this journey my mind became unfit for any minute observation. I only marked what I myself was forced to encounter. How I was sustained I am unable to conceive. My life was misery. Hunger, cold, and fatigue, had deprived death of all its horrors. My present sufferings I felt; what death was, I could only guess. 'I will endure every thing, in hope of living to smooth the closing years of my mother's life, and atone for my unkindness. Merciful God! support me.' These ejaculations were always the close of my melancholy musing; after which I felt a new invigoration, though, many times, my reflections were broken short by scenes of horror that came in my way. One, in particular, I found, after I came home, had been much talked of.

After we had gained the summit of Monte del Castro, and were descending, I was roused by a crowd of soldiers. My curiosity prompted me to go to it; I knew it must be no common occurrence that could attract their sympathy. Judge of the feelings which I want words to express. In the centre lay a woman, young and lovely, though cold in death, and a child, apparently about six or seven months old, attempting to draw support from the breast of its dead mother. Tears filled every eye, but no-one had the power to aid. While we stood around, gazing on the interesting object, then on each other, none offered to speak, each heart was so full. At length one of General Moore's staff-officers came up, and desired the infant to be given to him. He rolled it in his cloak, amidst the blessings of every spectator. Never shall I efface the benevolence of his look from my heart, when he said, 'Unfortunate infant, you will be my future care.'

From the few remaining wagons we had been able to bring with us, women and children, who had hitherto sustained without perishing all our aggravated sufferings, were, every now and then, laid out upon the snow, frozen to death. An old tattered blanket, or some other piece of garment, was all the burial that was given them. The soldiers who perished lay uncovered until the next fall of snow, or heavy drift, concealed their bodies.

Eventually they reached Corunna, turned at bay and after a successful rearguard action outside the town embarked for England in an absolutely pitiable state. Moore, famously, was fatally wounded in the proverbial hour of victory, and was succeeded only briefly by Davie Baird who was himself carried aboard one of the ships with a shattered arm very shortly afterwards. Baird recovered from the loss of the arm, but while a succession of postings on the home staff followed, it ended his active career. Not so his old regiment, although it was months before the 1/71st were fit for service again. In the meantime they were re-trained as light infantry, losing their tartan trews in the process but retaining their bonnets, albeit no longer with the distinctive ostrich feathers.

Thomas, in hospital, seems to have missed this alteration in the regiment's status, but he was passed as fit for duty again in time to join the expedition to the island of Walcheren on the Dutch coast. There he took part in the siege of Flushing (Vlissingen) and like so many of his comrades came down with the dread Walcheren Fever – a form of malaria. This saw him evacuated to hospital again at Bradburn Lees, where he eventually recovered but not, according to the *Journal*, until after the death of his friend Donald MacDonald, who had supposedly gone out to South America with him and shared the hardships of the retreat to Corunna.

This immediately raises an awkward problem so far as the *Journal* is concerned. There was no-one of that name, of course, in the August 1806 draft, yet Thomas says, 'He had come from Inverness to Edinburgh on foot, with no other intention than to enlist in the 71st. His father had been a soldier in it, and was now living at home after being discharged. Donald called it *his* regiment.' This might suggest Donald was actually William Farquhar, seemingly the only Highlander in the draft, if it were not for the fact that the rolls clearly show Farquhar served neither at Corunna nor at Walcheren. When Moore and Baird bravely marched into Spain they left a surprising number of men behind in Portugal.

Some of them were simply stragglers, while others, more legitimately were sick in hospital or were employed in various rear-party jobs. There were so many of them in fact that when Sir Arthur Wellesley returned to resume command in Portugal some months later, he was able to form two battalions of detachments from these men, which fought under him at Talavera on 28 July 1809. One of the men, serving in the 2nd Battalion of Detachments was William Farquhar, and alongside him interestingly enough was James Todd!

In fact none of the men belonging to that August 1806 draft died at Walcheren or any time shortly afterwards, and with Farquhar still in Spain the original ten candidates are thus reduced to four. One of them, Edward Floyd, eventually survived to claim the Military General Service medal for all of the battles described by Thomas, but he was an Irishman from Londonderry, not a young Scots lad from Edinburgh. Similarly William Mackee was not only Irish enough to claim his MGS as a Kilmainham pensioner, but, unlike Thomas, he came through the Walcheren campaign unscathed, only to be badly wounded at Waterloo and was in hospital at Brussels from June 1815 until at least the end of the year. Of the two remaining men, another Irishman, Joseph Mulholland[146] can also be eliminated: according to the regiment's quarterly muster rolls he qualified for additional pay in May 1808, indicating that far from being a fresh-faced young recruit, he had originally enlisted as long ago as 1801, when Thomas was just ten years old.

Thus, by an inexorable process of elimination we are left only with Joseph Sinclair, which is not to say, given the circumstances of his enlistment, that his real name may not have been Thomas after all. Significantly enough, not only did Joseph Sinclair go out with that draft to South America and come through the Corunna campaign, but the muster roll also records him as returning from Walcheren on board a hospital ship in December 1809, which means that up until that point in the story the experiences of Joseph Sinclair and the Thomas of the *Journal* correspond exactly – and uniquely.

However, that, of course, is not the end of it all. In September 1810 the 71st once again embarked for the Peninsula and in May of the following year Thomas – or rather Joseph Sinclair, as we should now call him – found himself at a small town on the frontier named Fuentes d'Onoro:

On the 3d of May at day-break, all the cavalry, and sixteen light companies, occupied the town. We stood under arms until three o'clock, when a staff-officer rode up to our Colonel, and gave orders for our advance. Colonel Cadogan[147] put himself at our head, saying 'My lads, you have had no provision these two days; there is plenty in the hollow in front, let us down and divide it.' We advanced as quick as we could run, and met the light companies retreating as fast as they could. We continued to advance, at double-quick time, our firelocks at the trail, our bonnets in our hands. They called to us, 'Seventy-first, you will come back quicker than you advance.' We soon came full in front of the enemy. The Colonel cried, 'Here is food, my lads, cut away.' Thrice we waved our bonnets, and thrice we cheered; brought our firelocks to the charge, and forced them back through the town.

How different the duty of the French officers from ours. They, stimulating the men by their example, the men vociferating, each chaffing each until they appear in a fury, shouting, to the points of our bayonets. After the first huzza the British officers, restraining their men, still as death. 'Steady, lads, steady,' is all you hear, and that in an undertone.

The French had lost a great number of men in the streets. We pursued them about a mile out of the town, trampling over the dead and wounded; but their cavalry bore down upon us, and forced us back into the town, where we kept our ground, in spite of their utmost efforts.

In this affair, my life was most wonderfully preserved. In forcing the French through the town, during our first advance, a bayonet went through between my side and clothes, to my knapsack, which stopped its progress. The Frenchman to whom the bayonet belonged, fell, pierced by a musket-ball from my rear-rank man. Whilst freeing myself from the bayonet, a ball took off part of my right-shoulder wing, and killed my rear-rank man, who fell upon me. Narrow as this escape was, I felt no uneasiness, I was become so inured to danger and fatigue.

During this day, the loss of men was great. In our retreat back to the town, when we halted to check the enemy, who bore hard upon us, in their attempts to break our line, often was I obliged to stand with a foot upon each side of a wounded man, who rung my soul with prayers I could not answer, and pierced my heart with his cries to be lifted out of the way of the cavalry. While my heart bled for them, I have shaken them rudely off.

We kept up our fire, until long after dark. About one o'clock in the morning, we got four ounces of bread served out to each man, which, [sic] had been collected out of the haversacks of the Foot Guards. After the firing had ceased, we began to search through the town, and found plenty of flour, bacon, and sausages, on which we feasted heartily, and lay down on our blankets, wearied to death. My shoulder was as black as a coal, from the recoil of my musket; for this day I had fired 107 rounds of ball-cartridge. Sore as I was, I slept as sound as a top, till I was awakened by the loud call of the bugle, an hour before day.

Soon as it was light, the firing commenced, and was kept up until about ten o'clock, when Lieutenant Stewart, of our regiment, was sent with a flag of truce, for leave to carry off our wounded from the enemy's lines, which was granted; and at the same time, they carried off theirs from ours. As soon as the wounded were all got in, many of whom had lain bleeding all night – many both a day and a night – the French brought down a number of bands of music to a level piece of ground, about ninety or a hundred yards broad, that lay between us. They continued to play until sunset; whilst the men were dancing, and diverting themselves at football. We were busy cooking the remainder of our sausages, bacon, and flour.

There was another day's fighting to come, and by the end of it, he recalled: 'We lost four officers and two taken prisoners, besides 400 killed and wounded,' which, as he went on to say, 'more than any words of mine, will give an idea of the action at Fuentes d'Onoro.' In reality they had 21 killed and 114 wounded over the two days, out of some 497 at the outset, although two officers were indeed taken prisoner together with 43 men. Once the inevitable sick and stragglers were factored in, the regiment was reduced for a time to little more than two hundred men, but once reinforced by a strong draft from 2/71st it soon took the field again and the *Journal* vividly describes the raid on Arroyo de Molinos at the end of October and the hardships of patrolling the frontier as Wellington prepared for the fast-moving campaign that would take the frontier towns of Cuidad Rodrigo and Badajoz. It must be from this point, however, that John Howell first started to rely upon the reminiscences of James Todd rather than those of Joseph (or Thomas) Sinclair, for, according to the 71st muster rolls, Sinclair missed the raid on Arroyo de Molinos because he was sick in the general hospitals – first at Abrantes and then Lisbon during the latter part of 1811, perhaps because like so many others he may have been suffering a recurrence of Walcheren Fever.

IX Officer and sergeant of the 43rd Highlanders; engraving by N. C. Goodnight after Van der Gucht. Although undated this is the style of uniform worn at the time of the Black Watch Mutiny

X An eighteenth-century view of Dublin from Phoenix Park – note the Highland officer in the foreground

XI Piper Clarke of the 71st at Vimeiro; print by Duborg

XII Rebels drilling by Gilray; contemporary satire on the supposed threat from Irish terrorists in 1798

XIII Troopers of the Royal Scots Greys; print after Charles Hamilton Smith, 1815. The trooper in front wears white breeches for a formal parade while the trooper at the rear has the grey campaign overalls worn at Waterloo. Black oilskin covers were also worn over the bearskins

XIV *Landing Troops and Guns*; print after Rowlandson, 1801. No location is given, but the date would suggest that Egypt may be intended – the mountains in the background would certainly rule out the Helder

XV Officers of the 92nd Highlanders; print after William Heath, 1820

XVI The Battle of Toulouse (1814); contemporary print by Heath depicting the last battle of the Peninsular War – an unnecessary one as peace had already been agreed

At any rate the 71st then spent most of the following year on outpost duty, thus avoiding the horrors of both the assaults on the fortresses and the great battle of Salamanca that followed. Only towards the end of the summer were they involved in the abortive siege of Burgos, but the next year opened with a seemingly unstoppable advance into northern Spain, effortlessly turning the French out of one defensive line after another and culminating in a terrific fight on the hills around the town of Vittoria as the retreating French turned at bay:

> Orders were given to brush out our locks, oil them, and examine our flints. We being in the rear, these were soon followed by orders to open out from the centre, to allow the 71st to advance. Forward we moved up the hill. The firing was now very heavy. Our rear had not engaged, before word came for the Doctor to assist Colonel Cadogan, who was wounded. Immediately we marched up the hill, the piper playing, 'Hey Johnny Cope'. The French had possession of the top, but we soon forced them back, and drew up in column on the height; Sending out four companies to our left to skirmish. The remainder moved on to the opposite height. As we advanced driving them before us, a French officer, a pretty fellow, was pricking and forcing his men to stand. They heeded him not – he was very harsh: – 'Down with him' cried one near me; and down he fell pierced by more than one ball.
>
> Scarce were we upon the height, when a heavy column, dressed in great-coats, with white covers on their hats, exactly resembling the Spanish, gave us a volley, which put us to the right-about at double-quick time down the hill, the French close behind, through the whins. The four companies got the word, the French were on them. They likewise thought them Spaniards, until they got a volley that killed or wounded almost every man of them. We retired to the height, covered by the 50th, who gave the pursuing column a volley which checked their speed. We moved up the remains of our shattered regiment to the height. Being in great want of ammunition, we were again served with sixty rounds a man, and kept up our fire for some time, until the bugle sounded to cease firing ...
>
> At this time the Major [Charles Cother[148]] had the command. There were not 300 of us on the height able to do duty, out of above 1,000 who drew rations in the morning. The cries of the wounded were most heartrending.

At the end of it all the narrator observed sadly that this:

was the dullest encampment I ever made. We had left 700 men behind. None spoke; each hung his head, mourning the loss of a friend and comrade. About twelve o'clock, a man of each company was sent to receive half a pound of flour for each man, at the rate of our morning's strength, so that there was more than could be used by those who had escaped. I had fired 108 rounds this day. Next morning we awoke dull, stiff and weary. I could scarce touch my head with my right hand; my shoulder was black as coal.

As usual the estimate of 700 killed and wounded was something of an exaggeration, for the battalion actually lost a total of 15 killed and 301 wounded. They were, however, the heaviest losses in the brigade and one of those wounded men left behind must have been Joseph Sinclair, for the muster rolls show him first in the field hospital at Vittoria, and afterwards at Bilbao. The account of the battle's aftermath and the retreat that followed must therefore have been supplied by Todd, although Sinclair did recover in time to take part in the later fighting in the Pyrenees, and in southern France up to the armistice.

Afterwards, safely back in Ireland at the war's end, he tells us he eagerly looked forward to his discharge, having served out the seven years for which he enlisted, only to be informed that those seven years could only be accounted from his eighteenth birthday. Thus, with some months still to run he was bundled on to a schooner and sent off to Flanders and Waterloo. In fact the muster rolls show that, precisely because his discharge was so imminent, Sinclair was transferred to 2/71st in December 1814, and therefore went nowhere near Waterloo.

That particular part of the story belongs in the next chapter, but as for Sinclair himself, the *Journal* simply ends with a letter announcing that he proposed to try his luck in Spain or in South America, which may be nothing more than a device by Howell to throw the curious off the scent and disguise the fact that 'Thomas' was really at least two, if not three, different men: Sinclair, Todd and Gavin. There is, however, an intriguing sequel: in 1848 the surviving veterans of all the wars fought between 1793 and 1815 finally received a Military General Service medal, and one of those who claimed it was recorded as *Charles* Sinclair of the 71st. He also received officially struck bars for Rolieia, Vimeiro, Corunna, Vittoria, Pyrenees, Nivell and Nive, but when the medal was catalogued in 1921 it also had another engraved bar for Monte Video, so whether the attribution to Charles rather than to Joseph Sinclair is a mistake in the list or reflects some uncertainty as to his real name, it is comforting to know that 'Thomas' lived to claim the medal he had earned all those years before.

~ 9 ~

Scotland Forever

The wars had seen the Highland regiments go to some strange places. While most of the 'Indian' regiments came home around the turn of the century, the 73rd was instead transferred from Madras to New South Wales in 1805 to serve as a garrison for Botany Bay and would not return home until 1816 – close on forty years after it first went out east as the second battalion of the Black Watch. In the meantime, of course, it gained a second battalion of its own, which went to Germany in 1813, narrowly missed the great Volkerschlacht – the Battle of the Nations – at Leipzig, fought at Gohrde and finished up the war in Holland. Similarly the 78th also stayed in the East Indies after Assaye, going on to Java in 1811; but the second battalion raised in 1804 was originally selected for light-infantry training under Moore and Mackenzie at Shorncliffe.[149] Had their training not been curtailed, when they were unexpectedly ordered to Gibraltar in September 1805, the 78th would therefore have become the Highland Light Infantry rather than the 71st. As it was, from Gibraltar they went to Sicily and to Calabria and stood in line to shatter the French assault in the surprising victory at Maida on 6 July 1806. Less happily, they then went on to Egypt and a minor disaster at El Hamet in 1807, but had another moment of glory in Holland in 1814, with a bayonet charge at Merexem – not so very far away from where the first battalion began its war all those years before.

Others had a quieter time – at first anyway. The 75th, for no apparent reason, was slow to recruit itself again after coming back from India and was only reckoned fit for a quiet posting to the Mediterranean and garrison duty in the Ionian Islands. The 72nd went out to the Cape with the 71st in 1806, but while Davie Baird let his old regiment go off on that filibustering expedition to Argentina, he held on to the 72nd and so they stayed in South Africa until 1821. The 93rd Sutherlands went out to the Cape too, but then in 1814 they were recalled for service in a new war against the Americans, and met their fate vainly trying to storm the entrenchments at New Orleans on 8 January 1815 – two weeks after that particular war had officially ended.

For the rest of them there was Walcheren and the Peninsula. At Orthes, towards the end of that particular conflict, according to Sergeant Robertson of the 92nd:

> Here the three Highland regiments met for the first time – namely the 42nd, 79th and 92nd; and such a joyful meeting I have seldom witnessed. As we were almost all from Scotland, and having had a great many friends in all regiments, such a shaking of hands took place. The one hand held the firelock and bayonet, while the other was extended to give the friendly Highland grasp, and the three cheers to go forward. Lord Wellington was so much pleased with the scene that he ordered the three regiments to be encamped beside one another for the night as we had been separated for some years, that we might have the pleasure of spending a few hours together.[150]

He was exaggerating, of course, about the degree of separation. The 92nd Highlanders were brigaded at the time with the 71st, who for some reason were seemingly not included in that convivial gathering. The third battalion in that particular brigade was an English one, the 50th Foot, but in 1812 for the first time there was a proper Highland Brigade, commanded by James Stirling[151] of the Black Watch, and comprising the 42nd, the 79th and the 91st. The latter was raised early in the war by Colonel Duncan Campbell of Lochnell as the 98th (Argyllshire) Regiment but a well-timed posting to the Cape in 1795 saw them escape being drafted and instead they were re-numbered as the 91st in 1798. Rather to everyone's surprise, despite still being overwhelmingly Scottish in composition, they were then marked down to lose the kilt in 1809, but nevertheless defiantly continued to regard themselves as a Highland regiment.[152]

All of them emerged from those years in Portugal and Spain with some credit, but it would only be fair to say that the reputation that they built up there was one of steady dependability rather than dash. That was exemplified by the Gordons at the Col de Maya in 1813 when a single wing of the regiment – just half a battalion – flung itself across a mountain road and for an incredible twenty minutes fought a whole French division to a bloody standstill, while men like George Bell of the 34th could only watch in awe:

> The 92d were in line pitching into the French like blazes, and tossing them over. They stood there like a stone wall overmatched by twenty to one, until half their blue bonnets lay beside those brave northern warriors. When they retired their dead bodies lay as a barrier to the advancing foe. Oh but they did fight well that day; I can still see now the line of killed and wounded stretched upon the heather, as the living retired, closing to the centre.[153]

There was a price to be paid, of course: out of less than 400 men who went into the fight that morning, 32 were killed and no fewer than 19 officers, 10 sergeants and 258 men were wounded – and that was just a taste of what was soon to come.

First, though, came anther peace: a very temporary one as it turned out, in the wake of Napoleon's first abdication and his exile to the Mediterranean island of Elba. A great congress at Vienna engaged itself in re-arranging Europe to the victors' satisfaction, while inevitably the British Army once again embarked upon the customary round of redundancies. Few regiments disappeared this time, since the wartime expansion had largely been achieved through the doubling of existing units rather than by raising new ones. Now most of the additional battalions began to be disbanded, or rather they were consolidated by discharging all the time-expired men, like Sinclair, together with the sickly ones, the lame and the bad characters, and then putting everyone else into the first (and now only) battalion of each regiment. The numbers of officers too were trimmed back by the simple expedient of placing the junior half of each grade on half-pay, which was bad luck for newly promoted officers who might have served long and hard as lieutenants in their first battalion only to be discharged before the ink on their captain's commission in the second was dry.

As before, there were some exceptions, or rather temporary stays of execution for some units, where the luck of the draw saw the senior battalion serving in some far corner of the globe, while the junior one was still engaged in doing something useful closer to home. Thus with 1/1st Royals and 2/1st Royals both serving in America and the West Indies, it was the third battalion that was spared long enough to fight at Waterloo. Similarly, with 1/73rd Highlanders still in Botany Bay, and 1/78th in India, their respective second battalions were still doing garrison duty on the Continent when war broke out again. Thus, by a curious and rather satisfactory coincidence, the Duke of Wellington's first regiment would stand with him in his last battle.

The 73rd, it has to be said, were now Highlanders in name only, for following the official loss of the kilt in 1809 the second battalion had largely been recruited from English militia units, just as the government expected. A rough analysis of the nominal roll for the regiment at Waterloo reveals that some 373 of the NCOs and men were English, and were largely drawn from the West Midlands, the Home Counties and Essex. Volunteers from the Irish militia accounted for another 142, and only 69 men were Scots; one man came from Tongue and a handful of others from the Aberdeenshire Militia, but most were from Dumfriesshire and the Lothians. Yet, despite the published intention that they should no longer be accounted part of the Highland establishment, they still appeared in the official Army List as the 73rd (Highland) Regiment.

Besides the 73rd, four other Highland regiments made it to Waterloo, and in their case there was no doubting their Scottishness. The 71st were there in Adams's Light Brigade of Clinton's 2nd Division, while the other three served in General Picton's 5th Division: the 79th in Kempt's brigade, and the Black Watch and Gordons under Sir Denis Pack alongside the 3/1st Royals and the 44th Foot.[154]

The story of Waterloo has been told far too often to require another retelling of its grand controversies. Suffice it to say that with all Europe ranged against him, Napoleon decided to strike north into Belgium and separately defeat both Wellington's army and the Prussians before their concentration was complete. The result was two battles on 16 June 1815; a hard-won Allied victory at the unimaginatively named crossroads of Quatre Bras, and a resounding Prussian defeat at nearby Ligny, which forced Wellington to pull back to Waterloo and fight hard there until the Prussians came back in at the eleventh hour and turned a doubtful

5   Major General Sir Thomas Picton, commander of the 5th Division at Waterloo, which included the 79th Highlanders in Kempt's Brigade and the 42nd and 92nd in Pack's

battle into a famous victory. It was also, of course, a remarkably bloody affair, yet curiously enough, if casualties are any guide, for most of the Highland regiments the earlier battle for the crossroads was far worse.

It didn't help that Sir Robert Macara[155] of the 42nd had for some reason fallen foul of Pack. In the early hours of 16 June the Gordons were paraded to the strains of 'Hey Johnnie Cope', played in traditional style by Pipe Major Alexander Cameron, but despite the row, the Black Watch were late in turning up and Macara was 'chidden severely' by 'Sweet' Denis before they all finally set off about 4 a.m. and halted for breakfast in the forest of Soignes, just to the north of Waterloo. According to Alexander Forbes of the 79th there was a general expectation that it was all a false alarm and that they would soon be ordered back. Instead, before the cooking was completed they were ordered forward again and soon realised they were marching towards the sound of the guns.

Ahead of them the battle had already begun – if the Dutch and Belgian troops holding the crossroads were brushed aside, the link between the Allied and Prussian armies would be broken. As the French pressure increased Wellington somehow found enough men for a localised counter-attack that quickly ran out of steam but at least cleared the way for the deployment of Picton's leading brigades along the eastern arm of the crossroads. In the hurry and confusion the battalions were thrown into line without regard to the usual rules of precedence and so Kempt's brigade was pushed out to the left, with the Camerons on the extreme end of the line, while Pack's brigade went on the right with the Gordons holding the right of the line by the crossroads itself, then the Black Watch, the 44th Foot and the 3/1st, who thereby took up the centre of the line.[156] No sooner were they settled into position than Pack was down on Macara once again: this time bawling him out for not yet having ordered his men to fix bayonets!

It was hardly a happy start to the day, and worse was to come. As soon as the two brigades were in position a strong skirmish line was thrown forward. According to Alexander Forbes of the 79th: 'The Light Companies of the . . . Brigade, to which were added the 8th Company and marksmen of the 79th Regiment, were immediately thrown out, when the action commenced.'[157] The other regiments presumably did likewise, each company deploying its own marksmen or skirmishers as well as the designated light company – once they were ready both brigades pushed forward only to suddenly find themselves under attack from French cavalry.

As the rest went forward, the Gordons were ordered to hold their position along the road by the crossroads, while 3/1st Royals were also held back in reserve by Picton himself. The result, as Sergeant Alexander McEween related, was that the Black Watch found themselves in an awkward position:

> The 42nd were not a quarter of an hour in the field before they were charged by the Lancers. They must have been at the time a little in advance of the Namur road, expecting the remainder of the Brigade to form upon them. The 44th moved up to the left instead of the right of the 42nd, its proper place. A few skirmishers were out in front. Lancers appearing as if reconnoitring.

Sergeant McEween said to his commanding Officer, 'Those are French Lancers.' The latter replied, 'No, they belong to the Prince of Orange!' Sergeant McEween said he was sure they were the 3rd French Lancers, whom he had formerly seen when a prisoner of war. Proposed to fire at them to see what notice they would take of the shot. He fired, and they immediately advanced against the 42nd. The skirmishers ran in with the cry 'Square, Square, French cavalry!'[158]

The Lancers overtook two Companies in the act of completing the Square. Several of the 42nd were cut off, but a portion of the lancers became hemmed inside the Square by the remainder of those two Companies, and were instantly bayoneted.

Part of the problem was that the fields into which they had advanced were covered with a tall crop of rye, which had largely concealed the approach of the cavalry, and in fact the 44th, next to the Black Watch, were still in line when they found the lancers coming at them from behind and only saved themselves by hurriedly facing about the rear rank and giving them a volley! For a time, indeed, French cavalry seemed to be everywhere. McEween himself was wounded shortly afterwards and so too was his commanding officer, Macara. But while McEween rolled into the comparative safety of a ditch, Macara was being carried off the field by four of his men when a party of French lancers rode up and murdered them all in cold blood. From that point on, no quarter would be given by the Black Watch – at Waterloo at least one party of surrendering Frenchmen was rhetorically asked 'Where's Macara?' before being shot down.

Further towards the crossroads the Gordons also found themselves attacked by cavalry. The lancers riding around the 42nd were only the scouts and skirmishers accompanying the heavy cuirassiers of General Kellerman, who had been tasked with punching their way through to the crossroads. According to legend they nearly got Wellington himself and would have killed or captured him had some of the Gordons not thrown themselves flat while he jumped his horse over them to safety.

Robert Winchester of the 92nd, however, told a more prosaic story.[159] According to him:

On the arrival of the 92nd at Quatre Bras, Lord Wellington then desired Colonel Cameron to form line upon the road, with his right resting on

6   The murder of Colonel Macara of the 42nd at Quatre Bras; one of a series of prints after sketches by Captain George Jones of the Royal Artillery published in 1820

the houses at Quatre Bras. His Grace took his station on foot, with his Staff, at the left of the Regiment. By this time the whole of the rest of our troops were warmly engaged with the Enemy. They then opened a cannonade on his Grace, his Staff, and the 92nd from several Guns posted upon the heights at the side of the road leading to Charleroi. The Duke ordered the Regiment to lie down under cover in the ditch, which was to our front at the edge of the road, which he and his Staff did also close to our left.

The French Cuirassiers soon after this, under cover of their Guns, came charging up the fields in front of the Regiment, *which still remained in line*. Lord Wellington, who was by this time in rear of the centre of the Regiment, said '92nd, don't fire until I tell you,' and when they came within twenty or thirty paces of us, his Grace gave the order to fire, which killed and wounded an immense number of men and horses, on which they immediately faced about and galloped off.

Shortly afterwards they formed again, and, accompanied by a body of Light Dragoons, charged up again in our front. They were all allowed to come within about the same distance as before, when we fired as formerly, and the same result was effected; causing great loss to them in killed and wounded. At this time a French officer of Light Dragoons, thinking his men were still following him, got too far to be able to retire by the way he had advanced, galloped down the road in the rear of our Regiment. The Duke of Wellington observing him, called out, 'Damn it, 92nd, will you allow that fellow to escape?' Some of the men turned immediately round, fired, killed his horse, and a musket ball at the same time passed through each foot of the gallant young Officer.

The officer, a Monsieur Burgoine, was taken prisoner of course and Winchester was agreeably billeted in the same house with him for some months afterwards, but in the meantime it was John Cameron of Fassfern's turn to fall.[160]

He was one of the originals. The son of Ewen Cameron of Fassfern and Lucy Campbell, he was originally articled as a lawyer, but when the war began back in 1793 he exchanged wig and pen for a sword as a second lieutenant in the Royal Scots Fusiliers and on 13 February 1794 was commissioned a captain in the then 100th Highlanders at the height of the feud with Erracht. Unlike many, he then stayed with the regiment all the way through what followed: in the Mediterranean; in Ireland in 1798; at the Helder in the following year and in Egypt as a major. Promoted lieutenant colonel in 1808, he led the regiment throughout the Peninsular War and was one of the nineteen officers wounded in the fight in the Pass of Maya.[161]

Now, as another French cavalry attack melted away under a withering fire from the Gordons, two strong infantry columns were seen coming up in support and, as Winchester recalled, Wellington ordered the Highlanders to charge:

We instantly leaped over the ditch, headed by Sir Edward Barnes and other officers of the Duke's Staff, and Colonel Cameron. We drove them in an instant behind some houses and garden walls, where they ran for shelter, from which we also speedily drove them. Here Colonel Cameron received his mortal wound, on which he lost the power of managing his horse. The animal turned round and galloped with all his speed along the road until he reached Quatre Bras, where Colonel Cameron's groom was standing with his led horse. The horse then suddenly stopping, pitched the Colonel on his head on the road.

He was got on a wagon and carried back towards Brussels with some of the other wounded, but died at the village of Waterloo and was buried there next morning by his foster brother, Private Ewen McMillan, accompanied by the regimental paymaster James Gordon, and a handful of other wounded men.

In the meantime the battle still ground on and more and more British and Allied troops were fed into the fight as soon as they came up. Colin Halkett's brigade, including the 73rd Highlanders, was marching to the battlefield by way of Nivelles, off to the north-west, and was still there at midday when Halkett at last learned the urgency of the situation. A forced march, some of it at a run, then followed, before they all arrived at the western side of the battlefield, at about 5 p.m., just as Pack's brigade was reaching the end of its endurance. The 44th and 3/1st Royals were consolidated into a single battalion under his personal command; the whole brigade was running perilously short of ammunition.[162]

'On our entrance to the battle,' remembered Tom Morris, 'we met a young man, a private of the 92nd regiment, whose arm had been taken off close to the shoulder, by a cannon-ball. On passing us, he exclaimed 'Go on, 73rd give them pepper! I've got my Chelsea commission!''[163]

It was hardly an inspiring entrance and accordingly, Halkett deployed on the west side of the road, just as Kellerman's cuirassiers came in again and disaster nearly ensued. Of the four battalions in the brigade, only one, the 30th Foot, stood firm and formed square in time. The 33rd Foot at first did likewise, but perhaps unnerved by the collapse of the 69th, who were ridden down while still trying to form up, they incontinently fled into the safety of the woods. The 73rd Highlanders did likewise, but in their case it seems to have been a calculated move by Colonel Harris on realising there was neither time nor space to form a proper square. Morris made no bones about what happened: 'A large body of the enemy's cuirassiers, who, coming so unexpectedly upon us, threw us in the utmost confusion. Having no time to form a square, we were compelled to retire, or rather to run, to the wood through which we had advanced.'

They were soon back in the fight again, but for many it proved too much and as Captain Mercer of the Royal Horse Artillery brought up his guns he had to force his way through an ever increasing throng of wounded men and fugitives streaming to the rear. Most were Dutch and Belgians, who had been fighting since early morning, but at one point he came across another wounded Highlander of the 92nd, this time still possessed of both arms but hobbling in obvious pain. Seating him on the parapet of a bridge, Mercer had his surgeon dig a musket ball from the man's knee. All the Belgian and Dutch fugitives around them were justifying their desertion in traditional style by declaring that all was lost, but the Gordon reassured the artilleryman: 'Na, na, sir, it's aw a damned lee; they war fechtin' yet an I left 'em; bit it's a bludy business, and thar's na saying fat may be the end on't.'[164]

There is something comforting about that Aberdeenshire accent coming so clearly down through the years, but the unknown soldier had the right of it. They were still fighting and it was indeed a bloody business. At the end of the day the crossroads was still in Allied hands but the cost for the Highland regiments was terrible.

When Macara of the 42nd went down he was succeeded in command by Robert Dick,[165] who was himself wounded almost immediately after. Command then devolved upon George Davidson,[166] but he too was fatally wounded just moments later and by the time the fighting ended that day 3 officers and 42 men were killed, and a further 15 officers and 228 men were wounded. The Gordons were hit equally badly. When Fassfern was shot, James Mitchell[167] took command only to be wounded almost immediately and was succeeded by Captain George Holmes. All in all the regiment lost 4 officers and 35 men killed, and 21 officers and 226 men wounded that day, although to place them in context that was still slightly fewer casualties than the regiment had lost in just twenty minutes at Maya!

Similarly the Camerons spent the day blazing away at any Frenchmen who came near them – once, mounting a local counter-attack and at another point forming square during one of the cavalry attacks. It is rather difficult reading the accounts of veterans to avoid the impression that by comparison with the adventures of the Black Watch and the Gordons their battle was a relatively uneventful one, but yet by the end of it they returned 29 killed and 274 wounded out of 440 officers and men who marched on to the field. Only the 73rd escaped comparatively lightly thanks to their relatively late arrival on the field, and returned just 8 dead and 52 wounded.

Those casualties aside, the battle ended optimistically with Wellington still in firm control of the crossroads, but ominously there was no word from the Prussians. Next morning, remembered Sergeant Robertson, Wellington asked the 92nd to kindle him a fire and sat beside it reading his newspapers while one of his staff, Sir Alexander Gordon,[168] went off in search of Blücher. He was soon back. The Prussians were in full retreat and for Wellington there was no alternative but to fall back towards Brussels and another crossroads on the field of Waterloo. If he would stand there, Blücher still had a last opportunity to unite the two armies by coming across country on the narrow road from Wavre.

During the withdrawal from Quatre Bras the sultry heat gave way to a violent and continued thunderstorm that lasted well into the night and ensured that everyone was soaked to the skin and thoroughly miserable. Daybreak however brought a change and by contrast Tom Morris of the 73rd managed to sound smug in describing how: 'By six o'clock we had a cloudless sky and a powerful sun, under the cheering influence of which, we began to clean our muskets for the coming strife. Having shaved myself and put on a clean shirt, I felt tolerably comfortable, though many around me were complaining of cramps and agues.' One of them was 'Thomas' of the 71st, who had completely missed the fighting at Quatre Bras, and instead spent two days marching and counter-marching, first in intense heat and then bucketing rain. 'During the whole night the rain never ceased,' remembered James Todd or whoever it was who told that part of the story to Howell. 'Two hours after daybreak General Hill came down, taking away the left sub-division of the 10th company to cover his recognisance. Shortly afterwards we got half an allowance of liquor, which was the most welcome thing I ever received. I was so stiff and sore from the rain I could not move with freedom for some time.'

While it is convenient to refer to the position they were now sitting on as a ridge it was nothing like that rocky mountaintop at Maya where the Gordons battled d'Armanac's division. Instead it was just a long line of rising ground athwart the Brussels road, just to the south of the little wayside village that gave the battle its name. The valley in front of it was broad and so shallow that no stream meanders across its floor to carry away the rainwater sitting on its heavy clay. Yet in military terms it was a good position, which had been used more than once to cover Brussels. It was large enough to contain the army, high enough to make a good defensive position, yet still invitingly accessible so that an attacker was more likely to try and come down the road rather than find a way around.

Immediately in front of the position were a number of stoutly built farm buildings on which to base an outpost line and channel the attacks into carefully prepared killing grounds. The most important was the Chateau d'Hougoumont, a walled complex of solidly constructed brick buildings, which guarded the army's vulnerable right flank. There were no Highland regiments there, but it is worth remarking that it was defended by Colonel James McDonnell[169] of the Coldstream Guards. A younger brother of Glengarry, he too had begun his career in the Strathspey Fencibles all those years before – but unlike his brother, he took his soldiering seriously enough to go on to serve with the 17th Light Dragoons and 78th Highlanders before transferring to the Coldstreamers and famously (with the aid of Sergeant Graham) closing the gates of Hougoumont.

Behind Hougoumont itself the troops were positively stacked up, with Cooke's guards division immediately to the north of the chateau, and Halkett's division with Tom Morris and the 73rd Highlanders on their left, reaching out to the Brussels road near another brick-walled farmhouse called La Haye Sainte. Alten's division, which included the 71st Highlanders, was in this area as well, but further back in the second line.

To the east of the Brussels road, the three kilted regiments were posted behind a convenient hedge lining the road to Wavre, which followed the crest of the ridge. This time it was Kempt's brigade on the right, then Bylandt's Dutch brigade, then Pack's – which had its three Scots battalions drawn up with the 3/1st Royals – on the right, the Black Watch on the left and the Gordons in the centre, while the brigade's fourth battalion, the 44th (Essex) Regiment, was detached in support of some Hanoverian Landwehr.[170]

Thanks to the rain, the mud that accompanied it and the general misery of all concerned, it was nearly midday before the battle actually began, with a probing attack on Hougoumont that rapidly escalated into a full-blown battle within a battle. Once that diversion was underway and Wellington's attention, so he thought, was firmly fixed on the right,

Napoleon launched all of his I Corps, led by Count d'Erlon in a frontal assault intended to punch straight through the Allied centre.

Instead, hit by a shattering counter-attack, delivered both by the Highlanders of Pack's brigade and by the Union brigade of heavy cavalry, d'Erlon's men were sent reeling back in confusion and were effectively knocked out of the battle for several hours. The dramatic gesture had failed and now it was to be a matter of sheer hard pounding and a test of endurance like no other.

Lacking sufficient infantry after the defeat of d'Erlon's corps, Napoleon now relied first on his heavy guns and then on his cavalry to achieve that breakthrough, and of all the Highland regiments at Waterloo, it was unquestionably Wellington's old 73rd who suffered worst. During the course of the afternoon they were to lose 5 officers and 49 men killed and 12 officers and 175 men wounded, with another 41 returned as missing out of a battalion that began the day almost exactly 500 strong. Necessity soon compelled the survivors to combine with the equally hard-hit 30th Foot, and for a time it looked as if the brigade might crumble under the pressure:

> A regiment on our right [the 33rd] seemed disconcerted and at one moment was in considerable confusion. Halket rode out and seizing their snow white colour; waved it over his head, and restored them to something like order; though not before his horse was shot under him. At the height of their unsteadiness we got the order to 'right face' to move to their assistance; some of the men took it for 'right about face' and faced accordingly, when old Major McLaine, 73rd, called out, 'No boys, it's "right face" you'll never hear the "right about face" as long as a French bayonet is in front of you.' In a few moments he was mortally wounded.[171]

The fourth son of Gilbert McLaine of Sallacastle on Mull, Archibald McLaine, if not quite one of the originals had been with the regiment since 1794, serving in the East Indies and at Botany Bay until promotion brought him home to the second battalion, and Waterloo.[172]

The 71st, having missed the carnage of Quatre Bras, were also paying for it now, according to 'Thomas':

> About twelve o'clock we received orders to fall in for attack. We then marched up to our position, where we lay on the face of a brae, covering

a brigade of guns. We were so overcome by the fatigue of the two days march that, scarce had we lain down, until many of us fell asleep. I slept sound for some time while the cannonballs, plunging in amongst us, killed a great many. I was suddenly awakened. A ball struck the ground a little below me, turned me heels over head, broke my musket in pieces and killed a lad at my side. I was stunned and confused and knew not whether I was wounded or not. I felt a numbness in my arm for some time ...

About two o'clock a squadron of lancers came down, hurraying, to charge the brigade of guns. They knew not what was in the rear. General Barnes gave the word, 'Form square'. In a moment the whole brigade were on their feet, ready to receive the enemy. The General said, 'Seventy-first, I have often heard of your bravery, I hope it will not be worse than it has been today.' Down they came upon our square. We soon put them to the right about.

Shortly after, we received orders to move to the heights. Onwards we marched and stood for a short time in square, receiving cavalry every now and then. The noise and smoke were dreadful. At this time I could see but a very little way from me, but all around the wounded and slain lay very thick. We then moved on in column for a considerable way and formed line, gave three cheers, fired a few volleys, charged the enemy and drove them back.

And so it went on for hour after hour. At one point Colin Halkett begged the duke to be allowed to take his men out of the line. "'It's impossible, Halkett,' said he. And our General replied, 'If so, Sir, you may depend upon the brigade to a man.'" Increasingly, however it was looking as if that literally meant to the last man. Captain John Kincaid, a Stirlingshire man who went through the Peninsular War in the famous 95th Rifles, certainly thought so:

The smoke still hung so thick about us that we could see nothing. I walked a little way to each flank, to endeavour to get a glimpse of what was going on; but nothing met my eyes except the mangled remains of men and horses, and I was obliged to return to my post as wise as I went. I had never yet heard of a battle in which everybody was killed; but this seemed likely to be an exception, as all were going off by turns.

Notwithstanding, Wellington stood and grimly held his position at Waterloo, counting on the arrival of the Prussians on his left. Gradually they did indeed make their presence felt, but Napoleon, refusing to admit defeat, launched his Guard in a shattering counter-attack against the Prussian-held village of Plancenoit, stabilising his endangered right flank there long enough to allow one last co-ordinated assault on Wellington's position with everything he had: horse, foot and guns – including the legendary Old Guard. While d'Erlon's battered I Corps again climbed the long slope towards the 5th Division, still holding its line along the Wavre road, the Old Guard was directed at the crumbling remains of Wellington's right. Halkett's brigade was now all but spent, and he had ordered the 73rd and his other battalions to send their shot-torn colours to the rear for safety. 'My boys, you have done everything I could have wished, and more than I could expect, but much remains to be done; at this moment we have nothing for it but a charge.'

And so they did. There was a shattering exchange of fire that saw the unsteady 33rd fall back in confusion once again, but the 73rd, with all their officers dead or wounded, still held their ground.[173] Nearby the Footguards, under Wellington's personal direction, were also pouring fire into the heads of the French columns, but it was Adam's brigade, including the 71st Highlanders, who came up to administer the final blow – sending both the Old Guard and, with them, the rest of the French army, tumbling back in demoralised confusion.

The battle was won, and by way of emphasising the fact Wellington ordered every man who could still walk or ride to go forward. Somewhere by the Brussels road Lieutenant William Torriano of the 71st Highlanders came across an abandoned French gun. It was still loaded and so he had it swung around and General Adam's ADC, Captain Robert Campbell, fired it at its former owners. By all accounts it was the last cannon-shot of the battle.[174]

In ordinary circumstances that cannon-shot would have provided an eminently suitable period to the history of the Highland regiments in the Napoleonic Wars, but it was of course completely overshadowed in the public imagination by a dramatic and ultimately controversial incident earlier in the day when, according to popular legend, the Royal Scots Greys had charged into battle with the Gordon Highlanders clinging on to their stirrups!

It happened when Count d'Erlon launched his I Corps in that massed assault on Wellington's supposedly weakened centre. At about

2 p.m. the huge and seemingly unstoppable French column advanced up the long slope towards Wellington's centre, scattering Bylandt's Belgians, who had already been thoroughly worked over by the French artillery. Only a thin and rather scattered line of redcoats lay stretched along the Wavre road before them. Victory must have seemed in their grasp; all they had to do was push through the hedges lining the road and there would be nothing but fugitives between them and Brussels. Instead, disaster struck.

One of the clearest and most important accounts of what happened next came from Robert Winchester of the Gordons, although he considerably exaggerates the size of Bylandt's brigade:

> At the commencement of the Action a Corps of Belgians of from 8,000 to 10,000 men were formed in line in front of the 5th Division, but soon after they were attacked and their skirmishers driven in on their line, the whole of them retired through the 5th Division, and were seen no more during the Action. After this the Enemy made several severe attacks on the 5th Division. About two or three o'clock in the afternoon a Column between 3,000 to 4,000 men advanced to the hedge at the roadside with leads from the main road near La Haye Sainte [to] beyond the left of our position. Previous to this the 92nd had been lying down under cover of the position when they were immediately ordered to stand to their arms, Major General Sir Denis Pack calling out at the same time '92nd everything has given way on your right and left and you must charge this Column,' upon which he ordered four deep to be formed and closed in to the centre. The Regiment, which was then within about 20 yards of the Column, fired a volley into them. The Enemy on reaching the hedge at the side of the road had ordered arms, and were in the act of shouldering them when they received the volley from the 92nd.[175]

The French had evidently fired rather hopefully into the shrubbery in an effort to clear it, then halted to reload before pushing through, but before they could do so something quite extraordinary happened. With the Allied front line crumbling, General Ponsonby's cavalry brigade, comprising the 1st (Royal) Dragoons; the 6th (Inniskilling) Dragoons and the 2nd (Royal North British) Dragoons, was ordered forward in a determined bid to counter the imminent French breakthrough. The

7   The Gordons and the Greys charging at Waterloo; print after Captain George Jones, RA. Published in 1820, but in all probability sketched within a year of the battle, this print – although not depicting any Highlanders clinging to stirrups – clearly shows the two regiments going in together.

8   The same incident from a slightly different angle. This print after Captain Jones depicts the dying General Picton being led from the field, while in the background can be seen the Gordons and the Greys advancing together. The signature on the right clearly bears the date 1816.

Royals and Inniskillings got into action first, then the Scots Greys and Corporal John Dickson came up behind the Gordons:

> Our Colonel shouted out: 'Now then, Scots Greys, Charge!' and waving his sword in the air he rode straight at the hedges in front which he took in grand style. At once a great cheer rose from our ranks and we waved our swords and followed him. I drove my spurs into my brave old Rattler and we were off like the wind. It was a grand sight to see the long line of grey horses dashing along with manes flowing and heads down, tearing the turf about them as they went. The men in their red coats and tall bearskins were cheering wildly and the trumpets were sounding the charge. We heard the pipes of the Ninety-Second playing in the smoke, and I plainly saw my old friend Pipe Major Cameron standing apart on a hillock coolly playing 'Hey Johnnie Cope are ye waking yet/' in all the din. All of us were greatly excited and began crying out 'Hurrah Ninety-Second! Scotland for ever! Many of the Highlanders grasped our stirrups and dashed with us into the fight.[176]

Ever since then historians have argued that it is an unlikely tale, and Dickson's account is certainly suspect in exaggerating the speed of the Greys advance. He was not the only one, however, to mention the Highlanders hanging on to the stirrups and that particular story emerged in print at least as early as 1844 in Captain William Siborne's *History of the Waterloo Campaign*, which was in turn based on a huge mass of correspondence gathered from veterans when making his famous model of the battlefield:

> As the Scots Greys passed through, and mingled with the Highlanders, the enthusiasm of both corps was extraordinary. They mutually cheered. 'Scotland for ever!' was their war-shout. The smoke in which the head of the French column was enshrouded had not cleared away, when the Greys dashed into the mass. So eager was the desire. So strong the determination, of the Highlanders to aid their compatriots in completing the work so gloriously begun, that many were seen holding on by the stirrups of the horsemen, while all rushed forward, leaving none but the disabled in their rear.

At first sight the trouble is that none of the Gordons' own accounts appear to substantiate that particular aspect of the story. Winchester's letter simply says that: 'The Scots Greys came up at this moment, and doubling round our flanks and through our centre where openings were made for them, both Regiments charged together, calling out "Scotland for ever" and the Scots Greys actually walked over this [French] Column, and in less than three minutes it was totally destroyed.' Similarly, Lieutenant James Hope told Clark-Kennedy of the Royal Dragoons that 'he never saw anything to equal the enthusiasm of both Corps when the Greys passed through the 92nd to charge – that they mutually cheered each other on – that the 92nd seemed half mad, and that it was with the greatest difficulty the Officers could preserve anything like order in the ranks.'[177]

At this point, however, it is worth recalling Winchester's statement that Pack ordered the Gordons to form four deep, instead of two, and then close to the centre – necessary because once each individual company had doubled up, big gaps or 'intervals' would be opened between them. As the cavalry came up behind the regiment the companies simply opened out again to their 'proper distance' and it was through these intervals that the Greys passed rather than forcing their way through the actual ranks. Once the cavalry were through there is then general agreement that the Highlanders followed closely after them; and Clarke-Kennedy of the Royals afterwards noted that: 'The [Union] Brigade was most gallantly supported by the Infantry, both in advancing and in retiring, by numerous small squares or parties of from ten, to twenty, or thirty men each, who came down the slope of the hill after us. Several of those parties were Highlanders, but whether 42nd, 79th, or 92nd, I cannot say.'[178] That other regiments, besides the Gordons, were involved is intriguing, but the reference to 'small squares or parties' is important for it clearly indicates that the battalion went forward without first closing the intervals between the companies – who were still four deep – not that discipline had completely broken down.

Thus far we have a pretty consistent picture of the Greys passing through the Gordons and then the Highlanders following after them, but there are also two other accounts by officers of the Greys that obliquely offer an explanation for the legend of the stirrup charge.

One, Charles Wyndham of the Greys, remarked in a memorandum that: 'Several [of the 92nd] went down the hill from the hedge with the

Regiment, and it was at this moment when the 92nd cheered the Greys, and cried, "Scotland for ever!"', while William Crawford recalled that: 'As we advanced we were met by a number of the 92nd Regiment, who turned and ran into the charge with us.'

Winchester, of course, placed the battalion some twenty metres back from the hedge when it all happened – moreover both Wyndham and Crawford appear to be talking about meeting a number of individuals, some of them falling back, rather than a properly formed unit. Now at Quatre Bras, as we have seen, when the 79th deployed for action, 'The Light Companies of the . . . Brigade, to which were added the 8th Company and marksmen of the 79th Regiment, were immediately thrown out.'[179] Over the twenty-odd years since the wars began in 1793 the British Army had learned the lesson of supplementing the designated light company with additional skirmishers, variously identified as flankers or marksmen, drawn from the ordinary battalion companies. Clearly the 92nd did so too, just as a matter of course, and it was these men whom the cavalry met and mingled with *after* passing through the main fighting line.

There was also another witness, Rough-Rider James Armour of the Greys, who must have been referring to these men when he wrote how some were bowled over, and recalled hearing someone shouting: 'I didna think ye wad hae saired me sae!' Being knocked about in this fashion strongly points to them being individuals, run down because they were not safely standing within the ranks of their companies – in fact Armour also went on to say that some Highlanders caught at the Greys' legs and stirrups to prevent themselves from being knocked over.[180]

At this point it is important to appreciate that the cavalry were actually moving relatively slowly. British cavalry it is true did have an unfortunate reputation for dashing at everything and behaving as if they were chasing a fox, but in this case they not only had to pick their way through the intervals in the 92nd battle-line, but then just twenty metres further on had to negotiate a hedge. James Anton of the 42nd recalled that it was a thick mass of thorns, which he and his kilted companions were very reluctant to struggle through, and while Corporal Dickson described his colonel jumping straight over it, none of the other cavalry eyewitnesses suggest this was done. Robert

Winchester of the 92nd, it will be recalled, even went so far as to say that the cavalry 'walked' into the French ranks.

It will not, therefore, have been unduly difficult for those scattered skirmishers – dodging about as the Greys rode over them – to grasp hold of the troopers' stirrups, not in order to be carried into battle faster, but, as Armour relates, simply as a matter of self preservation to keep themselves upright in the press.

Consequently, by thus examining all of the evidence carefully it is possible to at last reconstruct what really happened:

At the outset of d'Erlon's attack, most of the 92nd were lying down in two ranks about twenty metres or so from the hedge lining the Wavre road. In accordance with the standard tactical procedures of the time they will have been covered by a relatively strong skirmish line along the hedge itself, comprising both the light company and the additional marksmen drawn from the ordinary battalion companies.

As the French approached, Pack ordered the 92nd to stand up and to form four ranks deep. This was done by companies, with one half company dressing behind the other and the resulting gaps between each company were then closed by dressing in towards the centre. As they then prepared to fire a volley at the French, the skirmishers will have first thrown themselves flat, or else cleared off to the right and left, and then started to fall back and form behind the flanks – this was necessary to avoid disrupting the battle-line by rushing straight back. It was this movement that led some of the cavalry to wrongly believe that the 42nd and 92nd were retiring.

As the cavalry then came up from behind, the Highlanders opened out again to their 'proper' distance in order to allow the troopers to pass through the gaps between each four-deep company. This resulted in great excitement all round and the individual companies then followed behind the cavalry without first closing again to the centre. As Clark-Kennedy of the Royals described this happening, it would appear that elements of both the 42nd and 92nd were involved.

Immediately they had passed through the battle-line, the Scots Greys then encountered some of the 92nd skirmishers and it was these men, rather than the main body, who actually turned and ran in with the Greys – in some cases were seen hanging on to the stirrups, while the individual companies enthusiastically followed behind.

This then was the charge of the Gordons and the Greys at Waterloo. It was perhaps not quite the glorious 'Stirrup Charge', as immortalised in Stanley Berkeley's famous painting, and it did not necessarily involve all of the Gordons, but it happened – and more than any other single incident in the long wars that preceded it, it *made* the reputation of all the Highland regiments!

Epilogue

After all that, in March 1828 the well-known society diarist, Thomas Creevy, was justifiably able to crow that: 'We have an event in our family. Fergy has got a regiment – a tip top crack one – one of those beautiful Highland Regiments that were at Brussels, Quatre Bras and Waterloo.'[181] The appointment of 'Fergy' – or rather Lieutenant General Sir Ronald Craufurd Ferguson – to be colonel-in-chief of the 79th (Cameron) Highlanders was indeed a matter for some celebration. For twenty years and more, and in every corner of the globe, the Highland regiments had steadily been building themselves a reputation as good soldiers, and that reputation was finally cemented at Waterloo, perhaps by that one dramatic charge by the Gordons.

However, when Creevy was crowing about Fergy getting one of those 'tip-top' Highland regiments, he was referring to the kilted ones – as their popularity grew, the others, who had lost the kilt in 1809 through no fault of their own, quite naturally grew jealous and soon set about recovering the outward symbols of their Highland heritage.

The 71st had a head start, of course. The tartan trousers introduced by Pack had not lasted long, but they did keep their bonnets, albeit without the usual black ostrich feathers, and blocked up instead to resemble the cap worn by other light infantry units. When the rest of the army adopted a bell-topped chaco after Waterloo, they followed suit, although the body of their chaco was of blue cloth rather than black felt, and the diced band was retained around the bottom, along with a small flattened red tourie on top. It was still called a bonnet; in April 1834 they were also permitted to resume wearing Mackenzie tartan trews, while the officers were allowed the Highland scarf or shoulder plaid. With that they had to be content and it was not until 1947 that they finally regained their kilts.

In the meantime the 72nd had done one better, gaining both the title 'Duke of Albany's Own Highlanders' in 1823 and a suitably striking uniform to match their semi-Royal status (Albany being better known to history as the Grand Old Duke of York): uniquely combining Highland feathered bonnets with bright-red, Prince Charles Edward Stuart tartan trousers.

The 74th were next, designated as Highlanders once again in November 1845 and adopting a virtually identical uniform to the 71st with so-called Lamont tartan trews (which was really the ordinary army sett with a white overstripe) and the same style of bonnet or chaco worn by the Highland light infantry, rather than the feather bonnet sported by the 72nd. By this time the Duke of Wellington was the army's commander-in-chief and it was very sternly made very clear to Colonel Crabbe that this concession was entirely conditional on the regiment finding sufficient Scots recruits to justify the alteration:

> His Grace [the Duke of Wellington] cannot keep out of view the fact that it is found very difficult to complete the Highland Regiments already on the Establishment of the Army with Highland or even Scotch recruits and this state of things has rendered it occasionally necessary to extend their recruiting to other parts of the United Kingdom. As however Lieutenant Colonel Crabbe holds out sanguine expectations of being able to keep up the establishment of the 74th by means of its local influence in Scotland, the Commander in Chief yields to the Lieut. Colonel's assurances under that head, but with the direct understanding that should their expectations be disappointed, the expedients resorted to in the cases of the other Highland regiments similarly circumstanced, will be resorted to in the case of the 74th Regiment, that is efficiency of numbers must be maintained from time to time by the other means alluded to if that indispensable object cannot be attained by the exertions of its own recruiting parties.[182]

Wellington, clearly, was unconvinced and very reluctant to sanction the alteration in their status, but just for once he relented and grudgingly allowed them to become a Highland regiment again, perhaps because he remembered Assaye.

As for the others: in 1820 the 91st succeeded in having the word 'Argyllshire' added to their number, but it was not until 1864 that they became the 91st Argyllshire Highlanders. The change in title was a subtle one, but it was sufficient to justify the immediate adoption

9 An illustration from Cannon's series, depicting the 74th Highlanders in the 1840s; the uniform worn by the 71st at this time was very similar apart from the tartan and having buff facings rather than white. Note how the bonnet has been stretched and stiffened to resemble a chaco.

of Campbell of Cawdor tartan trews and pave the way to their later amalgamation with the 93rd in 1881 to become the Argyll and Sutherland Highlanders.

This was part of a general reorganisation of the British Army, which actually harked back to the Army of Reserve created during the French Wars, and saw nearly all of those regiments not already possessed of two battalions, paired off. The process was a complicated one, not helped by the intransigence of the Camerons, who refused to give up their unique tartan if paired with the Black Watch, but in the end it was carried through, although the Camerons were left without a partner.

First, the 42nd were instead joined with the 73rd (Perthshire) Regiment to become the *Black Watch*. This was quite an inspired move, for although no longer a Royal regiment nor even a Highland one, being predominantly English in composition, the 73rd were, after all, first raised in 1780 as 2/42nd. Similarly, up at Fort George the 72nd and 78th were combined and since both battalions had originally been raised by (different) Earls of Seaforth, they quite naturally and very happily became the *Seaforth Highlanders*. The 91st and 93rd, although once separated geographically became the *Argyll and Sutherland Highlanders*, and if they were normally referred to simply as the Argylls, their most celebrated battle-honour is the stand of the Sutherlands in that thin red line at Balaklava in 1854. Another odd, but conspicuously successful union was that of the 75th and 92nd to become the *Gordon Highlanders*. It was odd, because in some ways the 75th had never really been regarded as a Highland regiment and underwent the loss of the kilt with equanimity. By 1881 it bore the title 'Stirlingshire' but was to all intents and purposes an English regiment. Nevertheless it entered into marriage with the 92nd with some gusto, losing its own history almost entirely as it embraced that of its younger kilted partner.

The only pairing that failed was that of the two remaining Highland regiments; the 71st and the 74th, to form the *Highland Light Infantry*. Before the Camerons upset the carefully worked-out scheme, the former had been slated to join with the 78th, whose tartan they shared, and they resented having to double up instead with the 74th in a depot at Hamilton, just outside Glasgow, rather than in a 'proper' Highland recruiting area. The ill-feeling was warmly reciprocated and right up until the day '2HLI' were 'stood down' – disbanded – after the Second World War, they defiantly continued to refer to themselves as the 74th. They were, after all, the Assaye Regiment.

In fairness there was also another cause for complaint by both battalions. All of the other amalgamations paired a kilted and a non-kilted battalion and in every case, irrespective of seniority, it was the uniform – and indeed to a very large extent the identity – of the kilted

Epilogue

battalion that was adopted in its entirety by the new regiment. Thus, the 73rd adopted the kilt (and red hackle) of the 42nd; the 72nd gave up its red tartan trousers for the Mackenzie kilt of the 78th; the 75th enthusiastically changed from trousers to the Gordon tartan kilt of the 92nd; and the 91st discarded their tartan trousers for the Sutherland kilt. In the case of the HLI, however, both constituent battalions came to the union with tartan trousers – and to their dismay were forced to keep them. The only change was that 2HLI were reluctantly forced to adopt the Mackenzie tartan rather than the Lamont, and even then it took another twenty-odd years to sort out the details.

Ironically it was not until after the old 74th were disbanded that the HLI at last received official permission to resume wearing the kilt in affirmation of their Highland status – only to lose it again in their enforced amalgamation with the Royal Scots Fusiliers less than ten years later.

There has, however, been one final twist to the tale of how Scotsmen and Highlanders became synonymous. On 28 March 2006 all of the old regiments, both Highland and Lowland, officially passed out of existence: absorbed into a single Royal Regiment of Scotland. How long the constituent battalions will be able to maintain their individual histories and traditions remains to be seen, but all of them wear the kilt.

Appendix 1

The Beautiful Highland Regiments

The lineage of the Highland Regiments can be confusing, as the numbers allocated on their first raising could and did change, and in some instances the same number was allocated to different units – which were otherwise quite unconnected – in succession. A case in point being the old 71st (Fraser's) Highlanders, who were reduced in 1784 and two years later had their number re-allocated to what had until then been the 73rd (Macleod's) Highlanders, who in turn had their number re-allocated to what until then had been the second battalion of the Black Watch! Adding to the confusion is that word 'reduced', for strictly speaking redundant regiments were not disbanded – instead the rank and file were discharged and the regiment literally reduced to a cadre of officers, who were then transferred to the half-pay list. Thus, there was not only a new 71st (ex-73rd) Highland Regiment in the Army List after 1786, but there was also still a phantom of the old 71st Highland Regiment made up of half-pay officers with nothing to connect the two but their coincident numbers.[183]

In the biographical index below the various Highland Regiments taken into the line between 1739 and 1815 are listed first by number and then chronologically. For the avoidance of doubt, note that none of the regiments successively bearing the same number were connected in any way.

For the sake of clarity, disbanded units are identified thus: 64th (Loudoun's) Highlanders, while those still extant in 1815 appear as 74th (Highland) Regiment.

42nd Royal Highland Regiment: embodied 1739 as 43rd Regiment, but renumbered as the 'Forty-Twa' in 1748, and designated a Royal regiment in 1758. Second battalions raised in 1758 (reduced); 1778 (re-designated as 73rd Highlanders 1786); and 1803 (reduced 1814).

Uniform distinctions: buff facings to 1758 and thereafter dark blue; red hackle worn from 1795. Tartan was originally army sett (Black Watch) until 1745 when differenced by a red overstripe. This was borne at least until 1812, but seems to have fallen out of use during the Peninsular War.

64th (Loudoun's) Highlanders: raised by John Campbell, Earl of Loudoun, in 1745; served in Scotland and Flanders but reduced in 1748.

Uniform distinctions: white facings; a portrait of Colonel the Earl of Loudoun by Alan Ramsay shows a red sett, but there is evidence that the rank and file may have had a variant of the army sett with red and yellow overstripes. Officers' waistcoats were 'Rob Roy' tartan.

71st (Fraser's) Highlanders: raised by Major General Simon Fraser in 1775 with two battalions at the outset, although confusingly the regiment was so strong when it first arrived in America that the companies were pooled and then temporarily reorganised into three battalions. Reduced in 1784.

Uniform distinctions: white facings; tartan appears to have been the un-differenced army sett. A red feather or tuft appears to have been worn late in the war.

71st (Glasgow Highland) Regiment: raised by Lord Macleod in 1777 as 73rd Highlanders with two battalions; 2/73rd served at Gibraltar but was reduced in 1784. 1/73rd served in India and was re-designated as 71st Highlanders in 1786. Returned home 1797; served in Ireland 1800–5, then Cape of Good Hope and South America; Peninsula 1808–9; Walcheren; Peninsula 1810–14; Waterloo. Second battalion raised in 1803 but employed on home service only and reduced in 1814.

Uniform distinctions: buff facings; original tartan uncertain but probably army sett with red and buff overstripes, changing to red and white c.1798 – the Mackenzie sett but cut to display two vertical red overstripes on the kilt apron in contrast to the single centrally placed overstripe on the 78th kilt apron. Tartan trews adopted in place of kilt in 1808 and in following year bonnet denuded of feathers and blocked up to resemble chaco on adopting light-infantry role. Tartan trousers replaced by grey during campaigning in Spain and not re-adopted until 1830s.

72nd (Highland) Regiment: raised by Earl of Seaforth in 1777 as 78th Highlanders but re-designated as 72nd in 1786. Served in Channel Islands, then India to 1797. Served in Ireland 1800–5, then Cape of Good Hope to 1821. Second battalion raised 1803, serving in Ireland until reduced in 1814.

Uniform distinctions: yellow facings; painting of battle of Jersey shows un-differenced army sett. Lost kilt in 1809.

73rd (Highland) Regiment: raised in 1780 as 2/42nd but re-designated as 73rd Highlanders in 1786. Served in India to 1805, then New South Wales 1809–16. Second battalion raised in 1809; served in Germany and Holland 1813–14, and Waterloo; disbanded in 1816.

Uniform distinctions: as for Black Watch until 1786, then very dark-green facings adopted – Footguards officers complained that combination of dark-green facings and broad gold lace on officers' uniforms was too easily mistaken for their own. Tartan was presumably as for Black Watch, ie: army sett with single overstripe, but kilt was lost in 1809.

74th (Campbell's) Highlanders: raised by John Campbell of Barbreck in 1778 for service in North America; reduced in 1784.

Uniform distinctions: bright-yellow facings; no information on tartan but probably un-differenced army sett.

74th (Highland) Regiment: raised by Sir Archibald Campbell in 1787 specifically for service in India, but returned in 1805. Served at Walcheren 1809 and then Peninsula 1811–14.

Uniform distinctions: white facings; tartan may have been army sett with white overstripe as adopted in 1846. Lost kilt in 1809.

75th (Highland) Regiment: raised by Colonel Robert Abercromby in 1787 specifically for service in India, but returned in 1805. Subsequently served in Sicily and Corfu 1811–14.

Uniform distinctions: yellow facings; no information on any tartan worn before losing kilt in 1809.

Appendix 1

76th (MacDonald's) Highlanders: raised by Lord MacDonald in 1778 for service in North America; reduced in 1784.

Uniform distinctions: deep green facings; no information on tartan but probably un-differenced army sett.

77th (Montgomerie's) Highland Regiment: raised in 1757 as 1st Highland Battalion, briefly re-designated the 63rd Foot and finally re-numbered the 77th Foot. Served in North America and Caribbean and reduced in 1764.

Uniform distinctions: green facings, tartan unknown but probably army sett.

77th (Murray's) Highlanders: raised by Colonel James Murray in 1778 but reduced in 1783 without serving overseas.

Uniform distinctions: green facings; tartan may have been 'Murray of Athole'; army sett with single red stripe as for Black Watch.

78th (Fraser's) Highlanders: raised in 1757 as 2nd Highland Battalion, briefly re-designated the 64th Foot and finally re-numbered the 78th Foot.[184] Served in North America and Caribbean and reduced in 1764.

Uniform distinctions: white facings; tartan unknown but at least two officer portraits (Fraser himself and an unknown officer taking a pinch of snuff) show quite different unrecorded setts. It seems likely therefore that the rank and file wore the army sett while the individual officers pleased themselves. This may also have been true of the 77th (Montgomerie's) Highlanders.

78th (Seaforth's) Highlanders: see 72nd (Highland) Regiment.

78th (Highland) Regiment: raised initially with one battalion by Francis Humberston Mackenzie in 1793. Second battalion added but then consolidated with first battalion in 1796; served in Holland, Cape of Good Hope, India and Java to 1816. Second battalion again raised in 1804 and chiefly served Mediterranean and Egypt to 1813, then Holland and Belgium to 1815. Draft intended for first battalion also served at Walcheren.

Uniform distinctions: pale buff facings; army sett with two white and one red overstripe.

79th (Highland) Regiment: raised by Allan Cameron of Erracht in 1793, served Holland, Caribbean, Helder Egypt, Walcheren, Peninsula and Waterloo. Second battalion raised 1804–14 for home service only.

Uniform distinctions: green facings; unique 'Cameron of Erracht' tartan.

81st (Gordon's) Highlanders: raised by Colonel William Gordon of Fyvie in1778, but reduced in1783 without serving overseas.

Uniform distinctions: white facings; un-differenced army sett for kilts.

84th Royal Highland Emigrants: two battalions raised in North America as a provincial regiment in 1775, by Colonel Allan Maclean and Captain John Small, partly from discharged former soldiers and other Scots settlers in Canada and North Carolina. Served throughout revolutionary war and taken into line as 84th Foot but reduced in 1784.

Uniform distinctions: ordered to be same as for Black Watch, ie dark-blue facings and army sett with single red overstripe. Sporrans said to be made of racoon fur.

87th and 88th (Keith's and Campbell's) Highlanders: raised in 1759 by Sir James Murray Keith and (as explained in the text) originally intended as a single unit but split into two in order to create a regiment for John Campbell of Dunoon – a protégé of the Duke of Argyll. Served in Germany and reduced in 1763.

Uniform distinctions: dark-green facings; tartan was probably the un-differenced army sett, but as the first companies were originally raised as a reinforcement for the Black Watch it is possible that it had the single red overstripe.

89th (Morris's) Highlanders: raised by Colonel Staats Long Morris in 1759; served in India and reduced in 1765.

Uniform distinctions: no details are known and there is no evidence that kilts were worn in India.

91st (Highland) Regiment: raised by Colonel Duncan Campbell of Lochnell in 1794 as 98th Highlanders but re-numbered in 1798. Served at Cape of Good Hope 1795–1803, then Hanover 1805, Walcheren,

Peninsula and Flanders. Second battalion raised in 1803; served in Germany and Holland 1813–14.

Uniform distinctions: yellow facings; tartan was probably undifferenced army sett. Lost kilt in 1809 but wore tartan trews and blue bonnets at Walcheren.

92nd (Highland) Regiment: raised by Marquis of Huntly in 1794 as 100th Highlanders but re-numbered in 1798. Served in Mediterranean, Ireland, Helder, Egypt, Copenhagen, Walcheren, Peninsula and Waterloo. Second battalion raised in 1803 and reduced in 1814 without seeing overseas service.

Uniform distinctions: yellow facings; army sett with single yellow overstripe.

93rd Highland Regiment: raised by William Wemyss of Wemyss in 1800, served at Cape of Good Hope and then in North America. Second battalion raised in 1813 and served in Nova Scotia until reduced in 1816.

Uniform distinctions: yellow facings; undifferenced army sett.

97th (Inverness-shire) Highlanders: raised by Sir James Grant of Grant in1794 and reduced in Great Drafting of the following year.

Uniform distinctions: green facings, plain blue bonnets, tartan trews – army sett with single red overstripe.

98th Highlanders: see 91st (Highland) Regiment.

100th (Campbell's) Highlanders: embodied in 1761 from independent companies; took part in capture of Martinique in 1762, reduced in 1763.

100th (Gordon) Highlanders: see 92nd (Highland) Regiment.

101st (Johnstone's) Highlanders: embodied in 1761 from independent companies by Sir James Johnstone of Westerhall, but effectively employed as depot battalion providing drafts for 87th and 88th Highlanders; reduced in 1763.

Uniform distinctions: pale yellowish buff facings.

105th (Queen's) Highlanders: raised by William Gordon of Fyvie in 1761 with two battalions; served in Ireland and reduced in 1763.

Uniform distinctions: portrait of Lieutenant Colonel William Gordon shows bright-blue facings and nondescript tartan – presumably personal, like those worn by officers of Fraser's 78th.

109th (Aberdeenshire) Highlanders: raised by Alexander Hay in 1794 and reduced in Great Drafting of the following year.

Uniform distinctions: probably white facings, as per earlier 81st Highlanders, colonel's bonnet has green hackle. Rank and file probably had tartan trousers.

114th (Maclean's) Highlanders: raised by Allan Maclean of Torloisk in 1761 for service in North America, but never completed, and reduced in 1763.

116th Highlanders: raised by Earl of Breadalbane in 1794 and reduced in Great Drafting of the following year.

Uniform distinctions: white (or very pale yellow) facings; army sett with closely set double yellow overstripe.

132nd Highlanders and 133rd (Inverness Volunteers): both commenced raising in 1794 but never completed before drafting into 42nd in August 1795.

Uniform distinctions: black facings?

The foregoing list is confined to those Highland units that were actually allocated numbers. It is possible that other, rather shorter-lived battalions may also have considered themselves Highlanders. For example, Montgomerie's Royal Glasgow Regiment of 1794–5 was not officially designated a Highland unit, but his earlier West Lowland Fencibles wore tartan trews and feather bonnets, while he and his officers had kilts. It is likely therefore that the Glasgow Regiment did likewise.

Appendix 2

The Gordons at Waterloo

1 The battalion drawn up in a two-deep line at the commencement of d'Erlon's attack on a front of nine companies with the light company and marksmen covering their front

2 The battalion is ordered to double its ranks and close to the centre; as the first stage of which the left-hand platoon of each company files behind the right-hand company and the skirmishers start to clear to right and left.

3 The companies are now formed in four ranks with a platoon-wide gap between each.

4   The companies close the gaps to the centre and fire upon d'Erlon's men. The light company forms a platoon on each flank reinforced by the marksmen.

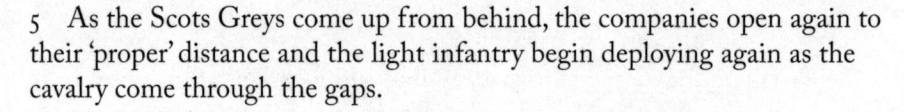

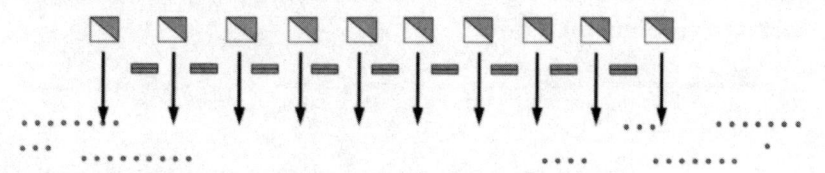

5   As the Scots Greys come up from behind, the companies open again to their 'proper' distance and the light infantry begin deploying again as the cavalry come through the gaps.

6   The Scots Greys attack d'Erlon's Corps, intermingled on the flanks with some of the skirmishers and followed by some or all of the other Gordons companies.

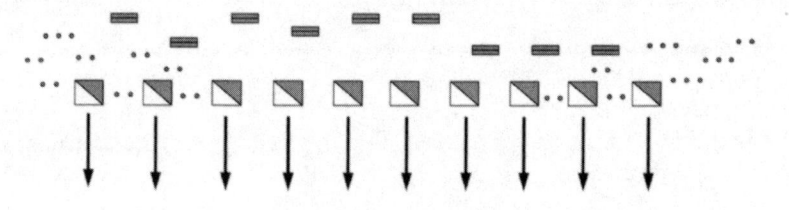

Endnotes

1 Quoted in Prebble, *Culloden*, 1961, pp. 34–5.
2 Munro, William, *Reminiscences of Military Service with the 93rd Highlanders*, London, 1883, p. 198.
3 The pedantic will of course point to a whole succession of Highland Independent Companies raised from 1667 onwards, but, unlike Wade's companies, all of them fell by the wayside and were either disbanded – or forgotten – or else absorbed into the ranks of ordinary regiments such as the Royals and the Royal Scots Fusiliers.
4 A tack was a lease and a tacksman therefore a leaseholder – and frequently a hereditary one.
5 'The day before the regiment was embodied at Taybridge, five of the soldiers dined and slept in my grandfather's house at Garth. The following morning they rode off in their usual dress, a tartan jacket and truis, ornamented with gold lace embroidery, or twisted gold cords, as was the fashion of the time, while their servants carried their military clothing and arms.' Garth, David Stewart of, *Sketches of the Highlanders of Scotland*, 1822, Vol. I, p. 242.
6 The significance of this claim was that in an age of near universal illiteracy a recruit was not legally considered to be properly enlisted as a soldier unless those clauses had been read and explained to him. They were also to be read to all soldiers every two months thereafter.
7 Anon., *General Wolfe's Instructions to Young Officers*, 1780, p. 21.
8 Prebble, John, *Mutiny* provides the best modern account of the mutiny, full of circumstantial detail, although, as ever, due allowance has to be made for his polemic style.
9 Another defector was Lieutenant Donald MacDonnell of Lochgarry, who commanded the Glengarry MacDonalds during the Rising.
10 The Black Watch have always been coy about their presence at Culloden. The Argyle Militia only accounted for four of the eight Highland companies in Cumberland's army; three others belonged to Loudoun's 64th Highlanders and the eighth was Captain Dugald Campbell of Auchrossan's Black Watch company.
11 Findlater to Duke of Newcastle, 8 July 1748. Bulloch, J.M., *Territorial Soldiering*, p. xxi.
12 In fact there was a considerable and quite confusing reshuffle of regiments, owing to the 'reduction' of Oglethorpe's 42nd Foot – which saw the Black Watch move up one step – and to the disbandment of ten regiments of army-controlled

marines, who had previously ranked as the 44th to 49th Foot. The new 43rd to 48th Regiments had originally been raised as the 54th to 59th Foot, while the new 49th was formed from Independent Companies serving in Jamaica. All of the regiments junior to the *old* 59th, including Loudoun's 64th, were disbanded.

13 Wolfe to William Rickson, Banff 9 June 1751 in Willson, Beckles, *Life and Letters of James Wolfe*, 1909, p. 141.
14 Quoted in McCardle, L., *Ill-starred General: Braddock of the Coldstream Guards*, 1958, p. 124.
15 The English or British establishment, maintained by an annual vote in the Westminster Parliament, included all regiments serving in Scotland and overseas.
16 *Hansard*, Parliamentary History, London, 1813, Vol. XCI, p. 98.
17 The most widely accepted tradition tells how he was leading his men towards Culloden when he met the first of the fugitives and, realising that all was lost, promptly turned around and marched straight back to Inverness with colours still flying and pipes playing. However, there is also an equally plausible local tradition that, having returned to the Highland capital, he at first made preparations to defend the bridge over the river Ness. What is less certain is who he proposed to defend it against. Although there is no evidence to support another story that a party of the Argyle Militia attempted to seize the bridge, at least one Jacobite fugitive did recall 'a brisk firing in the town which lasted a few minutes' – was Fraser trying to block the escape of his erstwhile Jacobite colleagues?
18 WO1/974 The Origins of the men are noted in a 'state' dated 9 March 1757 at Nairn:

Company commander	Men raised	Approved	Not Approved	Where Raised
Lieutenant Colonel Montgomerie	109	102	7	Atholl and Strathdearn
Major (James) Grant	230	230	-	Strathspey and Urquhart
Captain (John) Sinclair	110	-	110	Sutherland and Caithness
Captain Hugh Mackenzie	83	60	23	Glasgow and Ross-shire
Captain (John) Gordon	76	30	46	Edinburgh and Aberdeenshire
Captain Alexander Mackenzie	117	-	117	Perthshire and Aberdeenshire
Captain (William) McDonald	43	23	20	Edinburgh and Skye
Captain (George) Munro	112	112	-	Fairn Donald
Captain Roderick McKenzie	69	-	69	Kintail
	1029	557	472	

19 Garth, Vol. 2, p. 19.
20 McCulloch, I. M., *Sons of the Mountains*, 2006, provides the best account of the raising and subsequent services of both regiments. The second volume also contains an invaluable biographical dictionary of all the officers to serve in them.
21 WO34/41 f17, McCulloch, I. M., *Sons of the Mountains*, Vol. I:31, p. 40.
22 Confusingly the two Highland regiments were 'bumped' down the list after the decision was taken to bring a number of recently raised second battalions into the line as regiments in their own right. Although this conversion took place

after Montgomerie's and Fraser's Highlanders were taken into the line, all of the second battalions had been in existence for longer. Consequently they were accounted senior to the new Highland regiments, and so, for example the 2/4th Foot became the 62nd Foot and the 2/8th replaced Fraser's as the 63rd.
23 While this 'mark of Our Royal Favour' was bestowed after the disastrous fight at Ticonderoga on 5 July 1758, it predated the arrival of the news of the battle in London and was quite unconnected with the regiment's exceptional bravery there.
24 It could be argued that the 84th (Royal Highland Emigrants) could also be considered Americans as they were raised over there during the Revolution, but nearly all of the officers and many of the men were former members of the Black Watch and the 77th and 78th Highlanders, who had taken their discharge in America at the end of the Seven Years' War. Morris, on the other hand, was an American born and bred.
25 Bulloch, pp. 6–7.
26 Ibid., p. 12.
27 Ibid., p.98.
28 Ibid., pp. 32, 89–90.
29 Muster roll preserved at Gordon Castle – Bulloch,pp. 34–5.
30 Inspection report, 30 May 1775 (WO27), quoted in Strachan, Hew, *British Military Uniforms 1768–96*, London, 1975, p. 267.
31 The evolution of the British Army's infantry fighting tactics during this period is a substantial subject in its own right. Suffice to say that both theory and doctrine centred around the inescapable fact that the accurate range of a musket was only some fifty metres. It could be (and was) used at considerably greater ranges but not to any real effect. At the time when the Black Watch was first raised the dominant idea was to advance as close as possible to the enemy – sometimes as close as twenty metres, halt and commence firing by platoons. This was reckoned to be the most effective way of controlling fire over a long period, but it was realised in the 1750s that if, instead of halting, a single volley was fired by the entire battalion and followed up with a bayonet charge, platoon-firing simply could not kill enough of the attackers quickly enough to stop them. The British Army adopted this doctrine of 'volley and bayonet' with some enthusiasm and employed it throughout the period. It was certainly one that may have suited the Highland character, but it was quite unconnected with the introduction of Highland regiments into the Army.
32 The incident occurred on 19 October near Alfen and resulted in the capture of the greater part of the 37th Foot (Fortescue, J. W., *History of the British Army*, Vol. 4(1), p.311). The circumstances of the Geldermalsen affair are recounted by Stewart of Garth (*Sketches*, Vol. 2, p. 184–5) who also recounts how the French actually galloped along the road, with great fury, crying 'Choiseul, Choiseul'.
33 Captain, 50th Foot, 21 November 1776; major (brevet), 18 November 1790, serving at the time as ADC to Major General Dundas. He was no longer in the Army List by 1798.

34 Ensign, 42nd, 12 July 1773; lieutenant, 24 February 1776; captain 25 August 1778; major, 16 March 1791; promoted into 19th Foot, 31 December 1794.
35 Garth, *Sketches*, Vol. 1, p. 413. The Lieutenant Coll Lamont referred to was in fact Lieutenant *Colin* Lamont – at least one version of the Red Hackle legend, clearly influenced by a hasty reading of Garth's rather spare narrative, assumed the reference was to a Lieutenant *Colonel* Lamont and states that Major Dalrymple led the charge because Lamont had just been wounded! Lamont subsequently recovered and became a captain in the regiment on 1 September 1795.
36 It was more than likely the 71st, although the overstripes originally appear to have been red and buff – the regiment's facing colour, just as other regiments with yellow facings, such as the Gordons adopted a yellow overstripe in their tartan. Significantly, the officers of the 78th are reported to have frequently been in dispute with Wilsons over the colouring of their overstripes. The buff facings worn by the 78th were actually a milky white, in contrast to the brownish ochre worn by the 71st, and there may well have been some difficulty weaving a satisfactory shade of this into their kilts, hence the eventual adoption of a good clear white.
37 WO12/1883.
38 Fortescue, J.W. *History of the British Army* 4(1):212–3.
39 Barclays Bank in this case.
40 Guy, Alan J., *Colonel Samuel Bagshawe and the Army of George II*, London, 1985, p. 210.
41 Ibid. Just what the objection to chimney sweeps might have been is uncertain but both coal miners and seamen were notoriously prone to suffering from diseases such as tuberculosis.
42 Not to be confused with the quite different, and altogether more famous, Queen's Rangers, led by Colonel John Groves Simcoe.
43 PRO AO12/56 (American Loyalist Claims – Virginia).
44 Maclean, Loraine, *Indomitable Colonel*, pp. 74–7.
45 Much of the detail discussed here comes from Maclean, op.cit., although she appears not to have recognised the critical importance of first demonstrating that the funding was in place. In general it also has to be said that her biography, while extremely useful, is altogether far too indulgent and glosses over, ignores or is unaware of some of his less creditable proceedings.

Fassfern, incidentally, was one of those individuals whose name caused no end of problems; frequently being rendered as Fassiefern or Fassifern
46 Maclean, pp. 113–14. Dr A. Clerk, Kilmallie, to John N. Macleod of Saddell, 1877. There were no fewer than five Ewen Camerons enlisted in the Gordons in 1794, all from Kilmally. Two died while serving with the regiment, and one, who was already twenty-eight when he enlisted, was discharged in 1800. The two remaining were twenty and twenty-two years old respectively, but it is impossible (and not particularly relevant) to guess which of them was Clerk's informant. In fairness Clerk was a far from impartial chronicler, being the biographer of Colonel John Cameron of Fassfern.

47 Grant to Gordon, 16 February 1793. Fraser, G. M., *The Strathspey Mutineers*, pp.16–17.
48 Yonge to Gordon 2 March 1793. Bulloch, J. M. *Territorial Soldiering* : 143
49 Bulloch, pp. 168–9.
50 Maclean, p. 115.
51 Quite uniquely, the edition for that year contains all the headings for what was then officially termed the 79th (Cameronian Volunteers), but otherwise the page is quite blank – an oddity emphasised by the fact that a full complement of officers are listed for Paget's 80th and all the other regiments junior to the 79th on the pages following.
52 Fortescue, Vol. 4, pp. 302–3.
53 Garth, Vol. 2, p. 218.
54 Fortescue, Vol. 4, pp. 320–1.
55 Quoted in both Maclean and in Cannon's History of the 79th Regiment, taken from Erracht's own account. Maclean, pp. 133–5.
56 See Geggus, David, *War Slavery and Revolution: The British Occupation of San Domingue 1793–1798*, Oxford, 1982, for a more reasoned discussion of the problem.
57 Maclean, p. 144–5.
58 Once again Maclean ignores Erracht's ready acknowledgement of the feud with Locheil and attributes the 'conspiracy' against him to the malign influence of Fassfern, rather than to the chieftain whose authority Erracht openly admitted to challenging.
59 Amherst to Gordon, 24 January 1794, Bulloch, p. 193.
60 Loun (Scots): boy or young man.
61 Bulloch, p. 158, The samples do not survive, but logically the first would have run the yellow stripe through the blue ground, rather than the broad green checks. The third may have had a yellow stripe through both the checks and the blue ground.
62 Bulloch, p. 198. James Fraser of Gortuleg to Charles Gordon of Braid, 15 February 1794.
63 The stipulation in the letters of service that the majors should be appointed by the king was not to be taken literally, but meant that the gentlemen in question had either to be serving or half-pay officers and were not to be appointed directly from civilian life.
64 Fyvie, the son of the 2nd Earl of Aberdeen, was both the cousin and step-uncle of the Duke of Gordon and his younger brother, Lord George Gordon. The occasion of his threatening to skewer his nephew/cousin was during the week-long 'Gordon Riots' of 1780, which devastated much of central London.
65 Bulloch, pp. 39–40.
66 Ibid., p. 42.
67 Ibid., pp. 45–6.
68 Ibid., p. 101.

69 William Bell of Cocklarachie to James Ross (Factor at Gordon Castle), 25 January and 15 February 1778. Bulloch, pp. 42–3.
70 Bulloch, pp. 255–6.
71 Finlason, 11 March 1794, Bulloch, pp. 212–13.
72 Bulloch, p. 213.
73 Gordon Slade, H.; Craigston and Meldrum Estates, Carriacou, 1769–1841, *Proceedings of the Society of Antiquaries of Scotland*, 114, 1984.
74 Gen, Sir A. J. F. Reid, *Aberdeen Journal*, 11 December 1907.
75 Bulloch, p. 201.
76 *Morning Chronicle*, 1 September 1795.
77 Extracts from a surviving orderly book were published in *Journal for Army Historical Research*, Vol. LXXI, pp. 288, 281–3. On 16 June 1795 it was ordered that the full dress of officers was to be braided jackets, white cloth waistcoats and trousers, tartan hose and bonnets, with white hackles instead of the green formerly used. Nankeen trousers, short boots and round hats were permitted in undress. There are fewer references to the uniform of the rank and file, although they too were to have tartan hose. Mention is made of drab-coloured trousers in a context that suggests they were for undress or for fatigues, while references to white trousers being made up clearly relate to their impending embarkation for the West Indies. On balance it seems likely that they may well have had kilts, or at least tartan trousers.
78 Dundas to Huntly, 3 December 1796, *Scottish Review*, xvii, p. 130.
79 Todd to Cameron, 11 February 1797, *Scottish Review*, xvii, pp. 130–1.
80 Garth, Vol. 2, p. 312.
81 He can be seen wearing this uniform in a magnificent full-length portrait by John Singleton Copley. Traditionally the uniform, with its green facings, is supposed to hark at his service with the 77th, but the style unmistakably dates it to the 1790s. Moreover an unquestionably contemporary caricature by John Kay likewise depicts him in the same uniform and a copy of the painting in Ayr Council Chambers is unequivocally labelled as being Montgomerie in the uniform of the West Lowland Fencibles. Although there appears to be no surviving record of its clothing, it is also likely that his marching regiment – the short-lived Royal Glasgow Regiment – was similarly dressed in feathered bonnets and tartan trousers.
82 Prebble, John, *Mutiny*, p. 185.
83 Gordon, Pryse Lockhart, *Personal Memoirs*, Vol. I, pp. 150–1.
84 MacIntosh, H.B. *The Grant, Strathspey or First Fencible Regiment*, p. 44.
85 Gordon, Pryse Lockhart, *Personal Memoirs*, Vol. 1, pp. 150–1.
86 WO1/1059.
87 Garth, Vol. 2, p. 312. It should be noted that the British Army's records in this respect were very crude insofar as they recorded in general terms a man's place of birth but not his true nationality. A man recorded as being Irish or English would certainly have been born there, but could have Scottish parents and a Scottish

upbringing. The Duke of Wellington himself was of course caught out thus, for having been born in Dublin he was officially registered as an Irishman and upon being reminded of the fact famously retorted that a man might be born in a stable but it did not make him a horse.
88 Fraser, G. M., *The Strathspey Mutineers*, pp. 71, 73. Contrary to his carefully cultivated legend, young Glengarry clearly did not invariably wear Highland dress both in and out of season.
89 Lieutenant John Grant, (Jnr), 14 March 1794, Ibid., p. 87.
90 MacIntosh, H. B., *The Grant, Strathspey or First Fencible Regiment*, pp. 88–9.
91 Ibid., p. 105.
92 Sir James Grant to Lord Adam Gordon, Linlithgow, 21 March 1794 (Morning). Ibid., pp. 92–3.
93 *Rules and Regulations for the Formations, Field Exercise and Movements of His Majesty's Forces*, 1792, p. 128.
94 MacIntosh, H. B., *The Grant, Strathspey or First Fencible Regiment*, p. 95.
95 Ibid., pp. 105–7.
96 National Archives of Scotland, GD248/465/1.
97 National Archives of Scotland GD248/464/9.
98 MacIntosh, H. B., *The Grant, Strathspey or First Fencible Regiment*, p. 119.
99 This was a straightforward disciplinary matter in which a soldier confined for punishment was rescued by some of his rioting comrades, two of whom were afterwards executed. Once again the fact of the Strathspeys being a Highland battalion had no bearing on the causes or consequences of the trouble, and when viewed objectively, Altyre's handling of the incident was rather more commendable than otherwise.
100 Houlding, Dr John, 'Irish Army Orders' JSAHR LXXII 290, pp. 107–17.
101 Regimental Orderly book, in Mackay-Scobie, Ian, *History of the Reay Fencibles*.
102 WO25/748 T-V f36.
103 Although the arrest operation was run by the Dublin police chief, Major Harry Sirr, the 'muscle' was provided by a detachment of Dumbarton Fencibles, commanded by Captain Alexander Graham.
104 As such he was granted half-pay as adjutant (but not captain) when the regiment was disbanded; a privilege not otherwise extended to fencible officers unless wounded on active service.
105 In Ireland all the volunteer militia units, whether mounted or not, were termed yeomanry.
106 Stephens, Alexander, *The History of the Late Grand Insurrection*, 1805, pp. 246–50.
107 Ibid.
108 WO40/11 (Blanche's official report).
109 Ibid.
110 Garth, Vol. 2, p. 349.
111 Interestingly, another officer to come, albeit indirectly, from the Strathspeys was Sir James Grant's eldest son Frank. He had gone from the Strathspeys to be a

captain in his father's regular 97th Inverness-shire Regiment, but when it was caught up in the Great Drafting, he became a fencible officer again as major and later colonel of the Frasers!

112 The Royal Irish Artillery was at this time quite separate from the Woolwich-based Royal Artillery.

113 Musgrave, Sir Rich., *Memoirs of the different Rebellions in Ireland*, 1802, Vol. 2, p. 152.

114 Ibid., pp. 155–6. Who he was, or if indeed the incident ever happened at all, has never been established, and no-one else spoke of it at the time, but the 'brave Fraser sentinel' certainly provided a splendid subject for popular artists and entered into the growing mythology of the Highland regiments.

115 Raised by Henry Clavering in October 1794 and not to be confused with the earlier Argyle or Western Fencibles of 1793.

116 So called because instead of having a conventional gun-carriage, the barrel was mounted directly on to the bed of a light two wheeled cart or curricle, the shafts of which served as a trail.

117 Stephens, p. 316.

118 Musgrave, Vol. 2, p. 299.

119 Garth, Vol. 2, pp. 399–400.

120 Ibid. p. 242.

121 Although Morris's 89th was therefore the first regular Highland regiment to go to India, it should be noted that the independent companies that formed Boscawan's expeditionary force in 1748 were largely comprised of Jacobite prisoners and will inevitably have included a high proportion of Highlanders.

122 Lindsay, who also survived, afterwards wrote a lengthy – and surprisingly readable – account of their experiences. His narrative differs from the generally accepted version in suggesting that Baird did have the bullet extracted during his captivity, and, while confirming that the officers were fettered, makes it clear that they were not actually shackled together. An unknown number of the rank and file belonging to the two Highland companies were forcibly 'converted' to Islam and shanghaied into Tippu's forces. What became of them in the end is unknown. Lindsay's narrative may be found at <http://diarysearch.co.uk/diaries/Lindsay%20Diary.pdf>, accessed 4 October 2009.

123 Prebble refers to them as the Macrae Company, but Stewart of Garth was of the opinion that the reason why the mutiny was referred to as the 'affair of the Macraes' was that the whole regiment was loosely referred to as such. At any rate no particular company is singled out in contemporary reports.

124 Seemingly unaware of the enforced layover at St Helena, Stewart of Garth (and Prebble following him) write of the regiment being at sea for the entire ten months.

125 There they fought alongside one of the Company's sepoy regiments, the 8th Bombay Native Infantry. This was an elite unit formed by consolidating the grenadier companies of the other seven regiments and both they and the Highlanders got

on so well that they took to calling themselves the Third Battalion of the Black Watch!
126 Prebble (p. 140) quite wrongly gives the impression that the battalion was disbanded.
127 Garth, Vol. 2, pp. 164, 171–2.
128 Wellesley had changed his name from Wesley shortly after arriving in India.
129 It should be noted that this was indeed the name he was baptised with. His elder brother was also born a Mackenzie, but, as was not uncommon in those days, subsequently added his mother's name, Humberston, on inheriting her family's Lincolnshire estates.
130 Buff was a curious colour that varied according to regiment, from a pale cream to a rich brown ochre. It is possible that the 78th may in fact have been intended to have white facings but turned them into a 'buff' in order to avoid the usual practice of displaying the red cross of St George on their otherwise plain white regimental colours. Adopting the Ross-shire Buffs title may also have been intended to emphasise that their facings were not white but buff.
131 Commissions: lieutenant, 73rd/71st Highlanders, 1778; captain, 13 January 1781; half-pay, 1784; major, 78th Highlanders, 1793; lieutenant colonel, 78th Highlanders, 24 July 1793; colonel, 78th Highlanders, 3 May 1796; major general, 1802.

Notes: Fourth son of Colin McKenzie of Kilcoy and Martha Fraser, born at Tore, Ross-shire. Married Helen Anne Mackenzie 1785/issue. Adopted additional name Fraser in 1803. Served Gibraltar during Great Siege. Served Flanders 1794, commanding 78th at Nijmeguen and Geldermalsen, then Cape 1796 and India until 1800. Served Hanover 1805, then Mediterranean and Egypt; Sweden, Spain, and Walcheren. Died of complications following Walcheren Fever 13 September 1809. (Oxford Dictionary of National Biography)
132 The 94th were originally raised in 1793 as the Scotch Brigade; three battalions were recruited in the Edinburgh area but officered by men discharged from the old Scotch Brigade in the Dutch service. It is remarkable as being one of only two Scottish regiments raised at this period (the other being the 90th) that was *not* designated as Highlanders.
133 Wellesley initially reported he had captured sixty guns but later revised the total up to ninety. It is unclear, however, whether all of them were in the main gun line or whether the additional guns were found in the Maratha camp or in Assaye itself.
134 Wellesley to Monro, 1 November 1803. Supplementary Dispatches, 4, p. 211.
135 When awarded the Military General Service (MGS) medal in 1848, Todd was granted bars for Rolica, Vimeiro, Talavera, Fuentes d'Onoro, Vittoria, Prenees, Nivelle, Orthes and Toulouse. He also received the Waterloo medal.
136 Personal communication with Philip Haythornthwaite, who also points to another version of the story in *Military History Society Bulletin*, Vol. 1, no. 42, p. 219, in which Howell apparently stated that his source (probably Todd) presented him with pages of a journal that he had kept.

137 Ibid. – Howell admitted that 'the scene in the theatre was a real one but not in regard to Todd.'
138 WO12/7856–8.
139 Gavin's MGS had bars for Vittoria, Pyrenees, Nivelle, Nive, Orthes and Toulouse, and like Todd he was also a Waterloo man, but clearly his active service only spanned the years 1813–15.
140 Maclean, *Indomitable Colonel*, p. 180.
141 Sinclair, Sir John, *Hints Respecting the State of the Camp at Aberdeen, in 1795. With some Observations on Encampments in general; And an Appendix, on the Ancient Dress of the Scottish Highlanders.* I am once again grateful to Philip Haythornthwaite for drawing this pamphlet to my attention.
142 It is in fact clear that during the latter part of the war the overwhelming majority of infantrymen transferred from the militia and that individual recruits such as 'Thomas' were increasingly rare. It might also be noted that the majority, and certainly the best, of the 'soldiers' narratives of the war come from ex-militiamen like James Anton and Thomas Morris.
143 WO3/19:230.
144 Maclean, *Indomitable Colonel*, pp. 181–2.
145 WO3/47 Adjutant General's Memorandum 7 April 1809.
146 Not on the Military General Service medal roll.
147 Commissions: ensign, 18th Foot, 9 August 1797; lieutenant, 18th Foot, 18 July 1799; captain, 60th Foot, 21 November 1799; lieutenant and captain, 2nd Footguards, 9 December 1799; major, 53rd Foot, 8 December 1804; lieutenant colonel, 18th Foot, 22 August 1805; half-pay, Brunswick Fencibles, 5 March 1807; lieutenant colonel, 71st Highlanders, 7 January 1808; colonel (brevet), 4 June 1813.

Notes: seventh son of Charles 1st Earl of Cadogan, born 26 February 1780. Wounded at Buenos Aires; served Peninsula; initially as ADC to Wellington at Talavera, but then assumed command of 71st on their coming out; Fuentes d'Onoro, Alba de Tormes. Commanded brigade at Vittoria – killed in action there 21 June 1813. WO25/2964. Hall; *Oxford Dictionary of National Biography*.
148 Commissions: ensign, 71st Foot, February 1800; lieutenant, 16 July 1801; captain, 71st Foot, 25 March 1803; major, 9 March 1809; lieutenant colonel (brevet), 19 June 1812; lieutenant colonel, 71st Foot, 13 October 1814; lieutenant colonel, 2/83rd Foot, 24 October 1816; half-pay, 1818.

Notes: Served at Cape of Good Hope and Buenos Aires. Served throughout Peninsular War; slightly wounded at Vittoria 21 June 1813. Subsequently served in Ceylon. Died at Gloucester, 24 January 1855, aged sixty-eight. *Gentlemans Magazine*; Hall; *Royal Military Calendar*.
149 Garth, Vol. 2, pp. 257–8.
150 Robertson, Donald, *Diary*, p. 129.
151 Commissions: ensign, 42nd Highlanders, 22 April 1777; lieutenant, 3 August 1778; captain, 8 August 1792; major, 14 December 1796; lieutenant colonel (brevet),

29 April 1802; lieutenant colonel, 42nd Highlanders, 7 September 1804; colonel (brevet), 4 June 1811; major general, 4 June 1814. WO25/3998.
152 Analysis of the muster rolls (WO12) as late as January 1820 found 452 out of 572 rank and file were Scots and 29 out of 39 officers. See Henderson, *Highland Soldier*, p. 10.
153 Bell, *Notes of an Old Campaigner*, Vol. I, p. 104.
154 Two other Highland battalions took part in the campaign but were neither at Quatre Bras nor Waterloo: 2/78th were in garrison at Antwerp while the 91st belonged to the 4th Division, which was posted at Hal to counter any grand turning movement by the French.
155 Commissions: captain (late), 94th Foot, 16 December 1795; major, 42nd Highlanders, 14 November 1805; lieutenant colonel (brevet), 1 January 1812; lieutenant colonel, 42nd Highlanders, 16 April 1812.
  Notes: Minister's son, born at Fortingall in Perthshire and originally a doctor in the East India Company service before entering the army. Served Peninsula; badly wounded at Toulouse. Badly wounded at Quatre Bras and then murdered by Polish lancers while being carried from the field.
156 Had the brigade formed up in conventional fashion, 3/1st as the senior battalion should have been on the right and the 42nd the left with the 92nd and 44th right and left centre respectively. How they came to be so jumbled up on their actual deployment is unclear.
157 Lieutenant Alexander Forbes's account, in Siborne, *Waterloo Letters*, p. 357.
158 Siborne, pp. 377–8.
159 Siborne, pp. 386–7. Despite his name, Winchester was a Scot, born in Aberdeen.
160 Once again there is some confusion as to the spelling of his name. Most older histories refer to him as Fassiefern, but it is also rendered as Fassifern as well as by the more modern spelling of Fassfern.
161 Commissions: second lieutenant, 21st Fusiliers, 12 April 1793; lieutenant, Balfour's 93rd Foot, 30 October 1793; captain, 100th/92nd (Gordon) Highlanders, 13 February 1794; major, 5 April 1801; lieutenant colonel (brevet), 25 April 1808; lieutenant colonel, 92nd 23 June 1808; colonel (brevet), 4 June 1814.
162 Halkett, in Siborne, p. 321.
163 Morris, Thomas, *The Recollections of Sergeant Morris*, p. 69.
164 Mercer, A. C., *Journal of the Waterloo Campaign, Edinburgh 1870*, Vol. 1, pp. 250–1.
165 Commissions: ensign, 75th Foot, 22 November 1800; lieutenant, 67th Foot, 27 June 1802; captain, 78th Highlanders, 17 April 1804; major, 78th, 24 April 1808; major, 42nd Highlanders, 14 July 1808; lieutenant colonel (brevet), 8 October 1812; lieutenant colonel, 42nd Highlanders, 18 June 1815; half-pay colonel (unattached), 27 May 1825; major general, 10 January 1837.
  Notes: Served Sicily, Maida, Egypt. Peninsula – Busaco, Fuentes d'Onoro, Salamanca. Briefly succeeded to command of 1/42nd at Quatre Bras before being badly wounded. Colonel, 73rd Highlanders, 1845. Married Eliza Macnabb, 11 April 1818, but following her death in 1838 applied for further service. Commanded

centre division of Madras Army 1838 and temporarily commander-in-chief, 1841–2. Transferred to Bombay, commanded 3rd Division in Sikh War and killed in action at Sobraon 10 February 1846. (*Dalton; Hart(1840); Oxford Dictionary of National Biography*)

166 Commissions: lieutenant, 100th/92nd Highlanders, 16 June 1795; captain (brevet), 5 April 1801; captain, 42nd Highlanders, 25 September 1807; major (brevet), 4 June 1813.

Notes: Served Peninsula; slightly wounded at storm of Fort St Michael, Burgos, 19 September 1812. Wounded at Quatre Bras and died at Brussels. (*Dalton; Hall*)

167 Commissions: ensign, 100th/92nd (Gordon) Highlanders, 15 February 1794; lieutenant, 14 September 1797; major, 30 March 1809; lieutenant colonel (brevet), 3 March 1814; lieutenant colonel, 92nd (Gordon) Highlanders, 16 June 1815; retired from service, 1 September 1819.

Notes: Born Auchindaul, Lochaber and died there 1847. Served Mediterranean; Ireland, 1798; Helder, 1799; Egypt, 1801. Served throughout Peninsular War; wounded at Maya 25 July 1813. Served Quatre Bras, 1815; succeeded to command of battalion after Cameron of Fassfern killed, but was himself wounded very shortly afterwards. (*Bulloch; Dalton; Hall*)

168 Commissions: ensign, 3rd Footguards, 26 May 1803; lieutenant and captain, 3rd Footguards, 3 April 1806; major (brevet), 26 May 1810; lieutenant colonel (brevet), 6 February 1812; captain and lieutenant colonel, 3rd Footguards, 15 January 1815.

Notes: Third son of George Gordon, Lord Haddo. ADC to Sir David Baird (his uncle) at the Cape 1799 and in Egypt and at Corunna. ADC to Wellington in Peninsula and at Waterloo – badly wounded in Pyrenees 28 July 1813 and fatally wounded at Waterloo. (*Dalton; Gordons under Arms(196); Hall*)

169 Commissions: lieutenant, 1st (Strathspey) Fencibles, 1 March 1793; captain and captain-lieutenant (late), 101st Foot, 15 October 1784; captain, 17th Light Dragoons, 1 December 1795; major, 17th Light Dragoons, 1 July 1802; major, 2/78th Highlanders, 1804; lieutenant colonel, 2/78th Highlanders, 7 September 1809; lieutenant colonel, 2/Garrison Battalion, 21 February 1811; captain and lieutenant colonel, 2nd Footguards, 8 August 1811; colonel (brevet), 12 August 1819; lieutenant colonel, 2nd Footguards, 1825; major general, 22 July 1830; lieutenant general, 1841; general, 1854.

Notes: Third son of Duncan MacDonnell of Glengarry and Marjorie Grant. Died at 15 Wilton Place, London, 15 May 1859. Served at Maida, Peninsula and Waterloo. Wounded in defence of Hougoumont, where he and Sergeant Graham gained distinction by their closing the gate after the French got in. Commanded brigade of Guards in Canada 1838 and afterwards commander-in-chief until 1841. (*Bulloch; Dalton; Hart (1840);Oxford Dictionary of National Biography; Royal Military Calendar*)

170 There seems to have been some doubt about the 44th. At one stage during the fighting at Quatre Bras they were said to be reduced to just four effective companies and were consolidated with the 3/1st under Pack's personal command.

Yet they afterwards returned just 12 dead and 109 wounded; far less than any other regiment in the brigade.
171 Ensign Edward Macready, 30th Foot, in Lagden, A. and Sly, J., *The 2/73rd at Waterloo*, 1998, pp. 147–8. The 33rd Foot had red facings and so for a regimental colour carried a St George's cross on a white ground.
172 *Commissions*: ensign 73rd Highlanders 7 February 1794; second lieutenant 7 July 1800; lieutenant 21 July 1803; captain 14 May 1804; major 2/73rd 28 May 1812.
    Notes: Fourth son of Gillian McLaine of Scallastle, Mull, born 1777. Served India. Wounded at storming of Seringapatam 1799. Served New South Wales. Served Netherlands 1814. Died of wounds after Waterloo. Although Macready refers to McLaine as 'old', he died just two days after his 36th birthday!
173 The battalion was eventually taken over by the surviving major, Dawson Kelly, who had earlier been assigned to the staff.
174 Despite his name, Torriano was British; being the son of Captain Charles Torriano of the 30th Foot, killed at Toulon in 1793 and grandson of a Captain Torriano of the Royal Artillery, wounded at Laufeldt in 1747.
175 Winchester, in Siborne, p. 383.
176 Dickson's account in Low, E. B., *With Napoleon at Waterloo*, ed. McK McBride, London, 1911, pp. 137–48.
177 Siborne, p. 77.
178 Ibid.
179 Lieutenant Alexander Forbes's account in Siborne, *Waterloo Letters*, p. 357.
180 Alison, Sir Archibald, *History of Europe from the Commencement of the French Revolution to the Restoration of the Bourbons*, 1860, No. 14, p. 308.
181 *Historical Records of the Queens Own Cameron Highlanders*, Edinburgh, 1909, Vol. 1, p. 134.
182 Henderson, Diana, *Highland Soldier*, pp. 228–9, n19.
183 This odd state of affairs was equally confusing to contemporaries. John Blakiston was one of that surprisingly small band who obtained a commission whilst still an infant, and as he was too young to serve, was soon transferred on to the half-pay of the old 71st (Fraser's) Highlanders. Through a curious quirk in the regulations he was able to retain this half-pay commission when he entered the service of the East India Company as an engineer. There he commenced an action-filled career, which included serving on Wellesley's staff at Assaye, before returning home to enjoy the unusual distinction of being the only East India Company officer to serve in the Peninsula. As such he qualified in 1848 for the Military General Service medal and is to be found in the rolls listed under the 71st Highlanders – the Highland Light Infantry – rather than the old 71st.
184 This alteration was seemingly bitterly resented, for surviving memoirs continue to refer to the regiment as the 64th as least as late as the capture of Quebec in 1759.

Archival Sources

National Archives (Kew)

NA AO12/56   (American Loyalist Claims – Virginia)
NA WO1   In-Letters, Secretary at War
NA WO4   Out Letters, Secretary at War
NA WO12   Regimental Muster Rolls
NA WO25/748   Officers' service returns (comp. 1809–1810)
NA WO25/3998   General Statement of Field Officers Services
NA WO40   Secretary-at-War, In-letters and Reports

National Archives of Scotland

GD248   Seafield Muniments

Other Contemporary Sources

Anon., *General Wolfe's Instructions to Young Officers*, 1780
Cooper, Capt. T. H., *A Practical Guide for the Light Infantry Officer*, London, 1806
Hansard, T. C., *The Parliamentary History of England*, London, 1813
Rules and Regulations for the Formations, Field Exercise and Movements of His Majesty's Forces, 1792

Periodicals

Aberdeen Journal
Army List
Gentlemans Magazine
Morning Chronicle
Scottish Review

Correspondence, Memoirs and Journals

Anton, James, *Retrospect of a Military Life*, Edinburgh, 1841
Bell, George, *Notes of an Old Campaigner*, Tunbridge Wells, 1991
Guy, Alan J., *Colonel Samuel Bagshawe and the Army of George II*, London, 1985
Howell, John (ed.), *Journal of a Soldier of the 71st or Glasgow Regiment, Highland Light Infantry from 1806–1815*, Edinburgh, 1831

Lockhart Gordon, Pryse, *Personal Memoirs; or Reminiscences of Men and Manners at Home and Abroad*, London, 1830
Mercer, A. C., *Journal of the Waterloo Campaign*, Edinburgh, 1870
Morris, Thomas, *Recollections*, London, 1845
Musgrave, Sir Rich., *Memoirs of the different Rebellions in Ireland*, 1802
Peebles, John, *John Peebles' American War 1776–1782*, ed. I. Gruber, London, 1997
Robertson, D., *Journal of Sergeant D. Robertson, late 92nd Foot*, Perth, 1842
Siborne, H. T., *Waterloo Letters: A Selection from Original and Hitherto Unpublished Letters Bearing on the Operations of the 16th, 17th, and 18th June, 1815, By Officers who served in the Campaign*, London, 1891
Wellington, 1st Duke of, *Dispatches of Field Marshal the Duke of Wellington*, ed. J. Gurwood, London, 1834–8
— *Supplementary Despatches and Memoranda of Field Marshal the Duke of Wellington*, ed. 2nd Duke of Wellington, London, 1858–72

Secondary Sources

Alison, Sir Archibald, *History of Europe from the Commencement of the French Revolution to the Restoration of the Bourbons*, Edinburgh, 1860
Bruce, Anthony, *The Purchase System in the British Army*, London, 1980
Bulloch, J. M., *Gordons under Arms*, Aberdeen, 1912
— *Territorial Soldiering in the North-East of Scotland*, Aberdeen, 1914
Bumsted, J. M, *The Peoples Clearance: Highland Emigration to North America 1770–1815*, Edinburgh, 1982
Callaghan, R., *The East India Company and Army Reform 1783–1798*, Harvard, 1972
Dalton, Charles, *The Waterloo Roll Call*, London, 1904
Fortescue, J. W., *History of the British Army*, London, 1899–1920
Fraser, G. M., *The Strathspey Mutineers*, Kinloss, 2003
Garth, David Stewart of, *Sketches of the Character, Manners, and Present State of the Highlanders of Scotland, with details of the Military Service of the Highland Regiments*, Edinburgh, 1822
Geggus, David, *War Slavery and Revolution: The British Occupation of San Domingue 1793–1798*, Oxford, 1982
Gordon Slade, H., 'Craigston and Meldrum Estates, Carriacou, 1769–1841', *Proceedings of the Society of Antiquaries of Scotland*, 114, 1984
Greenhill-Gardyne, Lt. Col. C., *The Life of a Regiment: The History of the Gordon Highlanders*, Vol. 1, 1794–1816, London, 1901
Guy, Alan J., *Oeconomy and Discipline: Officership and Administration in the British Army 1714–1763*, Manchester, 1985
Hall, Dr John A., *Biographical Dictionary of British Officers Killed and Wounded 1808–1814*, London, 1998
Haythornthwaite, Philip J., *The Napoleonic Source Book*, London, 1990
— *The Armies of Wellington*, London, 1994
— *Waterloo Men: The experience of Battle 16–18 June 1815*, Marlborough, 1999

Henderson, Diana, *Highland Soldier 1820–1920*, Edinburgh, 1989
Houlding, John, *Fit for Service: The Training of the British Army 1715–1795*, Oxford, 1981
Houlding, Dr John, 'Irish Army Orders', *Journal of the Society for Army Historical Research*, Vol. LXXII, p. 290
Katcher, Philip, *King George's Army 1775–1783*, Reading, 1973
Lagden, A. & Sly, J. S., *The 2/73rd at Waterloo*, Brightlingsea, 1988;1998
Low, E .B., *With Napoleon at Waterloo*, ed. McK. McBride, London, 1911
Maclean, Loraine, *Indomitable Colonel*, London, 1986
McCulloch, I. M., *Sons of the Mountains: The Highland regiments in the French and Indian War 1757–1767*, New York, 2006
— *Highlander in the French and Indian War 1756–67*, Oxford, 2008
Mackay-Scobie, I. H., *An Old Highland Fencible Corps: The History of the Reay Fencible Highland Regiment of Foot, or Mackay's Highlanders*, Edinburgh, 1914
Mackintosh, H. B., *The Grant, Strathspey or First Highland Fencible Regiment 1793–1799*, Elgin, 1934
— *The Inverness-shire Highlanders, or 97th Regiment of Foot, 1794–1796*, Elgin, 1926
Millar, Simon, *Assaye 1803*, Oxford, 2006
Mullen, A. L. T., *The Military General Service Roll*, London, 1990
Musgrave, Sir Richard, *Memoirs of the different Rebellions in Ireland*, 1802
Oman, Sir Charles, *A History of the Peninsular War*, London, 1902–30
Pakenham, Thomas, *The Year of Liberty: The Great Irish Rebellion of 1798*, London, 1969
Philippart, John, *Royal Military Calendar or Army Service and Commission Book*, London, 1820
Prebble, John, *Culloden*, London, 1961
— *Mutiny: Highland Regiments in Revolt*, London, 1975
Reid, Stuart, *Wellington's Officers: Biographical Dictionary of the Field Officers and Staff Officers of the British Army 1793–1815 Vol.1 A–G*, Southend, 2008
— *Wellington's Highlanders*, London, 1992
— *18th Century Highlanders*, London, 1993
— *King George's Army* (3 vols), London, 1995–6
— *British Redcoat (1)*, Oxford, 1996
— *British Redcoat (2)*, Oxford, 1997
— *Highland Clansman*, Oxford, 1997
— *Redcoat Officer*, Oxford, 2002
— *Wellington's Army in the Peninsula*, Oxford, 2004
— *The Jacobite Army 1745–46*, Oxford, 2006
— *Queen Victoria's Highlanders*, Oxford, 2007
Siborne, William, *History of the War in France and Belgium in 1815*, London, 1844
Sinclair, Donald, *History of the Aberdeen Volunteers*, Aberdeen, 1907
Stephens, Alexander, *The History of the Late Grand Insurrection*, 1805
Strachan, Hew, *British Military Uniforms 1768–96*, London, 1975
Weller, Jac, *Wellington in India*, London, 1972
Willson, Beckles, *Life and Letters of James Wolfe*, London, 1909

Index

Abercromby, Sir Ralph 68–70, 73–4, 124–5
Abercromby, Robert 148
Anton, James 167, 200
Armour, James 200
Auchmuty, Sir Samuel 162–3

Baillie, Mackay Hugh, of Rosehall 118
Baird, David 142, 147, 149–50, 160, 171, 173
Ballyshannon 123–4, 130
battles
    Ahmednuggar 152
    Arklow 129
    Assaye 153–7, 204
    Ballinamuck 136
    Boxtel 69–70
    Buenos Aires 162–4
    Castlebar 130–5
    Cavan 135–6
    Col de Maya 182, 190
    Culloden 19, 23
    El Hamet 180
    Fuentes d'Onoro 174–6
    Geldermalsen 36–8, 151
    Maida 180
    Merexem 180
    Montevideo 162–3
    New Orleans 181
    Polilur 142
    Quatre Bras 184–91
    Seringapatam 149
    Talavera 174
    Tara, Hill of 125–9
    Ticonderoga 38
    Vimeiro 170–1
    Vittoria 177–8
    Walcheren 173
    Waterloo 191–202, 215–16
Beresford, William 162–3
Berkeley, Stanley 202
Black Watch *see* Regiments, 42nd Royal Highland Regiment
Blanche, Aaron 126–9

Cadogan, Colonel Henry 175, 177
Cameron, Alexander 184
Cameron, Allan, of Erracht 39–40, 55–75, 80, 167–80
Campbell, Sir Archibald 148
Campbell, Colin, of Stonefield 129
Campbell, Lieutenant Colin 152
Cameron, Donald, of Locheil 60, 64–5, 74–5
Campbell, Duncan, of Lochnell 82, 181
Cameron, Ewen, of Fassfern 60, 65
Cameron, John, of Fassfern 65, 80, 188–9
Cameron, John, of Kinlochleven 30–1
Campbell, John, Earl of Loudoun 19, 24
Campbell, John, of Barbreck 32
Campbell, Robert 195
Clarke, George 170
Clarke-Kennedy, Captain 199
Cornwallis, Lord 135
Cother, Charles 177
Crawford, William 200
Cumberland, William Augustus Duke of 20
Cumming, Alexander Penrose, of Altyre 107, 115–17
Cumming, Robert 111

Dalrymple, George 37
Davidson, George 190
Dick, Robert 190
Dickson, John 198
Dundas, David 36–7, 69
Dundas, Henry 48, 57–60, 94–5, 148

East India Company 57, 138–40, 148

Farquhar, William 164, 173–4
Ferguson, Sir Ronald Craufurd 203
Findlater, Lord 20
Finlason, William 82, 87–90, 92
Forbes, Arthur 184–5
Forbes, Duncan, of Culloden 2
Fortescue, Sir John 46–7, 55
Fraser, James, of Belladrum 131
Fraser, James, of Kincorth 130–4
Fraser, John 'Young Lovat' 110
Fraser, Simon, Lord Lovat 13–14
Fraser, Simon, Master of Lovat 22–3, 29–30

Gavin, Archibald 161, 178
Gordon, Lord Adam 66–7, 78, 80, 84, 100–1, 103–4
Gordon, Sir Alexander 191
Gordon, Dowager Duchess of 26–7
Gordon, George, Duke of 27, 31–2, 62–4, 76–81, 103–4
Gordon, George, Marquis of Huntly 67, 80–1, 90–1, 94–6
Gordon, James 189
Gordon, Jean, Duchess of 32, 66, 91–2
Gordon, Pryse Lockhart 64–5, 103–4
Gordon, William, of Fyvie 82–4
Gordon, Lord William 82–4
Grant, Alexander, of Sheuglie 139–40
Grant, Charles 140
Grant, Duncan 153
Grant, Francis William 111
Grant, Sir James, of Grant 41, 62–3, 78–9, 104–10, 114–15

Grant, John, of Glenmoriston 107–8, 114
Grant, Sir Ludovick, of Grant 24, 26–7

Haidar Ali 141, 149
Halkett, Colin 189, 194–5
Harness, William 155
Hay, Alexander, of Rannes 82–90, 92–4
Hely-Hutchinson, John 130–1
Holmes, George 190
Hope, James 199
Howell, John 161, 178
Humbert, Joseph 130, 132–6

independent companies 40–1, 47–8

Killala 130, 136
kilts 165–80, 181, 206–7
Kincaid, John 194
Kirkwood, Robert 24

Lake, Gerard 132–6
Leith, Alexander *see* Hay, Alexander
Leith, James 118
Lindsay, Hon. John 142

Macara, Sir Robert 184–7, 190
MacDonald, Simon, of Morar 79–80, 90
Mackay, George, of Bighouse 118–19
Mackenzie, Alexander 151
Mackenzie, Francis Humberston 39, 55, 151
Mackenzie, John, Lord MacLeod 32, 141
Mackenzie, Kenneth, Lord Seaforth 142–5
Mackenzie-Humberstone, Thomas 153
Maclean, Hector 125–6, 129
MacLeod, Lord *see* Mackenzie, John
MacPherson, Duncan, of Cluny 31
MacPherson, James 4
MacPherson, Rev. Robert 31
Martinique 73–5
Maxwell, Hamilton 31–2, 52
Maxwell, Patrick 157

Index

McDonnell, Alasdair Ranaldson, of Glengarry 106–7, 111–13, 116, 118, 192
McDonnell, James 192
McDonnell, John, of Lochgarry 32
McEween, Alexander 185–6
McGillivray, William, of Drumnaglas 27–8
McLaine, Archibald 193
McMillan, Ewen 189
Mercer, Cavallie 189–90
Mitchell, James 190
Molloy, Captain 126–9
Monro, Sir Hector 92, 141–2
Montgomerie, Hon. Archibald 22
Montgomerie, Hugh, of Coilsfield 79, 102, 104
Moore, Sir John 171, 173
Moray, Lord 27–8
Morris, Staats Long 26–7, 90
Morris, Tom 189, 191
Munro, William 2–3
Murray, Lord John 40
Mutiny, Black Watch 15–19
Mutiny, Leith 97
Mutiny, Portsmouth 98–9
Mutiny, Seaforth's (78th/72nd) 144–5
Mutiny, Strathspey Fencibles 108–17
Mutiny, West Lowland Fencibles 102–4

Nijmeguen 151

Orrock, William 155–6
Oughton, Sir Adolphus 145

Pack, Dennis 165–7, 183–5, 189, 192–3, 196, 201
Peebles, John 32–3
Picton, Sir Thomas 183–5, 197
Pitt, William, the Elder 21–2
Pitt, William, the Younger 48
Porter, John 135

Reay, Lord 118

Red Hackle 37–9, 42, 54
regiments, cavalry
  1st (Royal) Dragoons 196–8
  2nd (Royal North British) Dragoons 195–202, 215–16
  6th (Inniskilling) Dragoons 196–8
  19th Light Dragoons 157
regiments, infantry
  Coldstream Guards 192
  1st (Royal) Regiment 44–5, 183, 185, 189, 192
  14th Foot 90
  33rd Regiment 189, 195
  39th Regiment 140
  40th Regiment 162
  42nd Royal Highland Regiment 2, 13–20, 25–6, 28, 32–3, 36–42, 70, 75, 94–5, 97, 120, 181, 183–7, 190, 192, 199–200, 206, 209
  43rd Highlanders see 42nd Regiment
  44th Regiment 183, 185, 189, 192
  53rd Regiment 94
  60th Regiment 44
  64th (Loudoun's) Highlanders 19–20, 40–1, 209
  68th Regiment 99
  69th Regiment 189
  6th Dragoon Guards 132
  6th Regiment 132–3
  71st (Fraser's) Highlanders 29–32, 39, 52, 97, 147, 209
  71st (Glasgow Highland) Regiment 32, 41, 120, 141–2, 147, 149, 160–79; 193–5, 203, 207, 209–10
  72nd (Highland) Regiment 137, 142–7, 149, 169, 180–1, 203–4, 206, 210
  73rd (Highland) Regiment 120, 146, 149–50, 169, 180, 183, 189, 191, 193, 195, 206, 210
  73rd Highlanders (MacLeod's) see 71st Regiment
  74th (Campbell's) Highlanders 32

regiments, infantry (contd)
    74th (Highland) Regiment 57–8, 94, 120, 148–9, 154–7, 169, 204–7, 210
    75th (Highland) Regiment 120, 148–9, 169, 180, 206, 210
    76th (MacDonald's) Highlanders 32, 211
    77th (Athole or Murray's) Highlanders 98–9, 146, 211
    77th (Montgomerie's) Highlanders 22–5, 211
    78th (Fraser's) Highlanders 22–5, 211
    78th (Highland) Regiment 36, 55, 70, 98, 150–7, 166, 180, 183, 206, 211
    78th Highlanders (Seaforth's) see 72nd Regiment
    79th (Highland) Regiment 39–40, 55–75, 98, 137, 167–9, 181, 184–5, 190, 199, 203, 206, 212
    81st (Gordon's) Highlanders 83–6, 146, 212
    83rd Royal Glasgow Volunteers 97
    84th Royal Highland Emigrants 212
    87th (Keith's) Highlanders 26, 212
    88th (Campbell's) Highlanders 26, 212
    89th (Morris's) Highlanders 26–8, 78, 140, 212
    91st (Highland) Regiment 82, 169, 181, 204–6, 212–13
    92nd (Highland) Regiment 41, 65, 67, 76–82, 89–92, 94–6, 135, 137, 182, 184–90, 192, 195–202, 206, 213
    93rd (Highland) Regiment 137, 170, 181, 205–6, 213, 215–16
    94th Foot (Scotch Brigade) 153, 169–70
    97th (Inverness-shire) Highlanders 41, 82, 94, 213
    98th Highlanders see 91st Highlanders
    100th (Campbells) Highlanders 213
    100th Regiment see 92nd Regiment
    101st (Johnstone's) Highlanders 213
    105th (Queen's) Highlanders 213–14
    109th (Aberdeenshire) Highlanders 51, 86–9, 92–4, 98, 214
    114th (Maclean's) Highlanders 214
    116th Highlanders 98, 214
    132nd Highlanders 214
    133rd (Inverness Volunteers) 214
    Royal Glasgow Regiment 51, 98, 214
    Royal Regiment of Scotland 207
regiments, fencibles
    Aberdeen (Princess of Wales) Fencibles 118
    Argyle Fencibles 135
    Breadalbane Fencibles 41, 63, 66, 118
    Caithness Legion Fencibles 118
    Clan Alpine Fencibles 137
    Dumbarton Fencibles 129
    Fraser Fencibles 41, 130–6
    Glengarry Fencibles 116, 118
    Lochaber Fencibles 118
    Loyal Inverness Fencibles 41, 118
    Northern Fencibles 31, 62–5, 78, 84–5, 101–4
    Prince of Wales Fencibles 133
    Reay Fencibles 41, 118–19, 122–3, 125–9, 136
    Ross and Cromarty Rangers Fencibles 41
    Rothesay and Caithness Fencibles 41, 165
    South Fencibles 97, 103
    Strathspey Fencibles 41, 62–3, 78, 108–17
    Sutherland Fencibles 137
    West Lowland Fencibles 102–4
Rose, John 37

Scobie, John 125–6
Scots Greys see 2nd (Royal North British) Dragoons
Seaforth, Lord see Mackenzie, Kenneth

Index

Siborne, William 198
Sinclair, Sir John, of Ulbster 41, 165
Sinclair, Joseph 164, 174, 176, 178–9
Skelly, Francis 58
Stevenson, James 153
Stewart, David, of Garth 14, 38, 40, 100
Stirling, Thomas 33
Stirrup Charge 195–202, 215–16
Swinton, Samuel 156–7

Tarleton, Banastre 52
tartans 40–1, 62, 65, 78, 206
Tippu Sultan 142, 149
Todd, James 161, 164, 174, 176, 178, 191, 193–4
Torriano, William 195

Urquhart, David 136

Urquhart, James, of Craigston 89–90, 123–4, 130

Wallace, William 154–7
Watson, James 113–15
Wellesley, Arthur, Duke of Wellington 1, 36, 150, 152–7, 170–1, 187–8, 191–5, 204
Wemyss, William, of Wemyss 137
Whitelocke, John 163
Wight, Isle of 161
Winchester, Robert 186–9, 196, 198–9
Wolfe, James 18, 25
Woodford, John 101, 103
Wyndham, Charles 199–200

Yonge, Sir George 86
York, Duke of 72, 75

Other books on the Napoleonic Wars published by
Frontline Books include:

1809 THUNDER ON THE DANUBE
Napoleon's Defeat of the Habsburgs
John H. Gill
Volume I: Abensberg ISBN 978-1-84415-713-6
Volume II: Aspern ISBN 978-1-84832-510-4
Volume III: Wagram and Znaim ISBN 978-1-84832-547-0

ALBUERA 1811
The Bloodiest Battle of the Peninsular War
Guy Dempsey
Foreword by Donald E. Graves
ISBN 978-1-84832-499-2

DRAGON RAMPANT
The Royal Welch Fusiliers at War, 1793–1815
Donald E. Graves
ISBN 978-1-84832-551-7

NAPOLEON'S INVASION OF RUSSIA
Theodore Ayrault Dodge
Foreword by George F. Nafziger
ISBN 978-1-84832-501-2

SOLDIER OF THE SEVENTY-FIRST
From De La Plata to Waterloo 1806–1815
Joseph Sinclair
Introduction by Stuart Reid
ISBN 978-1-84832-561-6

THE WATERLOO ARCHIVE
Volume I: British Sources
Edited by Gareth Glover
ISBN 978-1-84832-540-1

A WATERLOO HERO
The Reminiscences of Friedrich Lindau
Friedrich Lindau
Edited and Presented by James Bogle and Andrew Uffindel
ISBN 978-1-84832-539-5

For more information on our other books, please visit
www.frontline-books.com. You can write to us at
info@frontline-books.com or at
47 Church Street, Barnsley, S. Yorkshire, S70 2AS.